W9-DDW-625

NEIGHBORHOOD
ORGANIZATIONS AND COMMUNITY
DEVELOPMENT

NEIGHBORHOOD ORGANIZATIONS AND COMMUNITY DEVELOPMENT

Making Revitalization Work

Neil S. Mayer

An Urban Institute Paperback

 THE URBAN INSTITUTE PRESS · WASHINGTON, D.C.

DISCARDED

WIDENER UNIVERSITY
WOLFGRAM
LIBRARY
CHESTER, PA.

Copyright © 1984
THE URBAN INSTITUTE
2100 M Street, N.W.
Washington, D.C. 20037

Library of Congress Cataloging in Publication Data
Mayer, Neil S.
  Neighborhood organizations and community development.

  Bibliography: p.
  1. Community development, Urban—United States.
I. Title.
HN90.C6M395 1984   307'.14'0973   84–17362
ISBN 0–87766–364–5

Printed in the United States of America

BOARD OF TRUSTEES
Carla A. Hills
  Chairman
Katharine Graham
  Vice Chairman
William Gorham
  President
Warren E. Buffett
John J. Byrne
Joseph A. Califano, Jr.
William T. Coleman, Jr.
John M. Deutch
Anthony Downs
Joel L. Fleishman
Philip M. Hawley
Aileen C. Hernandez
Ray L. Hunt
Robert S. McNamara
David O. Maxwell
Lois D. Rice
Elliot L. Richardson
George H. Weyerhaeuser
Mortimer B. Zuckerman

LIFE TRUSTEES
John H. Filer
Eugene G. Fubini
Vernon E. Jordan, Jr.
Edward H. Levi
Bayless A. Manning
Stanley Marcus
Arjay Miller
J. Irwin Miller
Franklin D. Murphy
Herbert E. Scarf
Charles L. Schultze
William W. Scranton
Cyrus R. Vance
James Vorenberg

 THE URBAN INSTITUTE is a nonprofit policy research and educational organization established in Washington, D.C., in 1968. Its staff investigates the social and economic problems confronting the nation and government policies and programs designed to alleviate such problems. The Institute disseminates significant findings of its research through the publications program of its Press. The Institute has two goals for work in each of its research areas: to help shape thinking about societal problems and efforts to solve them, and to improve government decisions and performance by providing better information and analytic tools.

Through work that ranges from broad conceptual studies to administrative and technical assistance, Institute researchers contribute to the stock of knowledge available to public officials and to private individuals and groups concerned with formulating and implementing more efficient and effective government policy.

Conclusions or opinions expressed in Institute publications are those of the authors and do not necessarily reflect the views of other staff members, officers or trustees of the Institute, advisory groups, or any organizations which provide financial support to the Institute.

Contents

Tables

Foreword

Neighborhood organizations initiated and controlled by local residents have in recent years begun the work of stabilizing and improving their own communities. With limited outside support, they seek to revitalize urban neighborhoods by building and renovating housing, creating new jobs and enterprises, reviving commercial activity, establishing community centers, and promoting energy conservation, often as part of broad strategies for community development. These neighborhood development organizations (NDOs) have chosen explicitly to target the benefits of their efforts to lower-income people living and working in their communities. And they have combined public and private resources of many kinds to finance their projects.

If NDOs are effective performers in their difficult task, government at all levels, and private institutions as well, may want to expand their support of NDOs. But a need for information exists. In the past little formal assessment was made of the progress or potential of NDO work. Nor was there much analysis of how supporters, and NDOs themselves, could best contribute to the success of NDOs.

Now, the research reported in this book carefully documents the often impressive performance of NDOs, based on the experience of nearly one hundred such organizations throughout the country. The author examines in detail how their records of accomplishment can be further improved, outlining the policy and program approaches that can contribute most to the effectiveness of NDOs. The lessons of their research offer guidance for NDO leaders and for sources of suppport, both about ways to expand NDO achievements and about the extent to which NDO work might sensibly be relied upon, and facilitated, in efforts to revitalize urban communities.

Government funds are stretched thin, and federal financing of urban revitalization has been sharply reduced in recent years. Decisions about
support for NDO activities from public and private sectors alike, along
with other choices about urban strategies, should be based on the kind of
practical information that this book provides.

William Gorham
President
The Urban Institute

Acknowledgments

Many people played important roles in producing this book. In conducting the research at The Urban Institute, Sue Marshall, who codirected the NDO project, contributed substantially to development of the data sets that were used in analysis and to overall project management. Marshall, Jennifer Blake, Maxine Edwards, and consultant David Carlson all conducted site visits that were crucial to the study; Blake and Edwards collected and prepared data for computer entry; and Blake performed many of the computations. Margery Turner gave extremely useful advice on computer programming when we ran into difficulties, and did some important programming herself.

The U.S. Department of Housing and Urban Development (HUD) provided funds for the research on which this book is based. At HUD, Howard Sumka, director of the division of Community Planning and Neighborhood Studies, was tremendously supportive of the study throughout its conduct and gave valuable comments on study reports and on a draft of this book. Former HUD staffers Joel Friedman and Alice Shabecoff, who were HUD's monitors for the study, offered helpful advice, comment, and support. Other HUD staff in Sumka's office and in the Office of Neighborhood Development were especially helpful in giving us access to needed program documents and in sharing information they had obtained about the neighborhood organizations in the study.

Valuable review comments on manuscript drafts also came from Raymond Struyk, Barry Checkoway, and Robert Hollister. Molly Ruzicka's editing greatly improved every chapter. Theresa Walker efficiently guided the publication process at The Urban Institute. Mykki Jones, Shirley Pearson, and others in The Urban Institute Support Center expertly typed the manuscript.

xv

Funds for the author's work in preparing the book from previous contract reports were provided principally by a grant from the Aetna Life and Casualty Foundation, augmented by Urban Institute general funds.

Special thanks are due the many people, both inside neighborhood development organizations and cooperating with them from without, who gave freely of their time to talk with us about the organizations' efforts and whose impressive work in troubled neighborhoods inspired this book.

Finally, Dusky Pierce, my wife, is simply by being herself the best support a person can have.

About the Author

Neil S. Mayer is an economist and senior research associate in the Housing and Community Development Center of The Urban Institute. His work has focused on the problems of revitalizing the distressed neighborhoods and economies of urban communities. His previous writings on the role of neighborhood organizations in community development include *Keys to Growth of Neighborhood Development Organizations* and numerous articles and papers. Dr. Mayer couples his policy research with hands-on experience in housing and economic development at the local level in California, where he now lives.

1

Major Issues and Findings

The Policy Context

Virtually every major city in America—growing, stable, or declining—harbors neighborhoods with intense economic and social problems. People with lower incomes, limited work skills or work opportunities, and other difficulties such as poor health or poor education are often concentrated in specific neighborhoods. The same neighborhoods have large stocks of deteriorated or deteriorating housing, stores threatened by declining business, and continuing losses of job-generating enterprises. Some of these neighborhoods are and have long been primarily homes for the very poor, while others are in large part working-class areas. A characteristic shared by all these neighborhoods is that the impetus for actions to preserve or restore healthy communities has been lost.

The conditions of these neighborhoods and the characteristics of their residents, together with the reluctance of outsiders to invest in such areas, form a circle of cause and effect that has proved difficult to escape in the quest for revitalization. Arguments have raged about whether public policy should deal with people or places, and about whether private actors' withholding of investment has precipitated, or has been a product of, deteriorating neighborhood circumstances. In the meantime, most distressed neighborhoods have not been revitalized, and new problem communities have continuously been added.

It is clear that neither the private nor the public sector has been successful in solving the problems of troubled neighborhoods. In an immediate sense, withdrawal of private investment has created many of the conditions—for example, rental housing needing repair—that distressed neighborhoods now confront. Some decisions by private profit-making actors in the past were in reaction to strong economic disincentives in the neighborhoods; others were based on inaccurate perceptions, discriminatory attitudes, or dissatisfaction with normal risks and profits in such neighborhoods when better opportunities arose elsewhere. Whatever the basis for private decisions, in many distressed neighborhoods the conditions that have discouraged private-sector activity persist, often in intensified form; and as a result, little private investment flows to them. Only rarely is private for-profit activity today leading to revitalization of troubled neighborhoods, and then it is often designed to serve higher-income newcomers rather than long-time residents.[1]

Public policy has also not been highly successful in stabilizing and revitalizing neighborhoods with concentrated problems. Some government programs, such as urban renewal, sought more to eliminate blighted neighborhoods than to address their needs. Other government activities, such as freeway building, have at times disrupted neighborhoods that previously functioned well. Public programs dealing piecemeal with specific neighborhood problems have been inadequate to break the circle of deterioration. Money for basic public improvements and services has often been directed to less distressed, more politically potent neighborhoods. And expensive incentives—for example, tax breaks and capital subsidies—designed to attract private investment to problem neighborhoods either have had little impact in overcoming more fundamental disincentives[2] or have been so costly as to help trigger their own demise.[3] In each of these types of interventions, government at all levels often has displayed limited knowledge of and sensitivity to neighborhood concerns and priorities.

In the past fifteen years, a third set of institutions—private, not-for-profit neighborhood development organizations (NDOs)[4]—have emerged as potential leaders in the process of neighborhood revitalization, with a growing capacity for undertaking development projects. Despite sporadic and often inadequate support, NDOs have taken increasingly responsible roles in many

---

1. Private action, sometimes publicly aided, by neighborhood homeowners to upgrade their homes for their own use has a better record in certain areas.

2. See, for example, Litvak and Daniels 1979, for evidence of failure of incentives to influence the decisions of private business enterprises on whether to locate in distressed areas.

3. The Section 8 housing-subsidy program for new construction of apartments for low-income people is a good example of a program that expended so many funds simply to attract private investors that it came to be considered too costly, and its legislative support evaporated.

4. NDOs are commonly known also as community development corporations (CDCs).

aspects of revitalization, including housing rehabilitation and construction, economic and commercial development, energy conservation, and the provision of community facilities (along with nondevelopment functions in human-service delivery, advocacy, and neighborhood organizing). Created and controlled by community people themselves, NDOs need not be "bribed" or cajoled into choosing troubled neighborhoods in which to pursue their efforts. Their projects are more likely to be designed to serve current residents than to produce only physical revitalization that benefits richer households and institutions at the expense of the local inhabitants. Ideally, NDOs also bring special knowledge of and sensitivity to neighborhood needs to their work, by virtue of their own local origins. And, for the same reason, they have a greater capacity to involve neighborhood people in revitalization activities—a key to the health of any neighborhood.

To some extent, outsiders have recognized the value of supporting NDOs and similar community-based organizations, because of the special advantages these organizations have in undertaking comprehensive revitalization efforts in distressed neighborhoods. In the private sector the Ford Foundation took the lead during the 1960s, supporting various community-based experimental efforts in its "grey areas" program and later funding a limited number of community development corporations (CDCs, functionally equivalent to NDOs) on a significant scale. In the public arena the U.S. Department of Housing and Urban Development's (HUD's) Model Cities program sought to involve community people as the shapers of comprehensive revitalization efforts, although few Model Cities programs ultimately concentrated on development work or built lasting independent institutions. In the late 1960s, at the urging of Senators Robert F. Kennedy and Jacob Javits, the U.S. Congress created the Special Impact Program within the Office of Economic Opportunity (OEO) to fund community-based organizations taking on comprehensive neighborhood development efforts.[5] This program and its successor (Title VII) in the Community Services Administration (CSA) supplied a modest number of organizations (annually about forty) with substantial levels of administrative and investment funds (substantial relative to other funding of community self-help efforts). The organizations were expected to produce job-creating enterprises and physical and other improvements in their neighborhoods, within the framework of comprehensive plans.[6]

---

5. The program began with multiagency involvement and a multifaceted thrust but quickly settled into the OEO with a CDC focus.

6. In revised and limited form, this program continues at present within the U.S. Department of Health and Human Services.

Many other community-based groups have taken steps toward becoming neighborhood "developers" in the period since the late 1960s. Some organizations that began as advocates, seeking responses from other public and private parties to neighborhood needs, have, in frustration, concluded that they can best take on the development work themselves. Especially during the second half of the 1970s, many new organizations were formed for the purpose of producing revitalization by conducting their own development projects. NDOs, new and old, took advantage of funds from expanding federal programs to invest in their communities, and they found increasing support from private foundations and lending institutions.[7]

NDOs certainly show signs of important accomplishments in stabilizing and improving their neighborhoods. A host of reports and articles in the NDO literature have cited "model" projects in which neighborhood organizations built or rehabilitated housing, generated new jobs, promoted local commercial businesses, and carried out other development projects, under difficult conditions that defied or discouraged other actors.[8] Many recent NDO efforts are concrete examples of cooperation between citizens and both the public and private sectors. Although observers across the political spectrum have lately spoken strongly about the importance of such partnerships, few actors other than NDOs have successfully conducted projects with public and private participation. NDO work has also stood alone in being directed to the needs of, and being controlled by, the low- and moderate-income residents of neighborhoods in need of revitalization.

Most NDOs have never been large-scale or consistent recipients of public and private support. Cutbacks in federal funding—in aid programs specifically for NDOs and in broader programs eligible for use by NDOs—have sharply reduced these organizations' abilities to serve their constituencies,[9] especially in combination with harsh national economic conditions. Funding reductions also threaten to force the dismantling of institutional capabilities (in terms of trained staff and so forth) that NDOs have developed in the course of their past work. The private-sector response has been insufficient to offset these losses.[10] Yet NDOs cannot serve people of limited means in troubled neighborhoods with dedication alone. Other resources, from outside the neighborhood, are required.[11]

---

7. Lending institutions most often financed projects where public guarantees ensured repayment.

8. See, for example, U.S. Department of Housing and Urban Development (HUD) 1980; and National Commission on Neighborhoods 1979a.

9. For details, see chapter 4 of this book; also Cohen and Kohler 1983.

10. See Cohen and Kohler 1983; also Salamon et al. 1983b.

11. Indeed, increasing the financial resources brought in from outside a neighborhood, and then retaining and expanding them within the community, is a fundamental NDO purpose.

Given their unique roles and approaches in serving troubled neighborhoods, NDOs' efforts may well be vital components of any successful neighborhood or broader urban revitalization process, and, if that is the case, they are therefore worthy of significantly expanded support and cooperation. A central question is whether NDOs fulfill their promise, effectively producing tangible results while benefiting and involving neighborhood residents and businesspeople. If NDOs do meet these goals, and thus deserve further encouragement, a second major question arises: how can the organizations themselves and their sources of support best build still more consistently successful NDOs capable of taking on greater efforts? Under the best of circumstances, resources flowing to NDOs will be limited—certainly in relation to the monumental tasks NDOs face—and those resources must be used well.

Finding the Answers

This book addresses the two primary issues just defined: assessing NDO performance and generating further NDO successes. Its purpose is to provide concrete information about whether and how to make NDO efforts a more fundamental, productive part of neighborhood revitalization policy and action.

To date, little systematic information about NDO efforts has been accumulated, especially information that might help direct action to promote their success. A large-scale, two-year study conducted by the author and others at The Urban Institute provided a rare opportunity to track and analyze in detail a large body of NDO work. This volume reports an array of findings, based directly on the results of that extensive empirical research, about the roles that NDOs can and do play in neighborhood revitalization and the ways to best ensure the effectiveness of NDO activities.

The study examined the work of nearly one hundred NDOs in major urban areas throughout the United States. Each had been a recipient, in 1980, of a federal Neighborhood Self-Help Development (NSHD) grant from HUD to help it undertake a specific development effort. The NDOs' experiences with those projects formed the data base of our research.

The NSHD program was created in order to improve the ability of community-based and community-controlled organizations to undertake neighborhood revitalization work, following recommendations of the *President's National Urban Policy Report* in 1978.[12] Grants totaling nearly $14 million were made in 1980 to 125 NDOs, 99 of them in urban areas. The

---

12. See HUD 1978.

grants were designed to provide funds for completing the planning and preparation of already well-defined development projects and/or for part of the
expense of actual implementation. In either case, NDOs were to obtain other
major resources in cash and in kind for the projects, from various public and
private sources and the neighborhoods themselves.

The experience of this large number of NSHD-grantee organizations
provided an enormously rich base from which to assess NDO activities and
performance, as well as to judge the value of well-designed outside aid to
them. Our study was able to examine the immense diversity of NDOs, their
projects, and their environments, and to take such differences into account
in drawing conclusions, while identifying important overall patterns of NDO
behavior. The study also traced the dynamics of project success or failure,
and of organizational growth, over an extended period of observation. As a
result, the research yields important lessons about ways of encouraging further
neighborhood-based efforts to revitalize and preserve the nation's urban communities, and about the accomplishments we can expect from these efforts.
In addition, it provides guidance for the most effective use of resources in
the current period of federal-funding cutbacks and other severe constraints.
The findings should be of interest to policymakers and program planners at
all levels of government, as well as to foundations, private businesses, and
religious and other institutions concerned with their communities' futures.
The findings should also be valuable to NDO leaders themselves as they
develop their organizations and projects, in addition to sources of technical
aid who assist and advise NDOs in that process.

This book provides answers to five principal questions.

1. What are the characteristics of organizations carrying out revitalization
   work and of the projects they undertook?
2. How well did NDO projects succeed as neighborhood revitalization
   efforts?
3. What factors were the prime determinants of NDO projects' levels of
   success?
4. How did NDO capabilities for community development work grow in
   the process of doing projects, and what limitations in capacity remain?
5. Based on answers to the first four questions, how should NDOs and
   their supporters go about further improving and expanding NDO records
   of successful performance?

In answering the first question, we examined the history, structure, and
skills of NDOs in our study; their ties to funders, other political actors, outside
experts, and residents; the extent of and trends in deterioration in their neighborhoods; and the types and scale of NDO projects, along with mechanisms

for implementing them. The descriptions provide a detailed view of community development work by neighborhood organizations. They also form a baseline for analysis—by outlining potential factors in NDO success (or failure) and by defining initial NDO capability from which capacity growth can be observed and measured.

Project success (question two) was assessed in numerous ways in the study. Principal among these were NDOs' performance in finishing proposed tasks, in producing planned outputs, in obtaining funds and nonmoney resources beyond their NSHD grants, in involving neighborhood residents, in assuring that project benefits extend to members of their own communities, and in contributing to longer-run revitalization strategies. The findings taken together provide a comprehensive measurement of how well NDOs can carry out development work and of the ability of NDO projects to remain sensitive to neighborhood needs. The results record the potential impacts of pursuing neighborhood revitalization policies that emphasize the role of NDOs—impacts that could be improved and expanded upon using other lessons of the study.

It is essential to any NDO policy and program to know what makes projects succeed or fail (question three). Our research analyzed the effects of a long list of potential success factors within six categories: internal NDO capabilities, relations with NDO communities and outsiders, economic and social environments from the national to the neighborhood level, types of projects, the structure of the NSHD grant program, and special combinations of the first five categories. Statistical and case-study analyses tested the links between each factor and the measured outcomes of specific projects. Armed with knowledge about the impacts of each factor on project success, NDOs can try to develop the capabilities and assemble the resources that most make a difference and can use such awareness to select projects that can succeed under the conditions given. Supporters are given a means of predicting projects' and organizations' outlook for success that they can use to choose which NDOs to assist and to provide them with the kinds of special aid that raise the likelihood of good results.

In order to answer the fourth question, we traced the capacity building that took place during the course of NSHD project work, the way such growth was typically encouraged and accomplished, and the remaining shortcomings in capability. The purposes of this analysis were to examine both the extent to which project experience in itself contributes to capacity and the manner in which its capacity-building value can be supplemented and enhanced by deliberate action within and without NDOs. Together with information about key factors in success, understanding of the capacity-building process can be used to focus efforts to strengthen NDO capabilities in neighborhood development. It can also be useful in assessing long-run potential for NDO work, by indicating how much growth in capacity is likely to occur as NDOs gain experience.

Finally, in answering question five, all the descriptive and analytic findings were integrated in order to outline a set of recommended actions designed to promote NDO effectiveness and growth. Recommendations include those for NDOs, as well as for their sources of support and guidance and for other institutions that may participate in their projects as business partners, investors, and the like. While these recommendations are extensive, they are necessarily a limited compilation of the many ideas about policy and practice that the study findings suggest and that are discussed throughout this book. Readers should use the specific study results to draw their own conclusions for action as well.

Research Approaches

Briefly, how were the key study questions addressed? As already indicated, the research for this book drew upon the project experience of ninety-nine urban NDOs nationwide (see appendix A for a complete listing of NDOs in the study). Written information on several key topics was obtained about all of the NDOs in the study, from materials they submitted as part of NSHD grant requirements. These materials provided data about basic NDO and project characteristics and about the more concrete components of project performance, which were then summarized quantitatively for presentation in this book. In addition, we formed hypotheses about which of the basic NDO and project characteristics affected project performance; we then tested these hypotheses by applying standard statistical techniques to the data for the ninety-nine NDOs.

In a second major line of study, a representative sample of thirty NDOs was selected from the list of all grantees (see appendix A for identification of NDOs in the sample and appendix B for a description of sampling methods). Each NDO in the sample was visited twice by research staff, once early in NSHD project work and once at or near the end of those project efforts.[13] Through extensive interviews and direct on-site observation, we gathered information about subtler aspects of NDO characteristics, their environments, and project performance. The two visits allowed us to see how NDO characteristics, which were assessed on the first site trips, affected the level of project results produced by the time of the second observation. The two visits

---

13. Note exceptions explained in appendix B.

also enabled us to observe directly the growth in NDO capabilities and knowledge during the period of NSHD project work.

Some information gathered about NDOs on site visits was recorded in quantitative form. It was used to describe the organizations in more detail and to test additional hypotheses about which factors affected performance. Other information was summarized narratively in site-visit reports for each NDO. Collectively, these reports were especially valuable in explaining why projects succeeded or failed (in conjunction with statistical analyses of this issue); and the reports helped trace the process of capacity building.

Finally, from the findings of all the statistical analyses and site reports, we derived policy and program lessons for NDOs and their supporters to use in generating future NDO successes. (For readers with an interest in study methods, appendix B presents more detailed information about data sources, means of analysis, problems encountered, and directions for future research.)

It is worth noting that the NDOs in the study, although numerous and diverse, do not perfectly represent the entire range of neighborhood organizations with an interest in doing development work. The NSHD program selected grantees based on competitive proposals from among NDOs meeting certain minimum requirements. Standards for selecting grantees included presentation of already fairly well-defined project plans, some history of past neighborhood work in the same field as the proposed project or a (sometimes loosely) related field, staff and management capacity to carry out the work, and established relations with neighborhood residents and local government (see appendix B for more detail).

Thus the study NDOs are on average moderately more sophisticated than the full range of such organizations. (A larger share of the latter are still at the stage of deciding whether to embrace development projects as a part of their desired agenda and are considering how to feasibly undertake them.) At the same time, the NSHD program deliberately avoided concentrating its grantmaking on the most mature community organizations, particularly those with major CSA funding (although it did not exclude them). The ninety-nine organizations in this study therefore best represent neither total newcomers to development nor the thin, most experienced layer of NDOs, but a broad range of NDOs in between.[14] If these organizations perform well, their success will suggest that there is substantial potential for expanded NDO work, both by these same NDOs as they mature and by others that are helped to develop similarly modest capabilities.

---

14. HUD seems also to have attracted more housing and fewer economic development projects than might be typical for all NDOs, although less sophisticated groups may generally do more housing work.

Relation to Other Research

This book, by using extensive observation and systematic analysis (statistical and case-study) to address the five questions cited previously, exceeds in scope and purpose most previous research about the development work of community-based organizations. In fact, much research on neighborhoods and their dynamics pays no explicit attention to NDOs. The NDO-related literature most commonly contains descriptions of the efforts of individual NDOs, calling attention to examples of model work deserving of emulation by other NDOs.[15] It should be noted that these descriptions play a valuable role in stimulating the thinking of NDO leaders and advisors about possible revitalization projects, and in sparking the interest of potential supporters. Other neighborhood research has looked at larger numbers of NDOs (and often other nonprofit groups), describing typical organizations, their work, and the variations among them.[16] Still other past writings have focused on the multiple ways that government and private institutions have been or could be more supportive to NDOs (and other neighborhood organizations).[17]

But none of these efforts systematically measures the level of NDOs' performance—in other words, the record of project success—with the broad implications of this performance for choices about the focus of effective neighborhood policy. And little of the past literature attempts to specifically link the observed characteristics of NDOs, their relations with outsiders, and their socioeconomic and political-policy environment with the success or failure of NDO work. Thoughtful exceptions in the literature[18] have been limited by the small study sample of NDOs that the researchers had the opportunity to observe. Moreover, research of these types has not been designed nor been able to tell us in detail which conditions and actions are most important to helping NDOs be productive and continue to grow.

Another line of NDO literature, written by participants knowledgeable in NDO work (NDO leaders and technical and financial supporters) does concentrate on the ''how to'' of successful project work and organization

---

15. Good recent examples, among many, include Bratt, Byrd, and Hollister 1983; Friedman 1981; HUD 1980; and New World Foundation 1980.

16. Valuable examples providing a guide to overall NDO activity for practitioners and policymakers include Cohen and Kohler 1983; National Commission on Neighborhoods 1979a; and The Support Center 1980.

17. Prominent examples are found in National Commission on Neighborhoods 1979b, for the public sector; and New World Foundation 1980, for the private sector.

18. See, for example, Bratt, Byrd, and Hollister 1983.

building.[19] The direct experience of such authors provides valuable insights into the process of creating effective neighborhood organizations. A drawback is the lack of data—outside of key examples, often from only one organization—to document NDO performance and the ties between NDO attributes and success. Such data could be used to generalize from the expert case-study observations, in addition to allowing other NDO actors to evaluate their own situation and to draw their own conclusions in light of the findings. A greater limitation, perhaps, is that expert practitioners rarely take (or have) the time to record systematically the important information they have gleaned in their work.

Two unpublished studies share the greatest kinship with the research approach used in this book. One, which proceeded almost simultaneously with our work, was a study of fifteen CSA-funded CDCs, conducted by the National Center for Economic Alternatives (NCEA).[20] The research, an evaluation of CSA's Title VII program of support, gathered detailed information about the CDCs' multiyear records of accomplishments, recording concrete outputs, leveraging of resources, and the like, comparable to measures reported in this book. One major difference was that the CSA-supported organizations studied were typically larger and older, a uniquely favored group that benefited from long-term Title VII funding on a substantial scale. A more significant difference, however, was NCEA's emphasis on outcomes, with less regard for determining what factors caused them, especially in terms of the internal characteristics of CDCs and of CDC links to other actors,[21] both of which are major foci of the analysis presented here.

An older study of OEO-supported (and then CSA-supported) CDCs, conducted by Abt Associates in the early 1970s, most closely parallels the research in this book.[22] Abt's analysis examined both the results of specific CDC projects undertaken and the causal connections between characteristics of organizations, their projects, and their environments on the one hand and project results on the other. This study captured CDC experience near the beginning of community-based organizations' involvement in development activities; of course, much has since changed as both the neighborhood movement and many individual neighborhood organizations have matured. Also, Abt's research had certain methodological shortcomings, in that it lacked both

---

19. See, for example, various observers cited in Cohen 1979; see also Hanson and McNamera 1981; McNeely 1982; and Moritz 1979.

20. National Center for Economic Alternatives 1981.

21. The effects of project type, the economic environment (to some extent), and very basic CDC characteristics (age, size, general "maturity") were given greater attention in the NCEA study.

22. Abt Associates 1973.

goals against which to compare CDC progress and adequate measures of important CDC characteristics, and also used statistical techniques whose requirements sometimes outstripped the availability of data and conceptual understanding. But a number of hypotheses pursued in this book—relating to the effects of NDOs' own characteristics, their environments, and the types of projects they choose on the NDOs' level of project success—are drawn in part from Abt's work.

In sum, the research reported here seeks to fill a significant gap in knowledge about the community development work of neighborhood organizations. It addresses a chain of related questions that are seldom treated together, regarding what NDOs and their projects are like, how NDOs perform, what determines their performance, how NDOs grow, and how they and other supporting institutions can further improve NDO levels of success and promote their growth. And the research couples quantitative information and statistical analyses with extensive case-study observations pertaining to a large and varied set of NDOs and projects, in order to answer those questions systematically.[23]

Key Findings

The major results of our NDO research can be readily grouped according to the five principal study questions outlined earlier. This section of the chapter summarizes those results. Each of the topics is discussed in detail later in the body of the book, accompanied by supporting evidence for the conclusions.

1. What Are the Characteristics of Organizations Carrying Out Revitalization Work and of the Projects They Undertook?

NDOs are best characterized by their diversity—in size, skill, experience, links to others, and their environments. For example, organizations in our study had annual budgets ranging from less than $10,000 to several million dollars; and some had no experience with development projects, while others had a track record of a dozen or more such efforts.

But some predominant patterns do appear. The largest number of NDOs are currently concentrating heavily on housing activities and are best categorized as nonprofit housing corporations, although many others have multifaceted development and nondevelopment programs, and some focus on

---

23. The research builds in part on hypotheses and findings of a previous study by the author, which drew lessons from twelve case studies about factors in NDO success and the process of their growth. That study is reported in Mayer, with Blake 1981.

nonhousing issues. Although the organizations have mixed histories, most are divided between those with backgrounds in advocacy work and those that have concentrated on doing their own development projects from the beginning. Most of the NDOs are of modest age (three to ten years old) and size (budgets of less than $500,000, staffs of less than a dozen).

NDOs do bring significant capabilities to their difficult tasks. Most have strong, talented executive directors; some level of experience with development projects; and strong support from neighborhood residents and board members. But they also have limitations. Often, NDO staffs have too few technically trained members, project experience is restricted to a few projects in a narrow spectrum of fields, and critical skills such as financial-feasibility analysis are lacking. For example, less than a quarter of NDOs in our study had more than a little previous experience with the type of project that NSHD grants supported, and nearly a third had none.

Many of the organizations substantially supplement their internal capabilities with technical assistance from beyond the neighborhood. They have successfully generated good relationships with public and private funding providers, whose resources are critical to their development work. But most still have work to do in generating additional forms of cooperation with the private business sector.

The projects NDOs undertook with NSHD funds are primarily in the housing rehabilitation area. More than half are solely of that type, and others have a housing rehabilitation component. Economic development ventures (with a focus on job creation) and commercial revitalization efforts (aimed at strengthening local business areas) each comprise about an eighth of the projects, with the rest scattered in new housing construction, community facility development, energy conservation and renewable energy sources, and mixtures of these categories. Total planned money expenditures for typical projects were in the range of $400,000 (not including the value of self-help labor), although this figure varied widely from project to project. Given the costs of development work, that dictated that projects had to be of modest scale (for example, the average housing rehabilitation effort planned to renovate less than fifty units).

Geographically, NDO efforts were most concentrated in the large cities of the Northeast, with even distribution of the others across north central, western, and southern regions (as defined by the U.S. Bureau of the Census). This northeastern focus matches, of course, the location of many of the older, lower-income neighborhoods of the country. NDOs' neighborhoods were also evenly distributed in terms of their predominant racial/ethnic groupings. The most consistent geographic pattern is that NDOs function in very troubled neighborhoods.

The overall picture, then, is one of NDOs with important but limited skills and resources, tackling ever difficult development work, in severely distressed environments where few others choose to invest and work.

2. How Well Did NDO Projects Succeed as Neighborhood Revitalization Efforts?

Despite difficult challenges, NDOs made considerable progress in carrying out the development projects they proposed. The great majority of projects produced important parts of their planned results, despite rising interest rates, declining public funding, and a generally worsening economic climate from the time that project planning began to the intended date of completion.

On average, NDOs had completed about 65 percent of the tasks they laid out for themselves by the time our study ended,[24] and more than half were still at work. Over two-thirds of the organizations had completed preparation tasks (planning, obtaining funding, and so forth) and were concentrating on project implementation (or had finished it).

Actual outputs were substantial, both on an absolute scale and relative to plans. Consider first the projects (almost half of the total) where all work that will be done is complete (though original intentions may not be met). Nearly all intended weatherizing and "solarizing" of homes has been finished. Over 80 percent of goals for housing rehabilitation—by far the most common project type—have been reached. A similar proportion of proposed community facilities has been completed. New housing construction and commercial space rehabilitation projects have reached about half their intended outputs; and economic development projects to create permanent jobs and efforts to assist private businesses have reached nearly 40 percent of initial expectations, despite very difficult economic conditions. NDOs' expectations for outputs as a share of intentions in still unfinished projects are in most cases modestly higher than the results of finished work for respective project types. Although expectations may be overly optimistic, overall accomplishments may ultimately be similar to those of finished projects.

Although progress has often taken longer than anticipated, concrete results are clearly emerging. Finished and unfinished projects together have already generated over 1,800 renovated housing units, over 200 weatherized homes and solar installations, more than 125 new housing units (and many more under construction), 4 community facilities, nearly 80 permanent jobs

---

24. The 65 percent figure reflects an adjustment to compensate for the fact that some projects were not originally intended to be finished by the last point at which information was collected about them.

in economic development efforts (not including jobs created as part of housing, commercial revitalization, and other work), over 80,000 square feet of renovated or newly built commercial space, 11 new NDO-owned ventures, and assistance to almost 50 businesses.

NDOs did nonetheless vary widely, within and among project types, in terms of their level of progress in producing direct outputs. Performance in the less successful kinds of projects was less than satisfying. Other components of the study focus on ways of making success more consistent.

NDOs were extremely successful in obtaining project funds from other public and private sources in addition to their NSHD grants. The median organization generated other monies roughly equal to three times the amount of NSHD funding, and a small number of highly successful NDOs lifted the average leveraging ratio to a value of over nine. Despite a deteriorating funding environment, NDOs were able on average to garner almost exactly the level of funds they had anticipated in their proposals. There were important variations, however, with nearly one-quarter of the projects able to pin down only half, or less, of their intended funds. Notably, a significant share of the money came from the private sector. A quarter of all non-NSHD funds were from private sources, and for nearly one-third of the study NDOs, a private lender or other private funder was the largest single source of (non-NSHD) project monies. This substantial use of private monies occurred in projects whose planning preceded the Reagan administration, with its strong private-sector emphasis.

NDOs were also widely effective in their NSHD projects in promoting self-help—that is, in promoting direct resident participation in planning and carrying out revitalization work. Residents were most active as members of NDOs' volunteer neighborhood-based boards of directors, where they helped to set policy and raise funds and offered their expertise and hands-on labor. But other residents not on boards of directors also played all of these roles, in addition to serving as paid permanent staff and project construction crew members. Self-help largely met NDO expectations, although these expectations were less well-defined and less well-measured than for some other results. The volunteer components of self-help may have accounted for somewhere in the range of one-tenth of total project resources.

No project result was more systematic than the success of NDOs in directing project benefits to neighborhood residents and businesspeople, especially those of limited means. NDO projects were deliberately designed to attain this objective, and they reached it consistently. New and rehabilitated housing was occupied and controlled by local people at costs they could afford; jobs generated went to neighborhood residents, especially neighborhood youth; commercial projects served local businesses and customers; and new public facilities were for direct community use. While this finding is unsurprising given NDO goals, it represents an important departure from many other publicly and privately sponsored revitalization efforts and emphasizes a singular role of NDO efforts.

NSHD-funded projects alone had only limited indirect impacts—that is, impacts on the behavior of other actors in response to NDO work. Many projects were still too newly complete (if indeed they were yet complete) and of too modest a scale to have important effects on others' decisions about housing investment, business locations, and so on. There were some modest effects of this type (for example, neighbors repairing their houses), and others may yet occur with time.

More important is the potential for a coordinated series of an NDO's projects to, together, produce neighborhood stabilization or change. Most NSHD projects appeared to bear a useful, logical relationship to broader NDO revitalization strategies and had potentially greater value in that context. But there is much we do not know about what constitutes an effective neighborhood revitalization strategy for any actor, and our study did not attempt to evaluate the appropriateness of overall NDO plans.

In sum, many NDO projects were highly successful in producing specific intended outputs, although housing, energy, and community development efforts were more successful than other types of projects. The organizations effectively leveraged NSHD grants, obtaining large amounts of other funds and nonmoney resources consistent with expectations. They were enormously successful in directing project benefits to people within their own communities and obtained some significant project assistance in the form of residents' self-help efforts. There is at least promise that continuing successful project work will contribute to broader improvements in the quality of community life, although many challenges and unanswered questions remain. Overall, there is ample basis on which to urge continued and increased support for NDOs' unique work, as a greater part of overall neighborhood revitalization policy and strategy.

3. *What Factors Were the Prime Determinants of NDO Projects' Levels of Success?*

A small number of characteristics within each of our six categories of success factors played especially important roles in project success or failure. Among internal characteristics—those residing in NDO staff, board of directors, experience, and structure—the most significant contributors to good performance were:

- A broadly skilled executive director, familiar with the process of doing community development work—although not necessarily explicitly expert in it—and effective in a diverse set of other roles that involve giving direction to work on other aspects of, and lining up resources for, such projects.

- A key staff member, in a position of major responsibility, with experience in and knowledge about development projects.
- An understanding of issues of project financial feasibility and of their importance.
- A track record of accomplishments in development and related neighborhood work that attracts outside support and helps provide other needed skills and experience.

Each of these characteristics had powerful impacts on the level of success of a large number of projects. To experienced observers of NDOs and perhaps to others, our identification of these factors as important may come as no surprise. The study verifies our expectations, and it establishes analytically the greater significance of these factors relative to other internal NDO characteristics—of management, teamwork, staff skills, and board participation—which also were found to play major roles in project success or failure in particular situations. Notably, study findings also reject a conventional notion: that NDOs' staff size, budget, age, visibility, and similar basic characteristics can be used as accurate predictors of performance, substituting for a more careful look at the organizations' capabilities.

Perhaps more important, this book's detailed findings about the major success factors (reported in chapter 4 but impossible to summarize adequately here) give a richer picture of their impact, which can be of practical use to NDOs and their supporters in improving NDO performance. Consider briefly, for example, "an understanding of project financial feasibility," cited in the preceding listing as critical to project success. Analysis showed that many NDOs were insufficiently aware of the need to assess, early on, whether planned projects were at all likely to produce revenues adequate to cover their costs. Some NDOs wasted valuable energy (and credibility) pursuing projects that could have been quickly recognized either as impractical or as requiring extensive subsidies that were ultimately unattainable—subsidies whose availability should have been investigated before the NDOs proceeded with other tasks. Our study found that NDOs' shortcomings in business planning and financial analysis were much more critical for economic and commercial development projects—where assessing potential markets for products, services, or space was key—than in housing work. And the research showed the inadequacy of relying solely on outside technical assistance to do financial analysis, a reliance that leaves NDOs without the ready on-staff capability to make quick assessments that are needed to select promising projects, to respond swiftly to changing financing possibilities, and the like. Each of these aspects of understanding project feasibility has implications for action by NDOs—in planning the steps in their projects, in selecting and training staff, in seeking technical and financial aid—as well as for outsiders—in assessing NDOs' requests for support, in pressing them for further information, in guiding them in project planning and selection, and in noting when special assistance is needed (needs that inexperienced NDOs might not recognize).

The body of this book provides specifics about the way factors affect performance and the implications of those findings for action for each significant determinant of success. Analyses of the key internal capabilities—the four mentioned earlier with greatest impact and others—have special significance, because these factors are potentially more responsive to NDOs' efforts to improve them than are most other conditions that affect NDOs' work.

The most important aspects of NDOs' relationships with others in influencing project success were:

- The level of support from their own communities for NDOs' projects and overall efforts.
- The quality of NDOs' working relationships with local government, particularly NDOs' ability to form genuine cooperative partnerships with both political officials and city staff.
- Access to competent technical assistance in specific fields where NDOs lacked their own expertise, especially when training of NDO staff was made a part of the assistance process.

Beyond these, several types of outside links that affect NDO ability to obtain funds for certain special purposes had substantial impacts on performance. Because most NDOs are (at best) very modest internal generators of funds, and many have notable limits in expertise and political influence as well, established, positive relations with the community and outsiders are of tremendous significance to NDOs' survival, their project efforts, and their growth. Again, the impacts of such factors and their implications for policy and action are discussed in depth in later chapters.

The difficult environments in which NDOs operate place a continuing drag on their ability to carry out revitalization work, in the same way that external conditions have discouraged other actors even from undertaking such work in the NDOs' neighborhoods or in similar contexts. During the period of our study, several external factors were especially prominent in determining the success, and often the basic feasibility, of projects. Prime among them were:

- Reductions in the availability of project funds from the federal government. These reductions not only directly decrease the funds available for project financing; they also often make it infeasible to use private financing, which usually needs to be combined with public subsidies to make projects work economically while still serving lower-income people.

- Rising interest rates.
- Declining general health of the national economy, in terms of business contractions, rising unemployment, and falling consumer spending, which in particular reduced the market for NDO services, products, and buildings below expectations.
- The troubled neighborhood circumstances in which many NDOs operate (regardless of turns in the business cycle).

Essentially, the worsening national conditions made even more difficult the already acute problems of working in depressed and declining communities. In an important set of cases, these external factors combined to overwhelm the impacts of NDO skill and dedication, stymieing a few projects entirely and markedly reducing the accomplishments of others. While NDOs need to more fully recognize the constraints these external conditions place on them, the most important lessons are probably for policymakers and potential supporters, who should interpret NDO performance in light of the factors NDOs cannot control and provide resources and assistance to try to offset them.

Project choices also had major impacts on ultimate success. In particular:

- Housing, energy, and community development projects fared better than commercial and economic development work, especially because of the greater difficulty in finding markets for, and lesser NDO experience and expertise in, the latter types.
- Relatively mature, better-equipped NDOs frequently selected projects so large and complex that even their capabilities were insufficient to handle them well.
- With care and resourcefulness, NDOs can choose projects that better fit with their particular circumstances and overall lines of work, significantly raising the likelihood of good performance.

The importance of project characteristics needs to be recognized by NDOs and their sources of support, so that together they can choose work that NDOs can handle successfully and can also generate extra assistance and development of capacity where project specifics dictate that additional skills and resources are required.

Certain combinations of characteristics across categories have special significance for project success as well. Three deserve separate mention:

- The extreme danger of NDOs entering into conflicts with city hall in instances where weak bookkeeping and other paperwork procedures leave them vulnerable to attack.

- The value of consciously assembling strong project teams not only from among NDO staff and boards of directors but also from outsiders, including funders, business partners, and technical experts—teams whose individual members may lack needed skills and credibility but who together can do project work well if they are selected to complement one another.
- The heightened negative impacts of deteriorating external conditions for financing projects, when these are coupled with internal weaknesses in financial analysis and in related staff and management expertise.

Many other combinations of characteristics also shaped performance, especially, for example, linkages between project types and other factors; important instances are noted in the text throughout the discussion of determinants of success.

Finally, the NSHD program itself contributed to project success in several ways, most importantly in:

- Promoting the leveraging of other funds, by funding the preparation tasks required in seeking other monies but giving limited money for implementation.
- Making project outputs more affordable to low-income residents.
- Keeping ultimately successful projects alive through long and difficult planning periods.

The program also contributed to capacity growth, by taking risks in project and NDO selection and by giving NDOs improved access to technical assistance. The special contributions of the NSHD program provide important suggestions for the structuring of other programs of NDO assistance.

Overall, the well-defined series of factors that were most powerful in shaping NDO project success provide a solid basis for action to improve performance. More-detailed descriptions later in the text identify the specific components of these factors that NDOs and their supporters can seek to affect and the ways they can go about making those changes. But even this chapter's summary review of primary factors makes it apparent that serious attention to the important determinants of performance singled out in our research can heighten NDO success.

4. *How Did NDO Capabilities for Community Development Work Grow in the Process of Doing Projects, and What Limitations in Capacity Remain?*

NDOs made major progress in building their capacities to effectively carry out development in the course of NSHD projects. The experience of project work itself, the visible results produced, the additions to staff and to the availability of technical experts, and the improvement of relationships with outsiders who participated in the projects contributed to the growth in capability. The overall result is a notably strengthened population of neighborhood groups, in terms of both community development and more general organizational capacity. The fact that the capacity building we observed was substantial yields a critical conclusion: NDOs have tremendous potential to become larger-scale, more effective development actors, if they receive proper nurturing and pay attention to building their own capabilities.

Capacity building was concentrated in four broad areas—two in internal capabilities and two in relations with the community and outsiders. Grouped in that order, these areas were:

- Increased staff expertise in all aspects of the development process. Improved skills in basic project planning, based on a better understanding of what makes up a development effort and of its difficulty, were especially noteworthy.
- Expanded track records of successful development projects. Experienced NDOs branched into new lines of work and less experienced ones greatly expanded their level of development accomplishments. Track-record growth was especially valuable in creating greater credibility and access to support for those NDOs with previously limited development histories.
- Strengthened relationships with community members, as neighborhood residents gained a better sense of how development activities work and saw their results.
- Improved and expanded connections with key sources of funding, principally as a result of delivering promised project products.

Additional capacity building took place in the operation of NDO boards of directors and spin-off organizations, in planning and proposal writing, in management capabilities, and in relations with technical-assistance providers and further outsiders. Learning by doing, working with outside experts, hiring of new staff, and other special efforts all contributed to growing capabilities. Actually doing real development projects with at least reasonably adequate support provided an excellent opportunity for growth. Funders should recognize the importance for long-term growth of aiding NDOs' early projects and of being patient about early performance.

Still, important advances remain to be made in building NDO abilities to do their current work well and to expand the scope and scale of their efforts. One major need for continued growth is in the development of good project directors, other than NDO executive directors themselves, so that work loads can be shared. Greater financial- and market-analysis expertise must be internalized. More NDOs must yet develop successful commercial and economic development projects. Better links to major private business sectors are needed for many reasons.

Equally important, capacity-building gains must be protected. If NDO resources drop precipitously owing to outside forces, newly trained staff will be lost, track records interrupted, and important gains in general will be made all too transient. One of the major costs of federal cutbacks to NDOs has been the loss of the capacity-building fruits of past experience.

5. *How Should NDOs and Their Supporters Go About Further Improving and Expanding NDO Records of Successful Performance?*

Major findings about factors in success and capacity building all have important implications for action by NDOs and their sources of support and cooperation. Broadly speaking, these actors should try to create more of the primary conditions that breed good performance, should focus on developing NDO capabilities in specific areas in which capacity building is feasible and still needed, should choose projects where circumstances suggest that success is or can be made probable, and should generate or provide extra resources when that is necessary in the face of special external difficulties and NDO weaknesses. This book's analysis suggests how those broad concepts should be made operational, by identifying success factors and their impacts and by understanding capacity-building processes and the means to trigger them.

Still speaking generally, NDOs must recognize that, because certain capabilities are so critical to project success, they must take the time to develop these capabilities and demonstrate them to others, even amidst the constant pressure of current work. That means, for example, consciously training project directors, involving boards of directors in decision making, and sharing planning with local governments, even though it might seem easiest in the short run for an executive director to "do-it-all" on his or her own. NDOs need also to recognize the constraints that other capacities, resources, and environments place on them and use that information to select and plan resource gathering and project implementation that can succeed. If, for example, an NDO is tackling an economic development venture for the first time, it needs to understand the special difficulties of establishing a market for products and services, it must seek out components of necessary business-planning expertise if it lacks them, it must press its funding sources for adequate initial capital to allow for slow start-up periods, and so forth. The specifics of these and many other prescriptions for greater NDO success are reported throughout the remaining chapters of this book, especially chapters 4, 5, and 6.

Sources of NDO support obviously need to focus their aid efficiently, because total NDO needs far exceed available resources. Elements of their strategies, again broadly described, should include:

- Using meaningful predictors of the probability of an NDO's success, similar to those success factors we identified, rather than simple measures of NDO size, visibility, age, and so forth, in deciding which NDOs to aid and how to aid them.
- Deliberately promoting funding of NDO projects by taking the risks of making early funding commitments themselves and giving money in forms (planning grants, subsidies that make the use of other funds feasible) that contribute to development of funding packages but insisting that NDOs use that first money to leverage other resources.
- Encouraging specific action by NDOs to improve their own capabilities, by giving money and technical aid for that purpose, by encouraging NDOs to pursue it, and by supporting projects that enhance NDO growth.
- Recognizing the limits of any community development organization's ability to serve people of limited means living in troubled neighborhoods, and providing realistic levels of support for NDO efforts to do that.

The last of these elements is a critical foundation for all the others. NDOs do good work in situations where other actors do not even try. They need and deserve support of many kinds—support that those conditions make inherently necessary. Within the context of this understanding, public and private policymakers can learn, from the research findings presented here, how to shape and target needed aid. Again, recommendations for action with respect to these and other policy elements are both implied and made explicit in later chapters of this book.

Organization of This Book

The remainder of this book is organized into five chapters. Chapter 2 describes NDOs, their projects, and their neighborhoods. Chapter 3 presents detailed findings about how well NSHD-supported projects turned out. Chapter 4 analyzes the factors that determined NDOs' varying levels of project success in community development work. Chapter 5 assesses capacity-building accomplishments, processes, and further needs. And chapter 6 examines more explicitly what NDOs and their supporters can do to encourage project success and future growth.

Readers may wish to give differing attention to various chapters. Some policymakers and program designers—in government and in private foundations, businesses, and religious institutions—might want to focus on the recommendations for policy and action in chapter 6, taking advantage of summaries of key sections within other chapters containing extensive analytic results, at least in their initial reading. NDO leaders and sources of technical assistance might take a similar approach, with additional attention paid to capacity building (chapter 5) and to more of the specifics of factors in success (chapter 4). Other researchers and policy analysts may have special interest in the analytic sections on NDO performance (chapter 3) and its determinants (chapter 4).

Nonetheless, this book is best understood when read in its entirety; and none of it is so technical that understanding of it requires special analytic training. A full reading provides a much better opportunity for the reader to draw his or her own conclusions about the meaning of observed NDO experiences for policy and action.

2

The NDOs and Their Projects

In order to make rational policy decisions about aiding the development project work of NDOs, potential supporters must have systematic
knowledge about the organizations, their neighborhoods, and the projects
they typically undertake. Such information provides a basis not only for
forming expectations about performance but also for defining needs for
aid, for projecting long-term NDO potential, and for understanding how
to contribute to NDO growth. Actors within individual NDOs can use
information about the capabilities and limitations of other organizations
and their project performance to plan realistically their own programs.
They may also be able to identify areas in which their programs need
strengthening.

This chapter presents detailed information about the ninety-nine NDOs
and projects that received NSHD support from HUD. The NDOs represent
well the spectrum of organizations and efforts in the field (see appendix
B). As winners of a national competition for HUD funds, they are on
average more accomplished in development than the typical neighborhood
organization with some interest in development. On the other hand, because
of both their number and the focus of the NSHD program, the NDOs are
not limited to the oldest and most sophisticated organizations in the country.
They reflect, as well, the growing body of community-based development
activity that was built on 1970s' opportunities and that now struggles to
continue in a more difficult current environment.

The three principal parts of this chapter describe the NDOs themselves, the environments in which they work, and the projects they undertook with NSHD aid.

NDOs

Who are the community organizations carrying out development projects in neighborhoods across the country? This section looks first at some basic characteristics of NDOs' organizational history, focus of work, and scale. It then assesses NDOs' internal skills and structure—staffing, management, board of directors, track record—and NDOs' relations with community residents and outsiders such as funders and sources of technical assistance. The last part of this section briefly summarizes the characteristics of "typical" NDOs and the extent of their diversity.

Basic Characteristics

The study population included NDOs of varying primary activities and structure. The largest share can be classified as nonprofit housing organizations, the main portion of whose work is in rehabilitating, building, and/or managing housing. Most of the rest of the NDOs are at the much more diversified end of the spectrum of NDO types: multipurpose organizations combining various development projects (not only housing) with work in human-service programs and/or advocacy. Table 1 presents the full distribution of organization types. Within the multipurpose category, more NDOs combine development and human services than any other mixture, but a substantial number are involved with development and advocacy or with all three areas.

Most NDOs in our study are between three and ten years old (table 2), reflecting, at the lower age range, the NSHD program's desire for some demonstration of past activity. More generally, the age concentration reflects the rapid expansion in the numbers of neighborhood organizations that have taken on development in the last decade.

NDOs' activity histories are diverse. The largest number are organizations that emphasized development from the start. But nearly as many had an advocacy focus at the outset, rather than doing programming themselves; and a significant share began with a focus on human-services delivery (see table 3). Current NDO organization profiles are highly correlated with their historical origins. Most nonprofit housing organizations started as development groups; more broadly focused neighborhood and multipurpose organizations have more diverse backgrounds; and coalitions and tenants' groups have their roots in advocacy work. These relationships are not surprising; many NDOs are still concentrating on interests that initially prompted community people to act together.

The scale of the NDOs' work is typically modest. Their median annual budget is less than $250,000, with many organizations much smaller than that, although some have budgets of several million dollars (see table 4). Most organizations are conducting less than a handful of major projects and programs of all kinds combined concurrently with their NSHD efforts. The number of concurrent development projects is fewer still; most often the

TABLE 1

TYPES OF NEIGHBORHOOD DEVELOPMENT ORGANIZATIONS (NDOs)

Type	Number of NDOs
Nonprofit housing organization[a]	46
Tenants' group[b]	3
Neighborhood organization[c]	11
Multipurpose organization[d]	31
Coalition[e]	8
Total	99

NOTE: Based on all ninety-nine NDOs with Neighborhood Self-Help Development (NSHD) projects.

a. An organization whose major function and purpose is the provision and service of housing.

b. An organization primarily composed of and designed to serve the occupants of a particular building or group of buildings.

c. An organization with either a single focus of development work *other* than housing or, in a smaller number of cases, with a mixed focus involving more than one type of development.

d. An organization that gives priority to development and to human services and/or advocacy activities.

e. An organization whose primary method of operation is through a formal, cooperative relationship of several neighborhood groups, perhaps with differing individual foci.

TABLE 2

YEARS SINCE NDO INCORPORATION

Number of Years	Number of NDOs
0–2	4
3–5	38
6–10	36
More than 10	21

NOTE: Based on all ninety-nine NDOs with NSHD projects. Also, some NDOs existed as organizations well before incorporation.

NSHD effort was the only development project in progress at the time of grant applications (see table 5).

Internal Characteristics

NDOs have a range of more subtle internal characteristics. This part of the chapter emphasizes elements of capability and structure that are likely to affect how well development projects progress. These elements can be strengthened (or strained) in the course of project work. The elements are assessed as they existed near the start of NSHD project work, and therefore form part of the baseline for analyzing factors both in project success and in the building of NDO capacity.

TABLE 3

NDO HISTORY

Historical Focus or Origin	Number of NDOs
Development	44
Advocacy	38
Human services	12
Community action agency[a]	4
Multipurpose[b]	1

NOTE: Based on all ninety-nine NDOs with NSHD projects.

a. An organization that was founded as a formal part of federal poverty programs under the Office of Economic Opportunity (OEO) or the Community Services Administration (CSA).

b. Balanced original focus among two or three of the development, advocacy, and human-services areas.

TABLE 4

NDO BUDGETS

Annual Expenditure ($)	Number of NDOs
Less than 50,000	15
50,000–99,999	8
100,000–249,999	24
250,000–499,999	10
500,000–999,999	9
1,000,000 or more	19
Total	85
No data	14

NOTE: Based on all ninety-nine NDOs with NSHD projects.

TABLE 5

NUMBER OF PROJECTS AND PROGRAMS CONCURRENT WITH NSHD

	Number of NDOs	
Number of Projects and Programs	*All Projects and Programs*	*Development Projects Only*
0	0	53
1	17	32
2	47	12
3–5	33	2
6–10	2	0

NOTE: Based on all ninety-nine NDOs with NSHD projects. NDOs reported current projects and programs somewhat differently in their written NSHD applications, raising some uncertainty about these data. Large organizations may have confined their listing to major projects with particular relevance to NSHD proposals, while others may have mentioned a wider spectrum of small efforts in order to better demonstrate capability.

As stated earlier, a clear picture of NDO characteristics is useful in formulating expectations about NDO performance and growth potential and in structuring NDO programs and aid. Suppose, for example, that in the future a certain skill is found to be critical to NDO success. If it is known that few NDOs possess this skill, program planners can reorganize NDO priorities to allow for the strengthening of that skill and can expect substantially improved NDO performance. Internal characteristics are of special policy interest in terms of both program success and capacity building, because they are often in large part under the control of NDOs and sources of aid.

The internal characteristics are grouped into seven areas:

- Track record—An NDO's history of undertaking projects of various kinds, viewed as preparation for carrying out the NSHD project tasks and as contributing to the organization's credibility when seeking participation by external actors.
- Key staff—The roles, capabilities, and experience of an NDO executive director and other staff with specific responsibilities in the NSHD project.
- Homework and short-term planning—Defined here as skills in activities such as proposal development, project planning and packaging, and presentation and follow-up with funders. Capability in these areas potentially is important in defining feasible projects, in preparing for their implementation, and in obtaining needed funds.
- Management—Includes abilities such as dividing responsibilities, identifying and responding to problems, managing consultants, estimating project costs and timing, and financial reporting.

- Board of directors—Who participates and what roles they play.
- Spin-offs and other organizational structures—How an NDO links itself with spin-off organizations in setting policy and managing projects.
- Planning—How long-range plans are formulated and by whom.

Some aspects of each of these seven areas of internal characteristics are relatively easy to evaluate quantitatively—usually by noting how many NDOs do and do not possess a particular attribute. When it is possible to quantify a characteristic, summary descriptions are reported here, even in cases where some judgmental decisions are required to differentiate between "strong" and "weak" or "much" and "little." In other instances, only narrative descriptions are feasible. Still other characteristics are very difficult to summarize across NDOs and are best described in connection with their specific impacts on project outcomes or in terms of specific capacity-building results. Such discussions are left for later chapters of this book. Finally, for certain NDOs, it was simply not possible to tell from our site visits and written materials how to assess some of their more subtle characteristics. Where that is the case, it is so noted in the discussion in the text, and findings reported here are based only on the organizations for which we have clear observations.

The bulk of our information on internal capabilities and structure is based on site visits to the thirty sample NDOs, because these characteristics, excluding track record, are not well revealed by written documents. With few exceptions, the numbers reported here present the appropriately weighted information from sample NDOs. As noted in appendix B, the sample is highly representative of the overall grant-recipient population of study NDOs.

The next several pages discuss the seven groups of characteristics in turn.

Track Record. Nearly all the NDOs have experience in carrying out some program or project[1] in their neighborhoods and in conducting development projects in particular.[2] The majority, however, have fairly modest development experience, and a substantial minority are taking on projects and roles of a type that is totally new to them.

Specifically, over 90 percent of the organizations have done some prior nonadvocacy work, including both human services and development, with

---

1. This is as opposed to having done advocacy work only or being new, untested organizations.

2. *Development projects* is used here to refer to housing, commercial, economic, community, or energy development efforts—as in the NSHD projects examined in this study—as opposed to human-services and related efforts.

TABLE 6

EXPERIENCE WITH ANY PROGRAM OR PROJECT

Experience Level	Percentage of NDOs
None	7
Little	39
Substantial	42
Some, but unclear how much	12

NOTE: Based on sample of thirty NDOs.

the numbers divided evenly between those with a little experience and those with more (table 6).

Similarly, over 90 percent of all NDOs in the study have at least some track record specifically in development, although this experience is often quite limited. The great majority of all study NDOs have carried out two to five development projects other than the NSHD project, including those currently under way (see table 7). A closer look at just the sample reveals that more than half of the NDOs were rated as having little, rather than substantial, development experience. Most often, those with little experience have been involved to some degree with one or two small-scale housing projects, while not necessarily acting as lead developers.

Nearly one-third of the organizations have no clear experience with the specific types of projects they are undertaking with NSHD money, and others are taking on partially new work within the context of multifaceted projects. Most of the rest have limited rather than major experience with their NSHD project type (see table 8). This range of experience is roughly consistent with HUD's assessment and apparent intent in selecting those NDOs for NSHD project grants. The department labeled half of the NDOs as having proven records in the same line of work and the other half as having demonstrated capacity to do NSHD work but in other kinds of program efforts or in similar

TABLE 7

NUMBER OF PAST AND CURRENT DEVELOPMENT PROJECTS UNDERTAKEN
(Other than NSHD)

Number of Projects	Percentage of NDOs
0	4
1	11
2–5	69
6–10	11
More than 10	4

NOTE: Based on all ninety-nine NDOs with NSHD projects.

TABLE 8

Experience in Development Projects of Same Type as NSHD

Experience Level	Percentage of NDOs
None	30
Little	44
Substantial	12
Some, but unclear how much	4
Some in part, but not all of multifaceted project	11

Note: Based on sample of thirty NDOs.

projects but of more limited scale. In addition, the current NSHD projects are similar in type to the major kinds of projects attempted by NDOs in past development work in only about 50 percent of the cases. Most instances where projects differ from past development work involve organizations with housing experience and tradition that are taking on other types of development.

Finally, NDOs both with and without experience in their chosen types of NSHD projects are playing new roles in the development process. Some that have previously been largely project sponsors and monitors are taking on developer responsibilities as part of the NSHD project. This is true particularly for organizations that have assisted in outreach and applicant processing for government-run housing rehabilitation programs and that are now taking full control of a project. Others with developer records are doing their own construction for the first time rather than contracting it out. A number are starting the first enterprises in which they are permanent owners seeking profits. Half, including many of the organizations with some history in their chosen project type, are taking on new responsibilities in one of these or comparable ways.

In sum, when their work is assessed in project-specific terms, most of the organizations have records of programmatic accomplishment, but many of them are confronting tasks that are new, or at least hardly routine. The limited experience of many NDOs clearly suggests that these organizations are facing difficulties already resolved by more experienced developers and that they need assistance and cooperation to compensate (the implications of their limited experience are examined in detail in later chapters). The limited track records serve also as an indicator of NDO potential: Other NDOs can expect to reach the NSHD grantees' levels of experience fairly quickly, while the grantees themselves still have much room to build competence through experience.

Key Staff. Most NDOs have staffs of modest size. The median number of staff was 11 at the time of grant applications (for all development and non-development activities, excluding—to the extent possible—temporary construction crews). One-quarter of the NDOs had only 2 to 5 staff members. Only about one-fifth had staffs of 35 or more, ranging to about 200 for the largest. It should be noted, however, that many NDOs experienced substantial staff cutbacks in the later part of our study period as public funding declined. The makeup of staff in key positions is important in any organization and especially in small organizations. Following is a more detailed look at the NDOs' staffing characteristics.

Typically, the NDOs' executive directors play major roles in a wide spectrum of organization activities, if not always in day-to-day implementation of development projects. For a third of the organizations, executive directors overwhelmingly dominate in a wide range of functions— not only in broad functions such as dealing with outsiders and strategy making but in project details as well. These directors are cited, for example, as "the whole show" or "the dynamo that makes the organization go" by people who deal with them. In another third of the NDOs, executive directors are extremely strong forces, but one or more other experienced people share significant NDO responsibilities—commonly handling general administration or a particular program area. In the remaining third, directors have some key functions, but others play equally or nearly equally central roles, especially in NDOs where the directors focus their attention on outside political and fundraising contacts.

Executive directors do not necessarily have extensive knowledge about or experience with development projects—particularly in younger but also in some of the larger, more established organizations. Indeed we judged just over half of the directors to have quite limited proven capability in this specific area, although virtually without exception they were bright, talented, energetic people who were skilled in other areas. Less than a sixth clearly had considerable experience in development when their NSHD-assisted projects began. The great majority, however, had acknowledged talents in generating ideas and in garnering funds, political cooperation, and community support for such work.

In many organizations, management of development projects is delegated to project directors other than the executive director. As table 9 indicates, nearly two-thirds of the NDOs have a separate project director; and in over half of these cases the actual delegation of project responsibility is substantial. Tasks such as fundraising/outside contact often remain largely with executive directors, however. Delegation is especially common for

TABLE 9

PROJECT RESPONSIBILITY

Responsibility	Percentage of NDOs
No separate project director	37
Project director with limited responsibility	26
Project director with substantial responsibility	37

NOTE: Based on sample of thirty NDOs.

executive directors with little experience in the development field; more than three-quarters of the directors in that category have appointed project directors.[3]

Project directors highly experienced in development are not easy to attract to small, insecurely funded organizations paying modest wages. Project directors in our study (focusing again on those other than executive directors) are generally intelligent and resourceful, but more than half had only modest levels of development experience, and more than another quarter had very little at the start of NSHD work. A fifth of the original NSHD project directors were fired, and another fifth either left early voluntarily or were recruited late.

Overall, most NDOs have at least some reasonable level of proven development capability and experience residing in either the executive director, a project director, or both (and several have substantial total development skill in-house). About one-fifth apparently originally lacked such expertise on staff and presumably have had to depend heavily on rapid learning by doing and on the skills of board members, coventurers, contractors, and other sources of technical assistance.[4]

Many NDOs have some further significant development expertise on staff in addition to executive and project directors. Most common are the nearly one-third employing construction supervisors with solid construction experience (and some others without such experience). A number have apparently competent housing managers, although in some cases their skills are involved so late in projects that it was not possible for us to observe them directly. A sixth of the NDOs have separate planners, financial packagers,

3. This reflects several different conditions: executive directors who choose permanently to focus on tasks other than managing development projects; directors who recognize their inexperience but who need to bring in other technical expertise until they can gain this experience; executive directors who are overloaded with other work; and perhaps other conditions.

4. For one-tenth of sample NDOs, we are less certain: It is known that either the executive director or the project director lacked proven development capability, but we do not have clear information on one or the other of these staff members.

or production managers (nonconstruction enterprises) with good skills.[5] In general, however, staff with financial project-planning skills are in short supply (as detailed in the next part of the chapter).

In sum, the vast majority of the NDOs in our study are headed by strong, able executive directors; but many of these leaders, by design or circumstance, have limited experience in carrying out development projects. Many delegate substantial project responsibilities to project directors, who more often than the executive director have at least modest development-project records. Collectively, these project directors and other staff have some significant skills for and experience in development projects in most NDOs. Nevertheless, experienced staff is generally thin, and skills are focused particularly in the construction end of development work. These summary statements notwithstanding, sharp variations exist among the individual organizations, variations whose importance for project performance is examined in chapter 4. Next is a review of specific skills possessed by NDOs for putting a project together.

Homework, Financial Analysis, and Short-Term Planning. Much important work in development projects consists of clearly laying out what work is to be done and the steps in implementation, determining project feasibility given various constraints, and communicating this information to other actors, particularly potential funding sources. The NDOs again differed sharply in their initial capability to accomplish these tasks. More than a third are well-skilled in proposal writing. However, another quarter are weak in this area (at least until NSHD funds allowed some staff expansion), and most of the latter use substantial outside assistance in drafting proposals.

Project planning—laying out in advance the project steps and the co-ordinated means to accomplish them—is a difficult capability to assess. In NDOs where it was possible to judge this component, a third of the organizations show strong combinations of skill in and attention to project planning, while two-thirds either show weaknesses in project planning or initially underestimated the importance of such tasks.

Especially lacking in the NDOs' staff planning ability is skill in analyzing financial feasibility of projects, determining the financing and other conditions needed to make projects workable, and outlining business plans and marketing strategies. Two-thirds of the NDOs for which we have clear assessments lack appreciable staff expertise in financial planning and marketing, and many fail to understand its value. Some NDOs have little specific knowledge about components of financial projections—for example, the cost elements of a given type of project or the initial capital required. A good number could

---

5. This includes partial overlap with NDOs that have construction managers as well.

neither develop a project pro forma on their own, including estimating costs and revenues over time, nor determine the financing terms necessary to make their projects viable. Moreover, few of the NDOs have specific skill in identifying or attracting customers.

The NDOs exhibit much greater capability in seeking project funding, in clearly presenting their intentions, and in following up with appropriate lobbying or responses to requests for further information. These skills have been noted for a majority of the NDOs, by people both inside and outside the organizations; for none of the NDOs were these considered major weaknesses.[6] In fact, several organizations were originally created primarily for the purposes of tracking the availability of financial resources and increasing their flow to specific neighborhoods, and they therefore excel in this role.

Overall, it is not surprising to find NDOs stronger in homework tasks requiring care, commitment, intelligence, and willingness to learn than in tasks requiring technical skill in finance and business that are generally founded in extensive development experience. Notably, some NDOs recognize their skill deficits in this area and are actively seeking technical assistance and strengthening in-house skills.

Management.   How do NDOs organize themselves to carry out development projects (as well as their other work), and what abilities do they bring to management tasks? These questions proved relatively difficult to address from site visits, which although extensive, gave limited opportunities to directly observe staff interactions, meetings of staff and consultants, and so forth. To make our description of management more concrete, information was gathered on a series of specific management components.

In general management approach, NDOs, like other organizations, vary significantly by size. Those with few staff and programs typically operate informally, with staff members attaining a good sense of where each project stands and lending a hand (or ideas) as needed. A major project or a major crisis in a project can command the full attention of an entire staff at least temporarily. As NDOs grow, they divide responsibilities among staff more rigidly, either by project or by project tasks or components (for example, in the latter case, housing rehabilitation versus housing management in the same set of buildings). The largest NDOs are more often comprised of divisions along these component lines, although usually certain designated individuals nonetheless had responsibilities for overall projects.

---

6. Some NDOs did, nonetheless, have troubled relationships with some important funders, especially local government.

Executive directors almost uniformly maintain prime (often sole) responsibility for outside contacts, while parceling out project implementation responsibilities. Logically, responsibility is often delegated more extensively when talented deputies and second-level managers can be found and/or trained, although the preferences of executive directors are also important determinants.[7] As indicated earlier, two-thirds of the NDOs have separate directors for their NSHD-aided projects, and most of these directors have substantial overall project control. Most organizations manage adequately to divide NSHD project responsibilities among project staffers. We have no clear findings about coordination of work through staff meetings and other mechanisms, except that staff meetings were neglected in some NDOs where key staff were overworked.

Overloading lead staff is a common management problem for NDOs. In a third of the organizations, either the executive director, NSHD project director, or both, clearly had more work and responsibility than he or she could fully keep up with over the long term. These managers were usually aware of the problem but felt that it was unsolvable.

An important way for NDOs to deal with staff shortages and gaps in staff technical experience is to work with technical-assistance providers, contractors, and coventurers; and many NDOs did so. In general, they manage and control these relationships effectively, often developing productive, continuing interactions. Over two-thirds of our observations showed good or (less often) at least adequate success in managing these arrangements. The process was smoothed by the fact that many sources of technical skill were eager to work with the NDOs, because they shared NDO objectives and specialized in serving community-based organizations.

Finally, proper financial accounting and reporting are necessary parts of successful management. Although their bookkeeping/accounting staffs are sometimes limited in formal training, over three-quarters of study NDOs have adequate or strong financial reporting capabilities in-house. A number of the rest farm out these tasks, with some loss in timeliness and flexibility but not in meeting basic requirements. In a few cases, however, inattention to careful recordkeeping practice put NDOs in exposed positions when questions arose. Also, many organizations with financial reporting adequate to meet funder requirements have limited ability to generate and use financial information in budgeting/managing their own operations.

On balance, study NDOs generally handle several elements of management well—delegating and dividing responsibilities, using technical assis-

---

7. In one large, well-staffed NDO, the executive director retained prime responsibility for all major projects and delegated project component tasks.

TABLE 10

PREDOMINANT COMPOSITION OF BOARD OF DIRECTORS

Composition	Percentage of NDOs
Neighborhood residents	44
Neighborhood residents and employees of local business agencies	23
Neighborhood residents and civic/professional people	18
Citywide professional and technical people	14

NOTE: Based on sample of thirty NDOS.

tance and contractors, and making basic financial reports. But a number lack the means to protect key staff from overload; and they are not as yet regular users of financial information in internal management processes. More visible management inadequacies might arise as NDOs grow in scale, but a shortage of resources for expanded staffing and project financing may remain more pressing problems in many instances.

Board of Directors. NDO staff in our study by no means operated in isolation. NDO boards of directors actively participated in revitalization projects and general organizational affairs as community representatives and contributors of skill and effort.

These boards are to a great extent based in NDOs' local neighborhoods. Two-thirds of the NDOs have boards comprised predominantly of neighborhood residents or, less often, of neighborhood residents and representatives of local businesses and social agencies (see table 10). Nearly another fifth mix representation of residents and civic/professional groups, and in many of those cases some members of the latter groups work or live in the NDO's neighborhood as well. Only a few boards are dominated by professional and technical people chosen on a more citywide basis. Board selection is balanced between election by the membership and election by the board itself (with several cases involving a mixture). In most organizations with significant representation from outside the neighborhood, some or all of the directors are chosen by the board.

The roles that boards play and the extent of their involvement are diverse. In a minority of cases, board functions are limited; for a fifth of the NDOs, board participation is largely ceremonial or passive. This situation is most often produced purposely by executive directors who feel that broad organizational goals have been long-since articulated and shaped by community sentiment and that staff, who are more expert and closer to ongoing NDO operations, should be left to pursue programs within that outline. In another sixth of the organizations, boards play a policy-setting role but not an active, forceful one. This occurs mostly in younger organizations where board members have little experience with or expertise in board functions.

But in over 60 percent of the NDOs, board members assume at least one and often several active and valuable roles. Two-fifths of all boards make important contributions in the areas of fundraising, lobbying, and providing contacts and credibility. Also in two-fifths of the organizations, board members play policy-setting and project-defining roles—for example, considering whether to accept or reject staff proposals for new projects, determining policy in cooperation with the executive director (usually by small boards of mostly long-standing members), and taking an active interest in narrower issues such as what kinds of tenants or activities will be included in a development project.

In close to a third of study NDOs, we find "working boards." Some of these are involved in actual project implementation on a day-to-day basis, while others supply major technical assistance in planning and analyzing projects and preparing proposals.[8] But more organizations are short on board technical expertise than benefit heavily from it. Finally, in nearly half of all organizations, the boards' participation is important in two or often three of the areas discussed earlier.

Generally, staff and board members are able to share work and responsibility harmoniously. Most of the NDOs that discussed board-staff relations with us have no problems, and many report effective, supportive relations and common views on how responsibilities should be divided. Often such positive relations were based upon board confidence in the executive director. Two organizations we visited had conflicts between the board and the executive director, resulting in one instance in the firing of the director and in the other in the changing of the board. In a few other cases, some board members have substantial concerns that staff were promoting too much dominance of development over other NDO activities, with accompanying rising staff salaries and NDO indebtedness.

Given the typical NDO's limited resources, a board of directors can contribute measurably to an organization's total capabilities, especially if the board compensates in areas where other actors are weak. Since most NDO boards are active in one area or another, the potential for such complementarity is substantial. But as is pointed out later in this book, it is necessary to nurture board participation in order to realize such benefits.

---

8. Of course, assisting in making financial contacts, doing day-to-day implementation tasks, and so forth may all be considered technical assistance as well.

Spin-offs and Other Organizational Structures. In the course of their work, NDOs create new organizational structures that either become independent from or remain linked to the NDO in varying degrees. The purposes of these spin-offs may be to give additional community people opportunities for control or influence; to separate types of activities in order to reduce participants' concerns that one activity will crowd out or conflict with another; or to retain control over new functions without losing nonprofit tax advantages. Among NDOs in the study, most were without complicated structures prior to their NSHD projects, but a fair number developed some kind of spin-off in the context of the project. In the early stages, however, these arrangements had limited impact on project functioning.

More specifically, at the time they began the NSHD projects, nearly two-thirds of the NSHD-grantee organizations had neither subsidiaries nor other spin-offs, nor were they spin-offs of other organizations. Another eighth had previously created only organizationally independent structures (housing and other cooperatives and separate human-service agencies). These latter NDOs provided contractual services to but did not control the independent organizations, which at any rate had no part in NSHD projects. On the other hand, a sixth of the NDOs already had subsidiaries (primarily construction or other development corporations) that were to be involved in NSHD-supported work. These structures were far more heavily controlled by the leadership of NSHD grantees, with boards that overlapped with NDO boards and staff. In one extreme case, the grantee is a board of directors only, and its subsidiary development arm runs the NSHD project, with part of the work carried out by that subsidiary's controlled spin-off. All of these various prior organizational arrangements showed no sharp effects on project work.

As mentioned, a substantial group of NDOs created new structures in the course of the NSHD projects. About one-fifth are spinning off cooperatives (all but one in housing) to give the direct participants ownership and control through their own boards; in several instances, the initiating NDOs will continue to provide management or other services to the cooperatives. One-sixth are creating for-profit or nonprofit subsidiaries, mostly as new job-generating enterprises. With the for-profit case, one apparent purpose is to preserve nonprofit status for the parent organizations, while allowing flexibility in profit-earning potential for the subsidiaries. (It is important for NDOs to retain their eligibility to receive foundation grants and tax-deductible contributions from other sources. For-profit subsidiaries can undertake surplus-generating business activities whose operation by NDOs themselves might jeopardize that "charitable" status.) Another purpose of establishing subsidiaries is to relieve parent boards (and to some extent staff) of the necessity of dealing with the specifics of enterprise operations, while creating more technically oriented subsidiary boards. In many instances the board and staff overlap between parents and subsidiaries is substantial, however, and some problems of staff overload have remained or intensified. Except for some parent-board tension about the appropriateness of profit seeking, few other problems were triggered by these new arrangements, at least as of our last site visits.

Planning. In addition to project-specific planning described earlier, NDOs develop broader plans for their neighborhoods, they choose strategies to accomplish them, and they select their proposed NSHD projects on the basis of those plans and strategies. The brief discussion here of the planning and project selection processes is limited somewhat by the fact that often important elements of broader planning either long precede or are separate from the NSHD project activities themselves.

Only a minority (perhaps one-third) of the NDOs have in recent years worked through major neighborhood planning processes. Some of these efforts have been elaborate, involving neighborhood residents and staff in assessing current conditions, in defining pressing needs, and in identifying specific targets of project opportunity. And several NDOs have long-range (three to five years) and one-year plans that they update regularly. More common than the elaborate processes are organizations that annually have retreats or at least extended meetings of board and staff members, in which the past year's activities are reviewed and broad directions and specific projects addressed for the coming year. But for many NDOs, ideas proposed by the executive director, board chairpersons, or key outsiders (technical aid or funding sources) serve for the processes of broad planning and of identifying project possibilities.

Regardless of the nature of the planning processes, the great majority of NDOs in the study have a well-understood revitalization focus or strategy. These strategies and the relation of NSHD projects to them are discussed separately in chapter 3.

Specific selection of projects is most often made principally by key staff, who identify opportunities within the outlines of revitalization strategies and submit suggestions to the board for review (see also previous discussion in this chapter under "Board of Directors"). Feasibility studies were performed in a number of cases in order to judge project potential or to compare alternative project sites. But more often project intents were previously developed or developing; and NSHD funds, sometimes together with coincidental, simultaneous availability of buildings, became part of the means to achieve them. In general, most of the NDOs do limited formal planning but have clearly delineated primary lines of work within which they hatch project ideas and pursue opportunities.

NDO Relationships with Their Communities and with Outsiders

NDOs, by necessity and design, draw heavily on outside resources to conduct development projects in their own neighborhoods. As has just been pointed out, many NDOs lack certain skills and expertise within their organizations (for reasons that include their desire to hire local residents and their inability to attract or pay for staff with extensive experience). Like other developers, they seldom can finance development projects internally and must seek loans and grants from outside sources—funds that are often repaid or reused (on a revolving basis) in other work but only over time. In many cases NDOs have as their central objectives, indeed their reasons for being, the bringing of additional resources to their long-neglected communities. Another of their central objectives is to involve local residents in decisions and actions that affect them.

For these reasons, NDOs' relations with outside actors who provide local participation, technical assistance, and financing are a critical factor in their abilities to perform their chosen development role. Like internal characteristics, relations with other actors are of special interest because they can to a significant degree be controlled or modified through the efforts of NDOs and their supporters. They can therefore be targets for policy and action, given an adequate understanding of the current quality of relations with outsiders and the importance of these relations to NDO success. Also like internal characteristics, relations with outside actors serve as indicators of NDO limitations and of areas of needed growth. The paragraphs that follow describe the nature and source of these relations at the time NSHD work began and look ahead to their potential importance in project performance (the latter is analyzed in depth in chapter 4).

Resident Support and Involvement.   The participation of neighborhood residents in multiple roles as board members, as voluntary contributors of direct labor and counsel, as paid employees at all levels, and in shows of support for organizations' activities is a central part of the work of NDOs. Residents' efforts on boards of directors were discussed earlier in this chapter; other self-help activities, which were an explicit goal of NSHD grants, are described in detail in chapter 3 as part of project outcomes; and the value of this participation to specific projects is analyzed in chapter 4 along with other factors in NDO success. The overall extent of cooperation NDOs enjoy from their communities is briefly noted here.

Community residents generally support NDOs' overall programs, and in many instances demonstrations of that broad support have been useful to NDO work. Two-thirds of NDOs enjoy strong support in their communities. Most of the rest have either broad but less active support (general approval but limited participation) or mixed support (often reflecting concern about personnel decisions or board-staff clannishness from a segment of the community). Only one organization in fifteen seemed in need of major improvements in its relations with the community.

Approval and participation seem to derive most often from the ability of NDOs to deliver benefits—housing, jobs, services—both directly and by pressuring others. But support is often dependent upon community organizing skills, past and present. Active support fell off in several cases when NDOs turned from advocacy to complex development projects. Indeed, the effort needed to maintain broad community contact and participation may not be readily sustainable while NDOs tackle development complexities. Visible project progress can help to retain community approval, but direct resident involvement in the NDO may suffer unless it is built into projects themselves.

As is detailed later in this book, community support is essential to NDO work—in obtaining funds, political cooperation, and volunteer labor—and can represent an important resource to help balance other NDO limitations and constraints.

Technical Assistance.   Approximately three-quarters of NDOs in the study were receiving major technical assistance for their NSHD projects by the time of our first visits. *Major* here means one of two things. Either the technical assistance supplies specific essential skills that were substantially or totally missing from an NDO's own staff; or the aid provider and the NDO establish a continuing consulting relationship that over time influences many aspects of the project's planning and implementation. As detailed earlier, many NDOs are limited in size and experience and do not incorporate on staff the full range of expertise needed for project development. Study observations show that NDOs attempt to fill many significant gaps in their own expertise with help from outside.

Technical assistance is defined broadly here to include the work of building contractors and other members of a development team, as well as that of outsiders in more advisory roles. Services from contractors, architects, and engineers are among the most common types of major technical assistance for the sample projects. Other technical advisors provided aid in project proposal writing, planning, and packaging; in project general management, reporting, and accounting; in additional aspects of project implementation such as real estate acquisition and management; and in organizational structuring, particularly the shaping of boards of directors and legal spin-offs. Each of these services is discussed in detail later.

Nearly all of the NDOs that receive no major project technical assistance nonetheless get project aid of a more minor type—either to supplement similar skills already present on staff or to bring unique skills to a secondary aspect of their project. Bookkeeper training, limited construction advice from materials suppliers, and guidance from solar energy or housing cooperative specialists on broader housing projects are examples of aid in these categories.

It is important to note that an NDO's use of major technical assistance need not indicate any internal shortcoming, particularly when the assistance provider is a building contractor, architect, engineer, or other development team member. Many successful, fully qualified private developers also obtain these services from the outside, because of the small scale of their needs in these fields or for simplicity in their own operations. Nor is this type of technical assistance appropriately sought from members of NDO boards of directors, except on an occasional advisory basis. The large commitment of time and resources required from development team members in most cases precludes using volunteers to provide these services. As with private developers, if the NDO adequately manages its development team, the strategy of hiring outsiders often makes good business sense. The same may be true for other specialized technical services in accounting or law. On the other hand, with some kinds of technical assistance, NDOs seek actively to internalize the skills in order to improve their own continuing project development capabilities. Many also prefer ultimately to do their own construction, in order to increase their control over employment and training opportunities, costs, and revenues.

Types of technical assistance.   Overall, all but one of the NDOs used technical assistance (major or minor) in connection with the NSHD projects, and many used multiple types.[9] One of the two most frequent forms of technical assistance (used by 50 percent of all NDOs) was advice, often on a continuing counsel basis, in outlining the steps in a development project and then in managing their actual implementation. The common use of this area of aid by NDOs reflects their limited development experience.

Equally common was contracting out for development team tasks. Half of the NDOs purchased outside architectural and engineering services, and two-thirds of those also contracted out for new construction or rehabilitation

---

9. We are deliberately focusing on technical assistance connected to the projects under study, rather than on assistance for general organization purposes or assistance linked to other NDO projects and programs; but some overlap is unavoidable.

work itself.[10] Other predevelopment and development assistance was obtained in relation to acquiring and syndicating properties; rental and cooperative housing management; marketing; and advice, workshops, or tool loans in the conduct of housing rehabilitation work. One-third of the NDOs received three or more of these types of technical assistance, sometimes from the same source.

Nearly half of the NDOs also received help in making fundraising contacts and/or obtained "inside information" about the kinds of activities foundations and other funders were likely to support. Such assistance generally is provided by board members who are in academia, local politics, the larger business community, and even city agencies in a few cases. The desire to develop these linkages is often a factor in the selection of new board members.

Accounting assistance—usually from private accounting firms or individual certified public accountants (CPAs)—was used by two-fifths of the NDOs during their NSHD projects. The work of these outside accountants included conducting annual audits, preparing annual financial reports for boards of directors, designing accounting procedures and journals for new spin-off organizations, and redesigning existing NDO accounting systems to meet reporting requirements of multiple funding services or multiple projects. In a few cases, accountants also assisted less experienced NDOs with budgeting and general contract reporting. In most instances, accounting assistance was sought by NDOs as a precautionary measure to avoid potential reporting and audit problems, from sources who gave periodic aid over several years as NDO accounting needs changed.

Legal counsel was used for one-fourth of the NSHD projects, often to accomplish a particular project task—for example, overseeing a complicated land transaction or drawing up incorporation papers for a development spin-off from a parent organization. In other cases, tax-law attorneys were hired to evaluate NDOs' assessments of potential for private-sector investment or syndication of properties, as well as alternative ways to structure construction company spin-offs.

One-fifth of the NDOs received proposal-writing assistance, usually specifically for the NSHD grant proposal. The scope of this assistance varied widely. A technical-assistance organization in a limited role simply reviewed

---

10. Note that even at the time of second visits to sites, not all projects had proceeded to construction, and it had not always been determined whether construction work would ultimately be contracted out. Original expectations for the full population of ninety-nine NDOs were that the organizations would split nearly evenly between those doing their own general contracting and those acting only as sponsor and developer. Even those acting as their own contractor often subcontracted specialized tasks. Three of the ninety-nine NDOs were sponsors only, it appears.

a proposal written by NDO staff. But in another case, a consultant largely designed an NDO project, wrote the NSHD proposal, and trained the executive director and staff in planning and directing the project's future.

About one-quarter of the NDOs received assistance in designing board structure and composition appropriate to the NDO's project role and resources, in training the board regarding its role, and/or in staffing the NDO specifically for the NSHD project. Such assistance was typically used by NDOs that were developing spin-off organizations, were relatively inexperienced in the development role to be assumed under the NSHD project, or had encountered major board-staff problems that a major funding source demanded be resolved through changes in board composition.

Clearly, technically skilled outsiders frequently took on substantial responsibilities in NSHD projects and related work. As is emphasized in chapter 4, their contributions (or lack thereof) were highly important to project progress.

Technical-assistance sources.   Who provides NDOs' technical aid? Overall, the thirty sample NDOs alone received technical assistance from more than one hundred providers, nearly 60 percent of whom were private individuals, firms, or banks and savings and loan associations. As already indicated, half of the NDOs brought private building contractors, architects, and/or engineers to their development team; and most of these, plus a handful of other NDOs, obtained other types of major technical assistance from the private sector.

Members of their own boards of directors provided technical assistance to about half of the NDOs, accounting for approximately 12 percent of the technical-assistance providers. The most important technical (that is, non-policymaking) contributions of board members to NSHD projects have been of two kinds: providing contacts with potential funding sources and providing direct assistance in such areas as accounting or construction-bidding procedures, when tasks were not so large that they required paid expertise.

Organizations that function primarily as nonprofit technical-assistance providers—for example, the Center for Community Change and the Support Center at the national level, and public-interest law firms and others locally—gave technical assistance to a third of the NDOs, accounting for approximately 10 percent of the assistance providers. Their assistance was directed toward numerous aspects of the NDOs' projects, as well as general organizational needs—project planning and proposal writing, reporting, accounting-system design, organizational structure and board training, and overall project management.

For a quarter of the NDOs, local government agencies—usually the local community development office—provided technical assistance for NSHD projects. Most commonly, city assistance was in the areas of land acquisition; building inspections; project planning and packaging; and attracting the participation of the Local Initiatives Support Corporation (LISC), banks, and others from the larger business community. For most NDOs, city technical aid is limited to one or a few of these areas. But local government can also assume an extremely active role. One NDO, for example, relied heavily on its community development department to break through red tape and to provide more specific assistance in several aspects of a housing rehabilitation project. In that case, the fact that the city provided a full-time liaison with the NDO for the project helped compensate for the lack of expertise in physical development on the NDO's staff and board.

Private foundations and state and federal funding sources are generally not major sources of technical assistance. Rarely, when one or two funders provided the bulk of continuing NDO monies, these actors lent staff to NDOs for detailed project planning and broader organizational consulting purposes. Of course, these sources also frequently provide the funds that allow other assistance to be sought.

NDOs in our study seldom used other neighborhood-based organizations for technical assistance, because the NSHD grantees are often better equipped than their counterparts to do development work. However, two NSHD grantees in the study sample are obtaining major assistance from other NDOs. One is patterning part of its housing rehabilitation project on another NDO's successful model, adopting specific procedures for its own use and channeling much of its local funding through the experienced NDO. Another NSHD grantee, though itself highly competent, has long relied on the financial-packaging expertise of a well-regarded and more experienced community development corporation for help with financing and syndications, and especially access to banks for private lending.

It is important to note that NDOs are by and large *buyers* of technical services. And since they are heavy users of technical aid, substantial funds are required for this purpose. Given the types of assistance used most frequently, the service is often needed early in the project, when it is less likely to be paid for out of project implementation loans and grants. Funding to purchase outside expertise thus deserves separate consideration by NDO supporters in shaping financial assistance.

Nearly 60 percent of NDOs in the sample do report receiving at least part of their assistance free, most commonly from or through board members (in NDOs that actively seek board members who have technical expertise or contacts with those who do). Free assistance also came from nonprofit providers whose overall work was paid for by foundation, labor union, and government sources, and directly from government and foundations. In addition, small contractors and private-sector professionals often either did not charge for every task performed for an NDO or charged below-market rate fees. NDOs can likely improve their access to low-cost aid by attracting skilled board participants and by fostering links to other such providers. Outsiders might usefully consider in-kind expertise as a form of support.

Relations with Funding Sources.   In general, NDOs intended to finance their projects with substantial funds beyond their NSHD grants. Because few NDOs are major generators of internal surpluses, they—like other developers—must find sources of outside support and investment. Establishing working relations with public- and private-sector actors to ensure an adequate flow of funds was a fundamental task for all organizations in our study. NDOs' relations with local, state, and federal governments and with private foundations and the business world are described in the paragraphs following. The manner in which these relationships might affect nonfinancial cooperation from the same sources is also discussed.

Local government.   Given local governments' potential roles in funding, approving, and assisting NDO projects, building and maintaining strong bonds to the local public sector are important elements of NDOs' effort to establish relations with outside actors. Most of the NDOs did exhibit these good relations. At the start of their NSHD grants,[11] approximately two-thirds of the NDOs, including several that were not expecting city funding for NSHD projects, appeared to have positive relationships with both elected officials (mayors and city councils) and pertinent departments of their local government. Positive relations with elected officials were most often based on NDOs demonstrating their ability to campaign for officials and bring neighborhood voters to the polls (provided these candidates were successful). Many elected representatives were eager to exchange cooperation for future electoral support. But in other instances, relations were built on credibility generated by NDOs' clear presentations of proposed projects, good track records with past projects, and success in gaining noncity funds in competitive circumstances.

The best relations with local community development offices and other city departments were developed when NDO executive directors consciously nurtured them, rather than relying on a supportive city council to pressure city departments into funding or other assistance. In general, NDOs tried to gradually build a track record and staff skills that would demonstrate to city

---

11. Study observations are likely biased upward from overall NDO experience by the NSHD program requirement that an NDO city's mayor must certify its project as consistent with city goals.

departments their ability to complete projects successfully and to handle money. They also worked at developing good interpersonal relationships with city personnel, expressing their interest in a mutually supportive partnership by means such as sharing project plans at an early stage and asking for city staff advice. These relationships commonly depend on the NDO executive directors (a nonabrasive personality is cited as key). Not unexpectedly, both elected officials and city staff also prefer to work with NDOs whose membership and organization use technical and legal avenues to bring about change rather than adopting confrontational strategies—though that does not mean an NDO's greatest impact necessarily lies in cooperation.

At the start of the NSHD projects, a sixth of the NDOs in the study had good relations with either local elected officials *or* city departments but not both. As is seen in chapter 4, links of both kinds have implications for NDO success. Another one-sixth had generally poor relations with their local governments as a whole, in most cases because of the hostility of mayors they had unsuccessfully opposed in recent elections or the indifference of those who viewed them as politically powerless.

State and federal government. Relatively little information was obtained in study interviews about the quality of NDO ties to state and federal funders, although the majority of study organizations anticipated funding from one or both sources for NSHD projects. Of the NDOs that discussed their state and federal relationships with some specificity, more than half had developed very good relations prior to their NSHD projects. How these long-term relations initially evolved is often somewhat unclear, but it appears that both track records and political contacts were important over the years. Several NDOs were former recipients of planning grants from HUD's Office of Neighborhood Development or had conducted previous HUD-funded projects. And, in terms of political support, some NDOs pointed to the role taken by their local governments and by their representatives in Congress to push through Urban Development Action Grants (UDAGs), Section 202 funds, or other federal funds that appeared stuck in the pipeline. Several NDOs had established a solid track record with state finance and development agencies, proving their ability to handle money and complete a project by successfully using a small loan or grant prior to the NSHD project.

Track records and political clout certainly provide no guarantees of funding, however. For example, one organization with a good record and a personal link to the Economic Development Administration (EDA) and to other agencies expected project funding that evaporated with EDA budget freezes and reductions. Another NDO was grateful to its city council and to its representative in Congress for active aid in the funding process, but it still took two years after an initial fund reservation to pry housing construction money from an uncooperative HUD office.

Like NDO relationships with local government, links at state and federal levels are changeable. For several NDOs, relations deteriorated during the early months of NSHD work, as a result of both external factors—for example, a political disagreement with an influential state senator—and internal ones— for example, inadequate fiscal management and accounting that resulted in an audit and a funding freeze. Another NDO made substantial staff changes to "get off probation" with a major federal funding source.

The private sector.   Overall, relationships between NDOs and the private sector seem positive but limited. Most of the NDOs for which we have information in this regard were on good terms with the private actors that were actively involved in their projects. But many NDOs seem to lack sub- stantial contact with other private actors whose participation could be valuable, and they have difficulty, moreover, creating new links of certain kinds.

In particular, NDOs often have good relations with neighborhood busi- nesses—such as suppliers of rehabilitation materials who give discounts and credit or local business operators who offer limited technical advice—and perhaps, also, with a fairly important charitable foundation. Most NDOs were working well with businesses that are major participants in their development projects—building contractors, partners or joint venturers, sources of tech- nical assistance, and clients. Although few NDOs relied on foundations as primary sources of project funds, many had some foundation support for projects or general administration. Many also anticipated major project fi- nancing from private lenders, and a few had corporate grants (though not for NSHD work). But, generally, relations with bankers and large-scale, influ- ential firms in the business community have been more difficult to establish. In a substantial number of cases, NDOs have recognized the desirability of involving business community leaders in a continuing way. Other NDOs, however, have shunned including private businesspeople on their boards or cultivating ongoing relations with technically and professionally trained out- siders, out of concern that community control over NDO work would be sharply reduced. Only a few NDOs had generally poor relations with the business community at the start of their NSHD project that led to problems; nevertheless, many NDOs had not fully exploited the benefits of working with private actors and were therefore missing out on valuable relationships.

Relations with the various categories of private-sector actors typically develop in differing ways. Neighborhood businesspeople are often attracted in much the same way as neighborhood residents—out of concern for their shared environment. Building contractors, partners, and customers or clients condition their participation on NDOs' businesslike attitude and performance and on direct economic advantages to them; and most actors of these types, many of whom are new participants in NDO projects, see long-term possibilities for continuing involvement.

Foundations, which often have already established relationships with the NDOs, look heavily to evidence of community support and to a track record. Lenders' participation was frequently encouraged by the Community Reinvestment Act to loan in NDOs' neighborhoods, as well as by the related advocacy work done by coalitions of community groups. In fulfilling their community obligations, lenders were interested in working with organizations with positive records of accomplishment. Sound ties with lenders and other major businesses in NSHD projects also generally required that some active project participants have reasonable financial expertise and that the way be smoothed in part by local government officials, board members with business contacts, or similar contacts.

In general, then, NDOs had good relations with the public sector at all levels and with foundations and certain local business actors, providing a basis for tapping these sources for financial assistance and other cooperation. The best relations were based on deliberate efforts by the NDOs to establish them and, except for new organizations, on NDOs' records of performance. Although political and other events outside NDO control heavily affect these relations, NDOs also have substantial room to shape their own connections to funders.

Summary of NDO Characteristics

Although the clearest generalization we can make about the NDOs we observed is that their characteristics vary substantially, a number of summary statements are warranted. These organizations, in setting out to gather needed resources for difficult projects in difficult circumstances, are mostly of modest scale and are far from luxuriously funded. The NDOs generally come to their tasks with important capabilities—primary among these are a strong executive director, at least some development experience, and support (in varying forms) from board members and neighborhood residents. But many have significant limitations as well. Their experience and technical skills are in most cases neither broad nor extensive. As a result, NDOs regularly face the problems inherent in undertaking projects new to them. And they have some specific weaknesses in the areas of financial-feasibility analysis, marketing, and business planning.

NDOs draw frequently on technical assistance—from board members, other neighborhood people, and outsiders—to supplement their internal capacities. They regularly employ outsiders both for continuing counsel and for specialized expertise. They have, in addition, developed continuing positive relationships with key sources of outside funding, without which most of their development projects would be impossible (even with the aid of NSHD grants), and have made connections with other development partners as well. But their links to some major elements of the private sector could well be strengthened in order to increase access to both technical and financial aid and cooperation.

Overall, we can expect NDOs to confront some problems with NSHD projects as a result of their limited resources, skills, and experience. But we can also see basic strengths for them to draw upon and potential for growth and improved performance. Both now and in the near future, NDOs clearly have ample needs for many kinds of assistance and cooperation, with which they might well produce much expanded results.

In terms of the dimensions just summarized, and in many other areas as well, individual NDOs differ markedly from each other. Moreover, specific strengths and weaknesses exist in a myriad of combinations. A major purpose in chapters 4 and 5 is to examine how those differences influence NDO performance and growth, given due regard for the environments in which the organizations function.

NDO Cities and Neighborhoods

In what kinds of local environments do NDOs perform their work? Study NDOs operate in a diversity of urban locations that nevertheless exhibit important consistencies from the viewpoints of assessing NDO performance and of shaping and supporting NDO efforts. The greatest number of NSHD grant recipients are located in heavily populated, older cities of the Northeast (see table 11). The rest are about evenly divided across the three other regions of the country as defined by the U.S. Bureau of the Census—the North Central region, the West, and the South (table 11). About half are from cities with populations of less than 500,000; the others are split between cities with under and those with over 1 million inhabitants (see table 12). The study NDOs are fairly evenly distributed along racial and ethnic lines—among neighborhoods with primarily black, Hispanic, and white populations and those with no predominant group (labeled "mixed" in table 13)—though largely black or largely white neighborhoods are somewhat more common.[12] The neighborhoods vary widely in density and in their split between rental and owner-occupied housing.

A factor common to the neighborhoods in which study NDOs function is the high level of likely problems they present to anyone trying to carry out development projects, and especially projects designed to benefit low- and moderate-income residents. In terms of the thirty NDOs in our study sample, for which we were better able to assess local environments, about half operate in neighborhoods where conditions for residents and businesses are clearly as trying as, or often substantially more trying than, anywhere else in the same city.[13] Poverty, unemployment, deteriorated and abandoned housing, a

TABLE 11

NDO PROJECTS BY CENSUS REGION

Census Regions[a]	Number of NDO Projects in Region
Northeast	44
North Central	23
West	15
South	17
Total	99

NOTE: Based on all ninety-nine NDOs with NSHD projects.

a. U.S. Bureau of the Census.

TABLE 12

NDO CITY SIZE

City Population	Number of NDOs
Less than 500,000	48
500,000–1 million	23
More than 1 million	28
Total	99

NOTE: Based on all ninety-nine NDOs with NSHD projects.

12. The tables describe the full population of study NDOs. The distribution of the sample of thirty NDOs is similar, but somewhat more sample NDOs are in small cities and fewer in very large ones.

13. We did not try to systematically quantify neighborhood conditions in this study. Census Bureau data were not yet available for 1980; 1970 data were badly out of date; and the variety of special-study information provided by NDOs in their applications could not be reasonably compiled and made consistent. We relied, instead, on the observations of knowledgeable observers and on our own direct, on-site observations.

TABLE 13

PRIMARY RACE OF PROJECT NEIGHBORHOOD

Primary Race	Number of Neighborhoods
Black	32
Hispanic	17
White	27
Other	3
Mixed[a]	20
Total	99

NOTE: Based on all ninety-nine NDOs with NSHD projects.

a. No single group constitutes more than 50 percent of the neighborhood population.

diminishing population often of advancing age, and declining or vacated commercial strips all characterize these neighborhoods. Many buildings would require major investment to be returned even to a safe, usable condition. Vandalism, theft, and, in a smaller number of cases, arson are serious threats to people and property. Social problems—including alcoholism, drug abuse, and mental illness—are common. A significant share of these neighborhoods are likely among the most troubled in the nation.

Many of the remaining half of the organizations work in areas that most Americans would describe as seriously troubled as well, containing many low-income residents, especially the elderly; often at least some vacant, boarded housing; and the like.

Less than a quarter of the organizations' neighborhoods are notably less deteriorated, showing stronger markets for housing in particular. In some of these instances and others as well, displacement of neighborhood residents by private revitalization or public investment is perceived as a serious threat in part or all of the neighborhood. Overall, for about two-fifths of our NDOs, gentrification/displacement is considered a near- or longer-term problem.

A strong indicator of the difficulty of undertaking the kinds of projects these NDOs pursue is the lack of comparable activity by other actors in the same neighborhoods. We had originally considered comparing conduct of NDO projects with that of other similar work in the same area, but we found no sufficiently similar undertaking at any of the sites to support such an analysis. In some neighborhoods little or no other investment was taking place; in others, there were no projects of the type the NDO chose (for example, there was residential rehabilitation but no commercial revitalization); and in still others, non-NDO investments served only higher-income populations in the same area. In addition, major public investments in several of these neighborhoods historically worked at cross-purposes with NDO goals:

most commonly, highway and street projects demolished neighborhood homes or isolated them from other parts of the city. Urban renewal projects in a few neighborhoods produced far more demolition than construction.

Unquestionably, the neighborhood conditions in which NDOs carry out their work will have strong impacts on their records of project performance. The specific impacts of these conditions are discussed in chapter 4. Whatever the level of competence—of internal capability and of relations developed with others—one should obviously anticipate lower rates of success in such environments than in most other locations. And, except in the very long term, local conditions are beyond NDO control. Good public and private policy will make allowances for the harsh environments NDOs confront in assessing their performance and will seek to provide NDOs with adequate levels of capability and resources to offset the unique challenges they face.

NSHD Projects

Within the broad field of neighborhood development, what kind and scale of work did NDOs set out to accomplish in the projects we studied? To provide a proper context for later discussions on how NDO projects turned out, why they succeeded or failed, and what impacts they have in their communities, it is important to have a clear picture of NDO project intents and design. Projects, after all, do not all demand equal capabilities, are not buffeted in the same ways by environmental conditions, and cannot offer the same potential benefits.

Project Types

We classified NDOs' NSHD projects into seven categories, six of which were based on separate primary intended outputs and the seventh of which included mixtures of the six. These categories are:

- Housing rehabilitation—Repair of rental or owner-occupied housing, including in some cases resale or cooperative conversion.
- Housing construction—Building of new residential rental or owner-occupied structures, including later resale or tenant or cooperative management.
- Commercial revitalization—Improvement of neighborhood commercial areas through rehabilitation or construction of retail and office space and assistance to commercial businesses.
- Economic development—Creation of permanent jobs and strengthening of neighborhood economic bases, by developing NDO-owned

TABLE 14

PROJECT TYPES

Type of Project	Number of NDOs[a]
Housing rehabilitation	56
Housing construction	3
Commercial revitalization	8
Economic development	13
Energy	2
Community development	5
Mixed	12
Total	99

NOTE: Based on all ninety-nine NDOs with NSHD projects.

a. These numbers differ from categorization for the purpose of sample selection, in which all mixed projects were assigned to some other category, and in which some projects were assigned to categories involving their less important outputs in order to provide a larger population to choose from in categories other than housing rehabilitation.

ventures or attracting other (mostly industrial) enterprises through rehabilitation or construction of appropriate structures and other aid.

- Energy—Residential weatherization or installation of solar energy devices.
- Community development—Creation of community facilities, such as parks or community centers, by rehabilitation or construction.
- Mixed—Projects where two or more outputs are intended, with reasonably equal emphasis.

By far the dominant focus of study projects (more than half of all projects) is housing rehabilitation, as indicated in table 14. This is not surprising. NDO neighborhoods are typified by deteriorated existing housing, and rehabilitation can provide immediate, visible benefits to local residents who help create and support NDOs. In some ways housing rehabilitation projects are simpler than other development work[14] and thus are more feasible for some less sophisticated organizations.

Nonetheless, nearly 45 percent of study NDOs are taking on NSHD projects predominantly or partly in the other areas of development work. These include the twelve mixed projects, which are usually (in ten cases) a combination of housing rehabilitation and some other output types—most often new housing construction (five cases) and/or commercial revitalization (six cases).

---

14. See chapter 4 for further discussion of project difficulty levels.

A brief further look at the three largest separate project categories—housing rehabilitation, commercial revitalization, and economic development—provides useful detail about the nature of these projects. The housing rehabilitation work was about evenly split between single-family and multi-family buildings. Great emphasis was placed on resident ownership and control and on dealing with vacant properties. The vast majority of single-family projects involved NDO purchase, rehabilitation, and resale to owner-occupants of homes, the bulk of which were not in current use. Nearly half of the multifamily rehabilitation projects anticipated establishment of tenant or cooperative management. (New housing construction projects also had a major homeownership and cooperative emphasis.)

Commercial revitalization projects were planned predominantly as renovations of existing buildings for commercial use, in a mixture of contexts. In some cases, NDOs intended to purchase buildings in their neighborhoods and rehabilitate them for use by the local businesses they planned to attract. They hoped these buildings would serve as catalysts to other commercial upgrading. In other commercial revitalization projects, NDOs were to help owners of existing commercial structures and businesses with building improvements and, less frequently, with technical assistance in marketing, seeking financing, and so forth. A smaller number of organizations selected constructing new retail and/or office facilities (for their own ownership) as their NSHD project.

Three-fourths of the economic development projects were to involve creation (or, secondarily, expansion) of NDO-owned ventures. These ventures were principally companies that would do housing construction, rehabilitation, and/or maintenance in conjunction with NDO housing improvement efforts, as well as for other clients. Most of the rest of the economic development projects involved renovation of structures that NDOs would acquire and later lease to businesses moving in from outside their immediate neighborhoods.

As could be expected, NDOs' project choices tend to reflect the types of organizations they represent. Our definitions of organization type are based in large part on the past focus of NDOs' efforts, and many groups are continuing in similar directions. As outlined in table 15, nonprofit housing organizations and tenants' organizations (along with coalitions) concentrated their NSHD work in housing areas, while multipurpose and other neighborhood organizations exhibited greater project diversity. These latter groups were less likely to have prior project experience of the same type as their NSHD work. Chapter 4 examines in detail how a variety of NDO characteristics interact with chosen project types and NDO environments to help determine success or failure.

TABLE 15

PROJECT TYPE BY ORGANIZATION TYPE

Organization Type	Housing Rehabil-itation	Housing Construc-tion	Community Develop-ment	Commer-cial	Economic Develop-ment	Energy	Mixed	Total
Neighborhood organization	4	0	0	1	2	0	4	11
Nonprofit housing	32	2	2	2	3	1	4	46
Tenants' organization	2	0	0	0	0	0	1	3
Coalition	8	0	0	0	0	0	0	8
Multipurpose	10	1	3	6	7	1	3	31
Total	56	3	5	9	12	2	12	99

NOTE: Based on all ninety-nine NDOs with NSHD projects.

Project Scale and Scope

NDO projects were on the whole of moderate intended scale, although they varied widely and, because of the high costs of development work, were expected to involve substantial funds and other resources. The median planned expenditure of all types of funds was roughly $425,000. These expected costs, however, ranged from about $90,000 to nearly $20,000,000. Because a small number of projects involved very large investments, the *average* expectation was well above the median: about $1.4 million.[15] Three-quarters of all NDOs planned to raise at least twice the amount of their NSHD grants from other sources. Further data on planned expenditures are presented in chapter 3, which compares actual funding experience with NDO expectations.

As is generally true for development work, it was anticipated that NDO projects would take substantial time to complete. More than two-thirds were scheduled to last over a year from the date they received NSHD funding. NSHD grants were awarded in two cycles—fifty-seven urban awards in June 1980 and another forty-two urban awards in October 1980. Project lengths were typically longer among cycle-two grantees (see table 16). This may well reflect the fact that projects were more likely to be selected for cycle one if they were already fairly far along in planning and packaging. Grant periods for cycle-two NDOs might then be somewhat more representative of the full

---

15. This figure also includes the value that NDOs attached to self-help and in-kind contributions by themselves and others.

TABLE 16

Expected Number of Months in Grant Period by Cycle

Number of Months in Grant Period	*Number of NDOs*		
	Cycle One	*Cycle Two*	*Total*
12 or less	28	1	29
13–18	23	12	35
19–24	6	19	25
More than 24	0	10	10
Total	57	42	99

NOTE: Based on all ninety-nine NDOs with NSHD projects.

expected period of project performance from initiation of plans to project completion.[16]

What level of specific project outputs was anticipated? The planned results listed in the following paragraphs naturally give the best indication of intended project scale. In interpreting figures for each planned output, however, it should be remembered that many NDO projects involved more than one activity. In addition to the twelve mixed projects, which include two or more roughly equal primary output goals, thirty other projects had intended results in addition to their primary one, including housing resale and cooperative conversion or smaller outputs from one of the six basic project-type categories. Some of these and other projects also involved plans for neighborhood job creation as part of accomplishing the primary goal. Thus many project plans were somewhat larger than the distribution of individual outputs suggests.

Intended levels of output for projects in major categories were as follows.

Rehabilitating housing. Seventy-three NDOs planned projects that included some rehabilitation of housing units. Expected project size averaged close to 50 units and ranged from less than 5 to nearly 500 units, with the majority of projects ranging between 10 and 50 units.

Building new housing. Twelve NDOs planned to construct new housing in projects ranging from 6 to 190 units and averaging about 55 units.

Revitalizing commercial areas. Sixteen NDOs planned to rehabilitate or construct new commercial spaces, averaging about 23,000 square feet in size. Rehabilitation projects ranged from an expected 1,000 square feet to 55,000

---

16. Even cycle-two project lengths might understate total project work periods, since the NSHD program required plans to be fairly well along. But this understatement would be balanced by the likelihood that cycle-two NDOs are on average less efficient than the total grantee group, because many of the top performers would have been selected in cycle one.

square feet and new construction from 3,600 square feet to 100,000 square feet. A dozen projects, primarily in the commercial category but also in economic development, were designed to assist new and existing businesses (not NDO-owned) with technical or financial aid, or both. The average project intended to help more than a dozen firms, but the range was wide, from one to thirty businesses.

Economic development. Twelve economic development projects intended to create an average of over fifty permanent jobs. These NDOs[17] expected to create (or expand) eleven NDO-owned ventures—seven construction/re-habilitation/maintenance companies, two fishing ventures, an adobe brick factory, and a bakery—and to build or rehabilitate three industrial centers in which other firms would locate. In addition, economic development projects were to create temporary construction jobs for neighborhood people in seven cases. And other types of projects (noneconomic development) were expected to generate at least temporary jobs in almost every case.

Energy. Three projects expected to weatherize an average of 45 housing units, and two projects were to install solar collectors in nearly 100 new housing units.

Community development. Five NDOs planned to develop community facilities: two health centers, two community centers, and a large-scale community garden.

Although many of the individual project plans are modest, the total expected output of NDOs in the study amounted to an impressive package of development work for neighborhoods where other investment is often limited (see table 17). Over 3,500 units of housing were to be rehabilitated, over 650 units were to be built, and more than 225 units were to be weatherized or "solarized." Over 150 businesses were expected to receive assistance, some 375,000 square feet of commercial space was to be built or repaired, and more than 625 permanent jobs were to be created in economic development efforts alone—in addition to the establishment of new ventures, industrial locations, and community facilities, and the creation of jobs as a side benefit of projects with other foci.

In sum, study NDOs undertook a diversity of development projects, whose moderate scale and predominant housing focus fit well with their past experience while still allowing them to extend into new areas and responsibilities. In total output and dollars invested, anticipated impacts were substantial. Chapter 3 reviews in detail what portion of the intended results have been realized to date or might yet be realized.

---

17. Two other NDOs changed their projects in midstream and indicated no planned jobs.

TABLE 17

TOTAL PLANNED PROJECT OUTPUTS

Type of Output	Level of Planned Output
Units of rehabilitated housing	3,544
Units of new housing	665
Rehabilitated commercial space (square feet)	235,164
New commercial space (square feet)	141,000
Businesses assisted	156
Permanent economic development jobs	634
Housing units weatherized	136
Housing units "solarized"	94
Community facilities developed	5
NDO businesses begun or expanded	11
Industrial facilities renovated or built	3

NOTE: Based on all ninety-nine NDOs with NSHD projects.

3

Project Outcomes

The NDO study provided an excellent opportunity to examine just how well NDO projects succeeded as neighborhood revitalization efforts. NDOs received NSHD grants for specific project purposes and were required to delineate in advance what they intended to accomplish. They also were expected to report regularly on the progress of their work. As a result, we were able to identify the NDOs' objectives and to track the results and impacts of their efforts.

We sought from the outset to measure a series of aspects of project performance. First is the set of direct results that projects produced as concrete indicators of project productivity—houses and apartments rehabilitated, jobs created, and so forth—and tasks completed in moving toward those outputs. Second and third are the leveraging of resources accomplished by the NDOs in the form both of money from sources besides NSHD and of self-help efforts by neighborhood people. Gathering these resources is a critical step in any significant NDO revitalization effort. A fourth measure is the distribution of benefits of project work. Ensuring that benefits go to current neighborhood residents and businesspeople, especially those of limited means, is a potentially important result of the development efforts of community-based organizations in particular—a goal often little pursued by other development actors. Fifth is the generation of indirect impacts, that is, positive actions by others in response to NDO work, and of still broader impacts on the aggregate quality of life in distressed neighborhoods. A sixth and final indicator of performance is the contribution of specific NDO projects to the organizations' overall strategies for revitalizing their neighborhoods.

Taken together, these measures yield a substantial picture of the achievements and potential of NDO development project work, especially in terms
of the stated goals of NDOs themselves and of their supporters. The findings
should be valuable to policymakers, public or private, in assessing the usefulness of NDOs as vehicles for neighborhood revitalization. In order to decide
the level of resources and effort to expend on NDOs, prospective funders and
providers of other forms of assistance and cooperation want to know how
successful NDOs actually are at producing development results, at bringing
together resources, at targeting benefits, and at contributing to broader neighborhood revitalization activity. To direct that assistance efficiently, supporters
want to be informed (among other things) of those measures of performance
in which NDOs excel or perform poorly and in what kinds of work. Measuring
performance is, of course, also critical for research purposes in order to
analyze the factors that determine level of success.

The first six sections of this chapter deal in turn with each of the
measures of performance just outlined. The final section summarizes performance in its multiple aspects. A further result of project work—the
building of NDO capacity to undertake future efforts—is the subject of
chapter 5.

Project Tasks and Outputs

How successful were NDOs in completing the project work they specifically set out to accomplish? We relied principally on two complementary
types of measures to assess project outcomes, each with advantages and
disadvantages. One is an index of the share of stated tasks that NDOs have
actually completed. In their NSHD grant instruments, NDOs specified the
major steps necessary to complete their work; it was thus possible for us to
evaluate how far along they were in carrying out those steps. The other type
of measure is the quantity of specific final outputs produced, relative to stated
intentions, for each type of project.

Tasks

In terms of the tasks accomplished, we grouped project steps into preparation and implementation tasks. Although the steps vary somewhat among
projects, they are generally similar within a given project type. For example,
a typical set of tasks for a housing rehabilitation project (in this case, rental
units) was:

Preparation:

1. Preparing a project management plan, including scheduling, staffing, and so forth
2. Staffing (hiring, training, or reassigning)
3. Securing additional project financing
4. Acquiring property

Implementation:

5. Rehabilitation
6. Tenant selection and training
7. Self-help (tenant management and maintenance)

We allotted up to forty points to projects for completion of preparation tasks and another sixty points for implementation.[1] After assigning a percentage complete to each project, we divided it by the percentage of each NDO's planned period of work that had elapsed. This roughly standardized our measure between projects that were and were not intended to be complete by the time we last measured their progress.

Such a percentage-complete measure has several advantages. It provides an index comparable across projects and project types and, at least approximately, between projects with earlier and later dates of anticipated completion.[2] It also yields a single measure even for projects with more than one type of output. But it lacks the clean and consistent objectivity of easily identified numbers such as housing units built.

Measuring the index of percentage complete in terms of original NDO expectations,[3] we find NDOs generally to have made substantial project progress. On average, NDOs completed nearly two-thirds (65.9 percent) of their planned tasks.[4] One-third of the organizations are virtually or entirely meeting full task expectations (see table 18). That is, thirty-three of the ninety-nine NDOs (in table 18, twenty-six plus seven NDOs) have completed 95 percent or more of the tasks they promised to finish by this time, and two-thirds are beyond the 50 percent level of accomplishment. (Note the convenient coin-

---

1. There is of course no single "scientifically correct" approach, but consistency is important, especially for analyzing why projects reached different levels of success (see chapter 4).

2. The mechanism for standardizing is only exact if we generally anticipate that an NDO should complete 1 percent of its work in each 1 percent of its period of project work—an improbable expectation.

3. The expectations referred to are those existing at the time NSHD awards were made.

4. The index takes into account partial completion of tasks and, as already indicated, compensates for the fact that projects with grant periods still in progress should not be expected to be complete.

TABLE 18
Index of Projects' Percentage Complete

Percentage Complete	Number of NDOs[a]
Less than 25	17
25–50	19
50.1–94.9	30
95–99.9	7
100	26
Total	99

Note: Based on all ninety-nine NDOs with NSHD projects.

a. Index is measured in terms of share of originally defined tasks accomplished, divided by share of grant period expired by the time of our last measurement.

cidence that because there are ninety-nine total NDOs, the absolute numbers of NDOs in tables that include the full population of organizations closely approximate percentages as well.) Moreover, nearly 70 percent of study NDOs have entirely completed all preparation tasks (not shown in table 18).

Some NDOs, recognizing problems as their projects proceeded, revised their work plans and their expected dates of completion. A parallel index of percentage complete based on both those kinds of revisions shows that half the NDOs are on or virtually on target and that average percentage complete is nearly 80 percent. Such a measure, of course, gives credit for recognition of difficulties but overstates NDOs' success in doing what they and NSHD grant reviewers had anticipated.

NDOs were not particularly good at finishing their tasks on time. Only one-third of projects on which work has ended[5] were completed on schedule, and only a quarter of those still under way expect to finish by originally scheduled dates (see table 19). As of July 1982, just over half of all study

TABLE 19
Timeliness of NDO Project Work

Finished Projects		Unfinished Projects	
On Time	Behind Schedule	Expected on Time	Expected Behind Schedule
15	30	12	37

Note: Based on ninety-four of the ninety-nine NDOs with NSHD projects. Information was inadequate for five of the NDOs.

5. *Finished* here means that work has ended, although in some cases not all intended work has been accomplished.

NDOs had requested extensions, and additional organizations not having made formal requests were nonetheless behind schedule in their work.[6] Typical extensions were for one-quarter to one-half of originally scheduled periods of performance and occurred in every project type.

The majority of extensions were requested because of delays in obtaining expected financing. The next-most-frequently mentioned reason was that of difficulty with property acquisition. Weather and project staffing problems also played a role in the delays. Delays of these frequencies and types may well mirror the experience of other, non-NDO developers. But rather than suggest that neighborhood organizations have performed poorly, the holdups indicate that NDOs and their sources of assistance should allow more time in initial project schedules for the inevitable problems that plague all development work.

Outputs

The NDOs to date have produced substantial concrete outputs. If we focus first on what we have termed *primary direct outputs*—the principal direct goal of each project—accomplishments thus far include more than 1,800 housing units rehabilitated, over 125 new housing units built, over 200 units weatherized or "solarized," more than 80,000 square feet of new or improved commercial space, nearly 80 permanent economic development jobs, and nearly 50 businesses assisted (see table 20). In addition, NDOs have largely finished building or rehabilitating four community facilities of various types and have created or expanded eleven business ventures of their own[7] (reflected in part in economic development jobs) to varying degrees of anticipated business volume.

NDO projects also generated what we called *other direct outputs*—direct results of the projects that were nonetheless not their primary focus. Such outputs generally included jobs in carrying out housing and other noneconomic development efforts. Unfortunately, we lack complete and precise information in this area, but it appears that several hundred temporary jobs were created at construction stages, especially in the many housing rehabilitation projects employing local people.

Returning to primary outputs, how should the quality of NDO performance be assessed? We judged success by the share of intended outputs that each NDO actually produced; that is, we simply computed the ratio of actual (completed) to planned outputs. The measure thus provides a clear-cut picture

---

6. Eighty percent of the extensions recorded were granted to the cycle-one grantees, whose projects had earlier due dates. Had the NSHD program continued at full administrative strength and had our study extended over a longer time period, the number of cycle-two extensions would likely have grown.

7. These ventures are owned by NDOs or their spin-off cooperatives or subsidiaries.

TABLE 20

SUMMARY OF ACTUAL OUTPUTS

Type of Output	Total Output	Average Output per NDO[a]
Units of rehabilitated housing	1,808	24.8
Units of new housing	127	10.6
Rehabilitated commercial space (square feet)	72,000	8,000.0
New commercial space (square feet)	9,700	1,385.7
Businesses assisted	49	4.1
Permanent economic development jobs	78	6.5
Housing units weatherized	122	40.7
Housing units "solarized"	94	47.0
Community facilities developed	4	N.A.[b]
NDO businesses begun or expanded	11	N.A.[b]
Industrial facilities built or renovated	0	N.A.[b]

NOTE: Based on all ninety-nine NDOs with NSHD projects. Data include primary direct outputs, as of March–July 1982, as defined in the text and distinguished from other direct outputs.

a. Averaged over the number of NDOs that planned to produce some output of this type. Many of these are still at work. In a few instances NDOs may have changed the type of output they intend to produce.

b. N.A., not applicable. In each of these cases, NDOs' output was one or zero.

of the NDOs' abilities to deliver on their stated intentions, upon which their NSHD funding was based. The measure's main shortcoming is that it leaves no adequate way to deal with incomplete projects, in which further outputs may well be forthcoming. This is especially important, for example, in apartment-building construction. In such projects it may be that no units are complete, although all are well under way. Another drawback of actual-to-planned output ratios is that they concentrate on a single project result (output) and do but reflect such things as NDOs' success (or lack of it) in reselling homes once they are rehabilitated. Because our percentage-complete measure handles these problems better, the two measures—percentage complete and actual-to-planned output ratios—are best used in tandem.

Forty-six of the ninety-nine total projects had ended (or virtually ended) their work by the time our observations ended in mid-1982. Table 21 summarizes the success of these just completed projects in meeting output goals. Data in the table are average ratios of actual to planned outputs across all NDOs intending a given type of output.[8]

---

8. Note that three types of outputs are not included in tables 21, 23, and 24 on actual versus planned outputs: community facilities, NDO businesses, and industrial facilities. We lack ratio measures for these outputs that are suitably comparable to the others in the tables, because we have essentially only discrete information—whether or not the facility or enterprise was put

TABLE 21
Ratios of Actual to Planned Outputs for Completed Projects

Project Type	Average Ratio of Actual to Planned Outputs[a]
Units of rehabilitated housing	.831
Units of new housing	.538
Rehabilitated commercial space	.458
New commercial space	.093
Businesses assisted	.367
Permanent economic development jobs	.394
Housing units weatherized	.971
Housing units "solarized"	1.000

NOTE: Based on applicable NDOs out of the ninety-nine NDOs with NSHD study projects.

a. Data are averaged across the actual-to-planned output ratios for each NDO with a completed project of that type.

NDOs were extremely successful in producing expected results in the residential rehabilitation, energy, and community development areas. The large numbers of organizations that planned to rehabilitate housing (thirty-two of the forty-six finished projects) typically delivered five-sixths of their intended outputs (table 21), and this number is expected to rise to nearly nine-tenths when final work is completed on the projects. The small number of finished energy projects were even more consistently successful, achieving almost precisely the intended results. The three community development projects on which work is ended created their community facilities largely as planned (not shown in the table).

The average NDO produced more than half its intended work on new housing construction (table 21), in the face of rising interest rates and reduced housing subsidies. Commercial revitalization projects generated typically somewhat less than half the outputs they had planned in providing space and technical assistance (except for the very weak performance of new commercial projects). Economic development efforts produced similar proportions of expected permanent jobs. While all nine of the finished projects that intended to create NDO-owned business enterprises did establish those businesses, four projects have fallen well short of objectives for the scale of operation intended, and one has fallen somewhat short (not shown in table 21). Commercial and economic development projects were likely harder hit than others by deteriorating external

into place—rather than expected versus actual size, revenue, and so forth. Separate comment is included in the text regarding these outputs, and the latter two outputs are reflected in the economic development job measure as well.

TABLE 22

DISTRIBUTION OF RATIOS OF ACTUAL TO PLANNED OUTPUTS FOR COMPLETED
HOUSING REHABILITATION PROJECTS

Ratios of Actual to Planned Units Rehabilitated	Number of NDOs
0–.5	7
.51–.94	6
.95–1	15
More than 1	4
Total	32

NOTE: Based on applicable NDOs out of the ninety-nine NDOs with NSHD projects.

economic conditions and reduced federal funding. These and other impacts of project type on project success are elaborated upon in chapter 4.

Even among projects producing the same type of output, success in generating intended results varied widely. Considering the predominant output type alone—housing rehabilitation—more than a fifth of the NDOs achieved only 50 percent or less of their goals, but almost half accomplished nearly or exactly their planned levels and another eighth exceeded their goals (see table 22). The reasons for these differences are dealt with extensively in chapter 4, in order to illuminate ways in which NDOs and policymakers can help to generate more consistently strong performance.

We also obtained information on NDOs' current expectations of final output for projects not yet finished. Such information is based upon HUD records in which NDOs notified the department in writing that they were revising the scale of their project, as well as on new schedules that we learned of from site visits or telephone calls.[9] As is clear from table 23, NDOs anticipate final results of unfinished projects that are in most cases modestly better than those achieved in finished work (compare with table 21).[10] The two projects to create NDO-owned ventures still in progress, as well as the remaining community development projects, are expecting outputs relative to plans similar to those completed as well. It is uncertain whether any of the

9. The expectations measure is somewhat biased toward optimism because some NDOs that we did not talk to have reduced project scale without notifying HUD in writing. But of the unfinished projects, most were either visited or telephoned by us.

10. Expectations for weatherized units are sharply lower. A single unfinished project has no expected output, whereas finished projects largely accomplished their goals. Of the two unfinished community facility projects, one has proven infeasible and has been abandoned in favor of an alternative project.

TABLE 23

RATIOS OF CURRENTLY EXPECTED TO ORIGINALLY PLANNED OUTPUTS FOR
INCOMPLETE PROJECTS

Project Type	Average Ratio of Expected to Planned Outputs[a]
Units of rehabilitated housing	.918
Units of new housing	.563
Rehabilitated commercial space	.595
New commercial space	1.000
Businesses assisted	.667
Permanent economic development jobs	.442
Housing units weatherized	0.000
Housing units "solarized"	No unfinished projects

NOTE: Based on applicable NDOs out of the ninety-nine NDOs with NSHD projects.

a. Data are averaged across the expected-to-originally planned output ratios for each NDO with an incomplete project of that type.

three industrial facilities will proceed, and, in any case, there are no finished projects of this type to compare them against.

Adjusting for possible overoptimism on the part of NDOs, we might anticipate final results that are at least not much worse than those for complete projects; but it is difficult to know. NDOs' high expectations for new commercial projects may be unrealistic, for example, given the experience of similar projects in which work is complete. On the other hand, those projects still in progress may be the ones for which financing is ultimately obtained, albeit belatedly, while the "finished" projects might be those that met impenetrable barriers (that is, work has stopped on them, with little accomplished, because of the barriers).

Finally, it is possible to analyze the relation of actual to planned outputs for all finished and unfinished projects combined. Such a measure would be representative of NDO accomplishments, provided no further outputs were produced beyond our period of study. In fact, however, we know from site visits that, for example, some apartment construction was almost complete and that, more generally, much work of all kinds was still actively under way (as of the time our observations ended). The overall ratios of actual to planned outputs therefore provide an understated lower bound for NDO success in delivering promised results.

Table 24 shows the average ratio of actual to planned outputs for all NDOs undertaking to produce each output type. Housing rehabilitation and energy projects have already achieved well over half their original goals. In

TABLE 24

Ratios of Actual to Planned Outputs for All Projects

Project Type	Average Ratio of Actual to Planned Outputs[a]
Units of rehabilitated housing	.556
Units of new housing	.179
Rehabilitated commercial space	.341
New commercial space	.040
Businesses assisted	.228
Permanent economic development jobs	.312
Housing units weatherized	.648
Housing units "solarized"	1.000

Note: Based on all ninety-nine NDOs with NSHD projects.

a. Data are averaged across the actual-to-planned output ratios for each NDO with a project of that type.

addition, 80 percent of community development efforts (not shown in the table) have completed or substantially completed their neighborhood facilities. Housing construction shows far less progress, in significant part because of projects still under construction. Commercial and economic development efforts experienced more limited success, by this measure as well as by the separate measures for finished and unfinished projects, than did housing rehabilitation, energy, and community development work.

A fact unrevealed by table 24 is that NDO-owned economic development ventures did quite well in achieving their goals. Most of these modest-sized ventures are functioning at a reasonable level in relation to plans. The low total number of permanent economic development jobs created compared to original intentions was primarily a result of failed economic development efforts of kinds other than NDO-owned businesses. In particular, the few NDOs that planned to renovate or build industrial facilities that would attract private businesses and would provide more jobs in their neighborhoods have shown little progress.[11] Apparently a variety of conditions have combined to make those projects infeasible to date, so that little progress has been made past the planning stages for many of them (see chapter 4 for causes of failure).

Other Potential Measures of Output

In the course of our study, we explored the possibility of comparing NDOs' direct project accomplishments with those of other actors in the de-

11. Because these weak projects were large, the average actual-to-planned output ratio is much higher than the ratio of total actual jobs to total planned jobs (.31 versus .12).

velopment field, as a supplement to the comparisons with NDOs' own planned objectives presented here. A primary requirement was finding examples of similar projects conducted in NDOs' or similar neighborhoods by other public or private actors. As mentioned in chapter 2, however, we were unable to find sufficiently similar projects to make such a study practicable. We had needed to get adequate specifics of project costs and outputs (for example, how substantial was the rehabilitation of a house) to enable us to make unit cost-of-output comparisons. Again, however, the data from basic study sources were not satisfactory for that purpose; and, given the lack of comparable projects, we did not endeavor to make the considerable effort to pursue more extensive information. These problems and other methodological complications and directions for future analysis are discussed at length in appendix B.

A further note regarding measurement pertains to long-range project accomplishments. Our study, though lengthy, was largely unable to examine the long-term operations of NDO efforts. We do not know, for example, how successfully (in fiscal or physical terms) NDOs will maintain the now-rehabilitated rental housing they own or how stable will be the jobs created in their new enterprises. Many of the factors that determine initial results will influence the viability of continuing operations as well (as is illustrated in chapter 4), but further problems and needs may arise as projects move well past the "production" stage. Certainly, NDOs and their supporters will have to give detailed attention to that aspect of development.

Summary of NDO Progress on Project Tasks and Outputs

Overall, NDOs were markedly successful in carrying out the direct project objectives they established for themselves. By the end of our study, the typical organization had already completed two-thirds of its planned tasks, and many NDOs were still at work. The bulk of the finished projects—namely those in housing rehabilitation—came close to meeting unit output goals, and smaller groups of community development and energy efforts had also reached almost all of their objectives. Housing construction and commercial rehabilitation efforts and NDO-owned business ventures achieved lesser but still significant success, while efforts to construct commercial buildings and to build or renovate industrial space and then attract private business were notably less successful. Expectations for continued progress on unfinished projects are substantial—roughly equivalent to outcomes for finished work—and the precise level of ultimate accomplishment will depend on whether NDOs still at work can meet or exceed the efforts of projects now finished. But the level of performance, given difficult conditions and objectives, certainly seems to call for continued support for NDO work. It also calls for further efforts to understand how best to expand their successes and to act systematically on that information.

The level of success varied widely, both within and between project types. Explanations and implications of this variation are detailed in chapter 4. The remainder of this chapter addresses the other aspects of project outcomes—leveraging, distribution of benefits, and broader impacts—each of which is a crucial element of the success or failure of an NDO project.

Leveraging

Raising needed project money is obviously a major component of any successful neighborhood development effort. Combining funds from multiple sources was an especially crucial task for NDOs in our study. NSHD grants were designed to provide funds for the later stages of project preparation and for only a part of implementation. Grantee NDOs were expected to obtain other funds (and nonmoney resources) elsewhere, both as a practical necessity and as a goal of the program. Success in leveraging—attracting these other resources—was thus a key aspect of project performance.

Leveraging performance is also a potentially critical indicator to policymakers of NDOs' abilities to play significant roles in meeting widely held public objectives. During the Carter presidency and again in the Reagan administration, much emphasis has been placed on marshaling private and public resources to support private action. NDOs try to perform exactly this function in the development field, and their NSHD projects comprise an array of concrete examples of such efforts. In judging the usefulness of supporting NDOs' work, policymakers will and should naturally view the leveraging accomplishments of these organizations as central elements for consideration.

NDOs were extremely successful in their leveraging efforts, raising non-NSHD funds totaling more than $112 million for the ninety-nine projects combined. In addition, NDOs received over $150,000 in in-kind goods and services and employed neighborhood self-help labor they valued at $6.7 million.

Funds were obtained from a long list of sources, including at least seventeen well-defined types[12] of grant givers, lenders, and investors—including federal, state, and local governments, and a variety of private-sector actors (see table 25). Private lending institutions provided the largest single share: $24 million, over one-fifth of the total. City government was next with nearly another one-fifth of all dollars. Federal participation summed

---

12. Funding sources also included other less precise categories, such as "other public."

to at least $30.7 million (about 27 percent of the total funds), but that total represents a host of separate programs.[13] The largest funding amounts from individual public programs were Community Development Block Grant (CDBG) loans and grants and Section 202 loans (nearly $10 million from each program). CDBG funds supported the most NDOs (forty-two), followed by money from private lenders, local governments, state governments, and the Comprehensive Employment and Training Act (CETA) program.

Projects frequently drew on funds from multiple sources. For example, a typical single-family housing rehabilitation program might draw on CDBG funds for acquisition and rehabilitation, CETA funds for part of labor costs in renovation, and savings and loan financing for resale—all complementing NSHD funds that covered a project director's and construction supervisor's salaries and a small piece of the rehabilitation budget.

The funding totals in table 25 represent very substantial leveraging of NSHD grant monies.[14] The median NDO raised over three dollars from other sources for each dollar of the NSHD grant. Table 26 presents the full distribution of leveraging ratios (in other words, ratios of non-NSHD to NSHD funds). Over 80 percent of the NDOs for which we have complete data had leveraging ratios of 1.0 or more, meaning that they at least matched each NSHD grant dollar. More than three-fifths of the organizations leveraged at least twice the amount of the grant, and one-fifth gathered over five times the NSHD total. On average, NDOs raised over nine times their grant amount from other sources, but this high average heavily reflects a few large ratios ranging to over 120 and is less reflective of overall experience than the median and distribution figures.

The scale of funding typically received by NDOs from each type of source was impressive. An analysis of the ten source types identified as providing funds for more than five projects reveals that the average award was more than $90,000 from each of these categories of funders and over $400,000 from nearly all of the most frequent sources (see table 27). Clearly, NDOs were able to obtain major blocks of funds for their projects. Despite NDOs' limitations, various combinations of NDOs' technical work, track records, political contacts, and other capabilities convinced individual funders to make large-scale investments in NDO efforts.

---

13. Neither the city nor federal totals include CDBG funds, whose source is federal and whose allocation choices are local.

14. The data in the paragraph represent only those NDOs for which we have complete funding information, resulting in leveraging ratios that differ somewhat from those implied in table 25.

TABLE 25
LEVERAGING BY SOURCE

Source[a]	Number of NDOs Receiving Some Funds or Other Resources	Total Value (Thousands of $)	Percentage of Total Money Leveraged
City[a]	35	21,508	19.1
Community Development Block Grants (CDBGs)	42	9,544	8.5
State	23	9,304	8.3
Comprehensive Employment and Training Act (CETA)	22	2,012	1.8
Economic Development Administration (EDA)	2	2,420	2.1
Section 312 (HUD)	6	2,694	2.4
Section 202 (HUD)	3	9,705	8.6
Section 235 (HUD)	2	785	0.7
Urban Development Action Grants (UDAG)	8	3,855	3.4
Other HUD	7	4,506	4.0
Community Services Administration (CSA)	7	792	0.7
Farmers Home Administration (FmHA)	1	2,500	2.2
VISTA	1	5	0.0
Other federal[b]	7	1,464	1.3
Various public[b]	4	7,604	6.8

Private lending institutions	37	24,562	21.8
Foundations	20	2,864	2.5
Religious organizations	1	75	0.1
Local Initiatives Support Corporations (LISCs)	6	935	0.8
Other private investors[b]	5	361	0.3
Other private donors[b]	3	78	0.1
Various private[b]	11	1,623	1.4
Various public or private[b]	18	2,861	2.5
Project income[c]	4	511	0.5
Total non-NSHD dollars		112,568[d]	100.0
In-kind (dollar value of goods and services provided)	10	151	
Self-help (dollar value of labor contributed by neighborhood people)	87	6,701	
NSHD funds	99	11,052	

NOTE: Based on all ninety-nine NDOs with NSHD projects.

a. The city category, as reported by grantees, likely includes not only direct city funds but also some federal (especially CDBG or CETA) and perhaps state money funneled through local government.

b. Contains funds not further specified by grantees.

c. Many NDOs did not report apparent income within this category, perhaps because the income came only after projects were set up.

d. In a few cases within many sources, we lack dollar amounts (data are missing), and the total is therefore understated.

How did NDOs' performance in leveraging compare with their original plans? Overall, the success level was again high. A great majority of organizations obtained enough money to proceed with their basic set of planned activities, albeit not always at the full original level. And on average, NDOs received almost exactly the amount of money they anticipated. Consider the ratio of dollars each NDO actually leveraged to expected levels of funding.

TABLE 26

ACTUAL LEVERAGING RATIOS

Leveraging Ratio	Number of NDOs	Percentage of NDOs (with Complete Data)
0	5	6.0
.001–.5	5	6.0
.5001–1	5	6.0
1.001–2	13	15.5
2.001–5	29	34.5
5.001–10	13	15.5
10.001–20	4	4.8
More than 20	10	11.9
Total	84	100.2
Incomplete data	15	

NOTE: Based on all ninety-nine NDOs with NSHD projects. Leveraging ratios equal ratios of non-NSHD to NSHD funds.

TABLE 27

MEAN AMOUNT RECEIVED FROM MAJOR LEVERAGING SOURCES

Source	Mean Amount (Thousands of $)
City	614.5
CDBG	227.2
State	404.5
CETA	91.5
Section 312	449.0
UDAG	481.9
CSA	113.1
Private lending institutions	663.8
Foundations	143.2
LISC	155.8

NOTE: Based on all ninety-nine NDOs with NSHD projects. The mean amounts are only for organizations that actually received money from the listed source. Some NDOs that planned to receive such funds did not in fact do so. Those zero amounts are not included in the averages.

TABLE 28

RATIO OF ACTUAL TO PLANNED DOLLARS LEVERAGED

Mean Ratio of Actual to Planned Dollars	Number of NDOs	Percentage of NDOs (with Complete Data)
0	5	6.0
.01–.25	11	13.1
.26–.5	7	8.3
.51–.75	4	4.8
.75–.94	8	9.5
.95–1	17	20.2
1.01–1.5	23	27.4
More than 1.5	9	10.7
Total	84	100.0
Incomplete data	15	

NOTE: Based on all ninety-nine NDOs with NSHD projects.

The mean ratio across all NDOs was .998. Nearly three-quarters of the organizations obtained at least half their anticipated funds; a majority achieved 95 percent or more of their expected funds; and over one-third obtained more than they had expected (see table 28). Although some of the highest levels reflect higher-than-anticipated costs rather than only successful fund seeking, the performance still seems very strong.

NDOs' likelihood of obtaining expected funds varied considerably, however, depending upon the sources they solicited. NDO success was high with state and local government, with the locally administered CDBG program, and with foundations, and lower with private lenders and a number of other federal programs (see table 29). Although some of this variation may reflect differences in funders' interest in supporting NDOs or in NDOs' abilities to meet funding standards, much of it no doubt is a consequence of declining federal spending and tightening conditions in private money markets. These issues are discussed further in chapter 4.

Also notable is the difference between leveraging success when NDOs had a clear expectation about where funds would be derived and when they did not. NDOs obtained little more than 10 percent of the money they had anticipated from sources that available information allowed us to categorize only as various and more than 100 percent of expected funds from more-explicit sources. One major part of this difference undoubtedly represents a measurement problem, however, in which planned funds from uncertain sources became actual leveraging from specific sources once we recorded their receipt.

TABLE 29

ACTUAL VERSUS PLANNED DOLLARS LEVERAGED FOR INDIVIDUAL TYPES OF
FUNDING SOURCES

Source	Mean Ratio of Actual to Planned Funds	Percentage of NDOs Obtaining at Least Three-Quarters of Planned Funds from the Sources[a]
City	1.22	69
CDBG	1.23	89
State	1.82	61
CETA	0.66	59
EDA	0.52	33
Section 312	0.51	50
Section 202	1.39	100
UDAG	0.56	38
FmHA	1.00	100
Private lending institutions	0.67	55
Foundations	1.29	80

NOTE: Based on all ninety-nine NDOs with NSHD projects. Sources include those providing 1 percent or more of all non-NSHD funds and that were specifically identified.

a. Among those NDOs that planned some funding from the source.

That also means that our other actual-to-planned leveraging ratios for specific sources are somewhat overstated. Nonetheless, supporters might want to press NDOs to identify specific candidate sources for financing at the early stages of projects, to ensure that realistic financing plans have been identified and are being pursued.

An issue of special interest, given recent directions in public policy, is the extent to which NDOs raised money from the private sector in particular. Almost two-thirds of all study organizations obtained some private funding specifically for their NSHD projects,[15] totaling over $31 million (more than $300,000 per NDO). For the average project, private funds provided nearly one-quarter of all financing, and for one-sixth of the projects the majority of funding was private, even with NSHD monies included in public-sector totals. These proportions differ little from original expectations. Private funds played a major role more often in housing projects where they supplied final mortgage financing than in other forms of work.

---

15. Others no doubt had private general support money that helped fund aspects of projects and associated overall NDO operations, but these funds were not specifically so designated.

TABLE 30

PRIMARY (LARGEST SINGLE) FUNDING SOURCES: ACTUAL AND PLANNED

Source	Number of NDOs to Which This Source Actually Provided Primary Funds	Number of NDOs That Planned to Obtain Primary Funding from This Source
Public		
City	17	20
CDBG	13	5
State	7	5
CETA	5	6
EDA	1	4
All other public	16	15
Subtotal	59	55
Private		
Private lenders	21	31
Foundations or religious organizations	4	3
Program income	3	4
Various other private	5	4
Subtotal	33	42
No identifiable non-NSHD	7[a]	2
Total	99	99

NOTE: Based on all ninety-nine NDOs with NSHD projects.

a. This number differs by two from the number of cases of zero leveraging in previous tables. The reason is that two cases in which we do not know how much money was obtained from a certain source, and have no other sources for which we do know a nonzero amount, have been included here. Other numbers in this table may be slightly imprecise if a source whose contribution we do not know actually provided more money than did those we know, because our computing approach selected the primary source among known-amount sources, even if some amounts were unknown.

In addition, a private-sector actor—usually a private lender—was frequently the greatest single source of project funds. As indicated in the first column of numbers in table 30, a third of all projects had a private source as their primary funder; and private lenders were more often the largest source than any other single public or private actor. Still, when actual and planned primary funding sources are compared (columns 1 and 2 of table 30), it is clear that expectations that private funding would provide the largest piece of project financing were somewhat less often met. This is most likely because high interest rates during much of the study period made the use of private loans difficult even when they could be obtained.

Overall, while public programs provided a majority of the funds, NDOs actively and successfully pursued private financing as well. It should be noted, also, that often the planning and fundraising for projects with extensive private funding preceded the Reagan administration, with its emphasis on purely private approaches.

Perhaps most noteworthy is that NDOs nearly always combined public and private financing. They used public monies—often grants or low-interest loans—to achieve lower expenses, making projects affordable to their constituents and feasible in their neighborhoods, and to absorb risks that private lenders would not take. In effect, the public funds made it possible for NDOs to pursue and use private-sector resources in meeting their objectives. This complementarity of funding is shown clearly to be a crucial aspect of work targeted to low- and moderate-income communities. NDOs in the NSHD program demonstrated an ability to achieve these public-private resource combinations on a large scale.

Self-Help

Active, direct participation—voluntary and paid—by neighborhood residents in planning and carrying out development projects is central to the work of NDOs. Such participation is an important objective in itself because it gives residents a sense of power and control, assures that project activities meet residents' real needs, and engages residents in productive work. It is, moreover, often a means to desired ends, in that it uses contributed labor (along with limited outside aid) to make community improvements available at a price residents can afford; and also maintains community resources for the benefit of neighborhood residents over the long term, by having residents own and/or operate them. NDOs are probably unique among development actors in having the potential to catalyze community self-help efforts in development projects.

Encouraging self-help efforts was an objective of the NSHD program, and each project we studied had an explicit self-help component. Furthermore, direct resident participation was widespread in the projects we examined.

Contributed labor of various kinds is a key aspect of self-help. As part of their project proposals, NDOs were required to estimate the expected dollar amount of such participation. The average anticipated value of contributed labor for all grantees was $66,000, about half the average value of NSHD grants themselves.[16] Actual average values reported were greater than anticipated, about $77,000, although these are probably somewhat overstated.[17] Even adjusting for overestimation, this is a significant component of overall project support, given that monies raised totaled less than $500,000 for the majority of projects. Also, we were able to document from site observations that at least the types of self-help activity that NDOs originally anticipated were in fact generally carried out, if not exactly in the form or at the level originally planned.

The element of self-help most frequently reported was participation by a neighborhood-based board of directors in planning, making decisions about, and monitoring projects. These and other important functions of volunteer boards, plus contributions to project success, are discussed extensively in chapters 2 and 4. To summarize briefly, board activity was frequently instrumental not only in shaping projects to meet community needs but in granting legitimacy to NDO work, in raising funds, in giving technical assistance, and in providing volunteer hands-on labor. Many executive directors took this participation as a matter of course, so much so that when we interviewed them, some had forgotten that board time had been their proposed self-help activity.

Broader (beyond the board) community support for NDO efforts—both vocal advocacy at key points and quieter continuing expressions—was also a fundamental element in raising money, in encouraging NDO staffs, and in granting legitimacy to NDO projects. Again, the specifics of such advocacy and its value to projects are detailed elsewhere in this book.

Primary attention is given here to direct involvement of nonboard community members in NSHD projects, rather than solely expressions of support. Residents took on a variety of project activities. In about a fifth of the projects, neighborhood residents contributed hands-on labor without direct payment, helping to build their own homes, create and maintain a community garden, or do demolition and finish work in building-rehabilitation efforts—both in buildings they would live in and ones that would provide homes, jobs, or other facilities to others in the neighborhood.[18]

---

16. This average included some paid labor and property that was funded from other sources already obtained by NDOs, although this was not originally intended by HUD to be counted in self-help totals.

17. This average likely overstates true self-help for two reasons. First, a significant number of NDOs probably reported as actual values what they had listed as planned values, without any real follow-up. Second, we assumed actual values matched planned values when we could find no information to the contrary.

18. Additional NDOs use volunteer labor in programs and projects other than those at issue here.

Attitudes of NDO staff differed sharply on the value of such labor. The NDOs that used self-help found it valuable and often essential to accomplishing project work at manageable costs; and they pointed to the side benefits of giving residents a sense of participation and control. A good example of this view is shown in the development of a community garden, for which there was a limited cash budget. The donation of many weekends of hard physical labor by teams of volunteers was critical to constructing the terraced garden on a steep hillside. Such labor also provided an opportunity for the direct involvement of many young people in providing a valued place for the community's older residents to raise vegetables. In addition, a number of senior residents took continuing responsibility for broader aspects of garden maintenance.

On the other hand, several project and construction crew managers said they deliberately avoided "sweat equity" labor because they found it too hard to direct into timely and efficient completion of work, particularly in projects with fewer unskilled tasks to perform. In this connection, NDOs profitably might try to identify those specific tasks in which volunteers are most useful. (For example, unskilled help naturally proved more adept at internal building demolition work and final cosmetic improvements than at performing major renovation tasks.)

Resident members of the six cooperatives being created among the thirty sample NDOs we visited were intended to take over varying levels of management. In the housing cooperatives, initial participation levels were disappointing (residents were inclined to perpetuate tenant-landlord types of relationships), but improvements were made with experience and training. In another project, volunteers operated a newly established fish market, providing more free labor than planned when early revenues were short.

The least successful aspect of self-help in terms of meeting goals was participation by nonboard residents on project advisory committees, an aspect that far more NDOs planned to set up than actually did. But active board participation in planning and oversight, sometimes in specially created project committees, substituted well, except that participation was less wide. The project advisory committees were often established at HUD's insistence as part of NSHD program requirements. A possible lesson of the experience with this directive is that NDOs should be selected for support based on fully demonstrated commitments to community participation and then should be given fairly broad leeway in structuring participation mechanisms.

In about half the NDOs, various other forms of volunteer work were contributed (again aside from board-member activities). These most commonly involved free construction management and training from local contractors; resident block watches against fire and vandalism; tenant participation in policy-setting oversight of housing management and maintenance; volunteer work in finding housing with rehabilitation potential and recruiting owners or tenants; and extra, unsalaried work by NDO staff. Other efforts included general counsel on development strategies from a local developer, commercial design consultation from area merchants, and use of energy and housing-repair tool libraries by residents to improve their own homes. (To date, however, tool library use has fallen short of anticipated levels.)

Residents were also heavily involved as paid staff in NSHD project work. Over half the NDOs used local-resident crews in temporary rehabilitation and construction jobs and as the intended permanent workers in newly created construction-related enterprises. Many NDOs thought of the employment and training opportunities for local people as prime elements of their projects. Particular concentration was on hiring neighborhood youth, to give them skills and to help reduce social problems.

Furthermore, NDOs' permanent staff were often hired from their immediate communities. Of the nineteen sample NDOs for which we have clear information, a dozen have staff drawn primarily or entirely from the neighborhood, and another four have staff that are a strong mix of neighborhood and nonneighborhood people. The participation on staff by long-time neighborhood activists contributes substantially to the legitimacy and support NDOs have in their communities; again, this often reflects NDOs' job-provision, training, and career-opportunity goals. A number of people who gained their first development experience on NDO staffs found jobs in that field in city hall, private enterprise, or other NDOs; and remaining NDO actors, while feeling the losses, were pleased by their success.

In sum, self-help was a significant component of NSHD project work for board members and other community residents. The self-help efforts contributed to project success and affordability, to a sense of control, and to the skills and incomes of participants.

Beneficiaries of NSHD Projects

Who benefits from the NDOs' work on development projects? The distribution of benefits is an important issue. Many public and private efforts to upgrade neighborhoods have been controversial, in large measure because of the population they were perceived to serve. Frequently, it has been charged that newly incoming, wealthier residents, businesses, and developers have benefited, while the original residents of "renewed" neighborhoods have been pushed out or neglected. Neighborhood organizations, which, at least in concept, are created and controlled by neighborhood people, certainly might be expected to serve the present residents of their communities. NSHD grants were intended to assist projects that did just that.

With nearly absolute consistency, the NDOs we visited are indeed serving neighborhood residents and local businesses with their NSHD projects.[19] Furthermore, these NDOs take special pains and incur special costs to guarantee that benefits are targeted in that way. *All* housing rehabilitation and construction efforts provided improved quality housing to low- and/or moderate-income people from the NDOs' own communities. A majority of the housing rehabilitation projects involved restoring vacant, boarded units for rental or homeownership; often these units had been slated for demolition or were doomed to continued disuse. Grants, direct subsidies, and favorable-rate financing were obtained by the NDOs to ensure that rents or ownership carrying costs for restored buildings were within the range of affordability of neighborhood people with limited means. Priorities for occupancy were also given to such residents.

A smaller set of housing efforts rehabilitated occupied (or largely occupied) rental structures. In each case (with one possible partial exception),[20] the clear objective was to hold any rent increases to levels that current tenants could and would willingly pay for the improved units. Our observations indicated that the objective was attained, through a combination of hard work at low wages, subsidies,[21] and deliberate limitations on the extent—and thereby the cost—of rehabilitation work. In one special case, for example, rent-delinquent tenants were hired to help make repairs, thus enabling them to stay. Efforts were made to minimize the disruption caused by rehabilitation activity during occupancy, including moving tenants temporarily into vacant units in a building when feasible. Newly constructed units were also priced to meet the needs of neighborhood residents. Energy conservation and renewable energy sources (solar) were used to keep down operating costs to residents of new and renovated housing.

In sum, neighborhood residents were served rather than displaced by housing improvements to their neighborhood, because NDOs established this as a critical objective and took direct action to achieve it. NDOs assessed what costs local residents could afford as owners or renters and

---

19. Nonsample NDOs in the grantee population also consistently proposed projects that would benefit local people, but we could not verify actual beneficiaries for places we did not visit.

20. In one instance, it is unclear whether and how landlords receiving low-interest loans were restricted in the levels of postrehabilitation rents.

21. At least two projects need further grants or subsidies to protect tenants and project finances over the longer term.

then undertook to assemble the resources that would allow affordable housing to be made available. In a number of cases, projects were made more difficult by the efforts to provide affordable housing—requiring, for example, the complex marshaling of funds from multiple sources or extensive marketing of homes to lower-income people when wealthier customers were available.

As indicated earlier, in nearly all housing projects, some form of housing ownership within the neighborhood was established or preserved, whether individual homeowner, cooperative, or NDO ownership. A major purpose was to ensure control over long-term affordability, protecting residents against housing cost pressures that market forces might later bring to bear (or in some instances had already generated). The ownership efforts were undertaken despite difficulties in involving people without ownership experience in, for example, running a cooperative. And in several cases owners were helped to invest their own "sweat equity" labor in completing work on their homes, in order to make ownership more financially feasible. As mentioned earlier, tool lending libraries were also developed to facilitate further home repairs by neighborhood people.

In addition, a number of housing projects were specifically designed to serve groups of low- and moderate-income people with special needs. These included skid-row residents with alcoholism and other social problems, elderly and handicapped people requiring appropriate housing design, and large families who are often neglected in other housing developments. The extra costs of serving lower-income people generally and these people in particular should not be disregarded in assessing the effectiveness of NDO efforts.

Economic development efforts similarly concentrated their benefits on people with limited incomes and special needs. Jobs created in NDO enterprises were systematically filled with unemployed and underemployed neighborhood people—most often neighborhood youth. Many housing and commercial rehabilitation projects were carried out at least in part by construction crews from the neighborhood, as mentioned earlier in our discussion of self-help. In most such cases, the jobs had a built-in training component; inexperienced low-income youth were taught skills and work habits that could earn them either permanent NDO jobs or employment elsewhere. In some cases, trainees had a history of social problems. Indeed, some economic-development venture efforts were planned outgrowths of NDO job-training and social-service work. A good example of such an effort was the creation of a maintenance and rehabilitation company to employ youth in a community disturbed by alcoholism and drug abuse, in which previous recreation and counseling programs had proved inadequate.

CETA funds and other subsidies were used to make it feasible to hire unskilled workers, while providing goods and services to people of limited means at favorable cost levels.

Commercial revitalization and construction efforts were tailored to serve unmet local needs and to aid local (current and would-be) business-people. In seeking commercial tenants, NDOs carefully assessed the types of goods and services that were needed within the community, although they gave consideration to strategies for attracting customers from a wider area as well. Local businesspeople were involved in project planning, and provisions were being developed to give technical and sometimes financial assistance to local small businesses coming into the projects or operating nearby. Arrangements were made for space for local service agencies as well as for profit-making businesses.

Community development projects provided new facilities—urban gardens, community meeting places, and social-service centers—to neighborhood residents and organizations, not to outsiders. Often these were in locations where the absence of adequate facilities had long been recognized and previous improvement efforts had failed.

This consistent NDO focus on benefiting neighborhood residents is in marked contrast to the activities of other actors in NDOs' communities. A number of these neighborhoods are suffering the damaging effects of past public investment—especially in the form of highways. Currently, several communities are facing efforts by private owners to redevelop properties for use by new and wealthier residents, or to hold vacant properties off the market until that opportunity arises. Non-NDO investment that is taking place is invariably designed for gentrification. Unfortunately, an unintended impact of NDO work in a few cases has been to encourage such behavior by improving the most blighted properties that discouraged other neighborhood investment. In addition, NDOs are confronting rising real-estate costs and decreased availability of property for their own efforts, or they are attempting to anticipate these developments in areas near revitalizing central business districts and the like by securing property ownership.

Policymakers and experts may disagree about whether to try to revitalize troubled neighborhoods for the benefit of current residents or to attract people of more substantial means as residents, employees, and customers. What is clear is that NDOs are critical actors in targeting benefits to the people who today directly experience the problems of troubled communities. Given consistent past failures by others to direct development to serve these people, either in their present neighborhoods or after they have been displaced, that role is of major consequence.

Indirect Impacts of NSHD Projects

NDO efforts to revitalize their communities—repairing their houses or apartment buildings, investing in businesses, and so forth—can potentially encourage other actors to participate in neighborhood improvement. NDO projects may also have effects for their actual participants, beyond the immediate benefits of a job or a better home. These two kinds of results of NDO work are referred to here as *indirect impacts*.

Not surprisingly, NSHD-funded projects have to date had limited indirect effects, because at the end of our study, most projects were either unfinished or recently completed. Potential responses by other actors to the visible results of NDO work had not really had time to form. For example, local business-people would generally want to see whether an NDO's newly rehabilitated commercial area generated a reasonable level of customer patronage before making improvements in neighboring stores. Also, many NDO projects are small in scale. (As an illustration, the average number of housing units rehabilitated by the end of our study that were part of NSHD projects planning work of that type was 25, while the number of units needing repair in neighborhoods reporting that statistic averaged over 1,500.[22]) Individually, modest projects often will not by themselves reverse neighborhood psychology and "investment" behavior, although the prospects are improved in a number of cases where activity is highly concentrated.

Some important indirect impacts have appeared nonetheless. Again the focus here is on the results of our thirty sample projects, for which we were able to examine indirect impacts more adequately.[23] First, property owners in the vicinity of a small number of NDO housing rehabilitation projects have begun to make at least cosmetic improvements in apparent response to the NSHD projects. The fact that in the two most visible instances NDOs have done their work on the modest number of vacant houses in the neighborhood has likely helped to generate indirect effects. In a few other cases, housing rehabilitation in neighboring properties seems to be the result of a mixture of NDO work, public-sector actions, and broader market forces. As indicated earlier in our discussion of project beneficiaries, these indirect impacts are occasionally negative in terms of NDO objectives, because other owners make improvements in order to attract higher-income residents from other locations.

Second, NSHD housing projects in two other instances are promising to have major wider impacts of other kinds. One limited-equity housing coop-

---

22. Data for units in need of repair are of varying vintages and from differing sources.

23. Primarily, this examination took the form of discussions with knowledgeable observers: NDO leaders, local government planners, and private contractors.

erative effort helped to establish the limited-equity approach, initially viewed with some skepticism in the NDO's home city, as a good way to attack a community's problems in preserving affordable housing; the project also established the NDO's credibility as a developer.[24] This experience has opened opportunities both for this NDO and for other actors to develop further projects of this type in cooperation with public and private partners. In another neighborhood, the NSHD project is part of a larger city-NDO effort that will repair and rehabilitate a substantial portion of the neighborhood's total housing stock.

Several commercial construction and repair projects show significant potential for spin-off effects. NDOs have taken on the first step in commercial revitalization of a number of difficult locations. They hope to spur investment in neighboring stores if they succeed in attracting new customers and changing the neighborhood's image in potential customers' minds.

NDO projects have had important indirect impacts for neighborhood people in terms of the nonmaterial aspects of their lives. For example, an urban garden gave many elderly people, formerly confined to their single-room apartments and hotel lobbies, a place to socialize, enjoy the outdoors, and be productive—with widely perceived benefits to their mental health and general well-being. In another instance, some of the alcoholics and other troubled people given a new home in a rehabilitated hotel showed, on average, better social behavior "on the street"; this was believed to be a reflection of their pride and cooperation in the new quarters. In addition, young job trainees more often stayed at work and out of trouble—an intended purpose of many NSHD projects—and may have gained longer-term benefits in outlook, beyond immediate job skills. And in many neighborhoods, community members gained a somewhat greater sense of control over their lives and environments by planning and overseeing project work. This sense of control was developed not only by NSHD projects but also by past NDO work, and it is hoped that it will be strengthened by future NDO projects as well.

Indeed, this notion of a continuing process is of broad importance in assessing indirect impacts. While a single project may be too small to have indirect effects of its own, it may be part of an overall strategy that may genuinely change a neighborhood's character. For example, several NDOs have as their objective protecting their neighborhoods against displacement

---

24. In limited-equity cooperatives, residents own shares in a building—for which they pay a small initial sum—that entitle them to residency as long as they wish. They make continuing payments to cover financing and operating costs. When they move out, the price at which they can sell shares is limited to their initial payment plus a modest gain, and the building mortgage is untouched. The resulting fixed-financing costs make such cooperatives cheap over the long run.

pressures, while improving housing conditions. One NDO in particular is given great credit for stabilizing its community through a mixture of advocacy and development work. Its NSHD project, to purchase and rehabilitate an apartment building, is a substantial but by no means isolated addition to past efforts to limit intrusive growth by neighboring institutions (universities, particularly), to slow rent increases, and to expand nonprofit ownership. The relation of NSHD projects to NDO strategies is discussed separately in the next section.

Finally, a critical indirect impact of NSHD projects is the building of NDO capacity to do future work. Since, as has been emphasized, no single project can turn around a neighborhood, increasing the potential for future NDO successes is an important part of the revitalization process. NSHD projects had extensive indirect impacts on NDO credibility, expertise, and ability to sustain themselves, as is detailed in chapter 5. In addition, the success of NDO projects in neighborhoods where deterioration is the familiar pattern may more broadly spark effective revitalization efforts by other actors.

NSHD Projects and Broader Revitalization Strategies

Many NDOs do not have elaborate or formal long-range planning processes, as indicated in chapter 2. But the vast majority of NDOs do have their own revitalization approach or focus, which is shared by the leading actors in each organization. The strategy may be written and rewritten as boilerplate for proposals, exist in long-standing ancient lists of objectives, be largely an oral tradition, or be neatly documented in multiyear plans; but in most cases it is well understood by participants with whom we talked.

It was difficult to gain a good sense of NDOs' revitalization approaches from the written NSHD grant proposals only. NDOs tended to make comprehensive lists of their objectives, rather than describing a true focus, averaging over four objectives' each in such general categories as employment and housing rehabilitation. We obtained clearer information by discussing objectives with the NDO leaders we visited. The most common NDO objective is to stabilize neighborhood housing—protecting against further deterioration, demolition, and/or gentrification by establishing community and resident control over neighborhood housing and by rehabilitating and maintaining it within the means of current residents. Other objectives commonly include focusing on the needs of neighborhood youth for training and jobs to help them deal with various social problems or emphasizing delivery of a spectrum of life necessities (food, decent housing, health care, and so forth). These sample-based findings are consistent with data on the most frequently expressed objectives for all ninety-nine grantees.

For nearly 80 percent of the NDOs, the projects we studied fall neatly within the NDOs' chosen revitalization foci. Indeed, about one-fifth involved continuation, speedup, or expansion of projects already under way in the NDOs' main line of work—for example, selecting an additional set of single-family homes to buy and repair in the same neighborhood. Another one-third were newly started housing rehabilitation and construction projects that fit within established NDO strategies for housing stabilization. Several others followed NDOs' past orientations toward job training and enterprise generation—including starting businesses to employ trainees where only training had occurred before. Still others dealt with improving already acquired buildings.

Departures from past revitalization strategies were made largely by human service and advocacy-oriented groups seeking to meet further neighborhood needs for housing and economic development. Even these, however, need not be seen as deviating from NDOs' revitalization strategies, although they may involve modifications of them. In fact, the departures often reflect the interrelatedness of neighborhood problems—for example, the need to generate jobs as well as services in order to deal with social problems—or the necessity of "doing it yourself" in some cases when pressuring or cajoling others into making development investments seems fruitless. But development-oriented NDOs frequently also took on specific types of development projects that differed from their past work, although fitting within their strategies. Included in this category are the several housing rehabilitation-oriented NDOs that established construction companies—categorized as economic development ventures because of their jobs focus—to do housing rehabilitation in their own neighborhoods (previously this work was contracted out). Such extensions of lines of development work are discussed further in chapter 5 in connection with track-record capacity building.

More generally, the relationship of NSHD projects to revitalization strategies was by no means limited simply to whether current projects matched past ones. NSHD work made a variety of deliberate contributions to overall revitalization efforts: for example, creating jobs by supplying building materials linked to NDOs' own construction projects, earning revenues in development work to offset funding losses in primary social-service activities, and providing additional types of facilities in the immediate neighborhood vicinity where past NDO work of other types had been located. Many projects were designed to establish records of accomplishment that would lead to related work that NDOs sought to make their focus; to serve as visible showpieces that would establish broad credibility for NDO efforts; or to demonstrate the validity of an NDO's approach to neighborhood problems. Linkages of these last three types between NSHD projects and NDOs' strategies are also detailed in chapter 5. These strategic links notwithstanding, a significant number of projects are best seen as capitalizing upon specific opportunities within the context of overall neighborhood needs and goals.

Analysis of our data indicates that the linking of NSHD projects to revitalization strategies apparently had a modest positive benefit for the projects themselves, in terms of likelihood of success. But the effect was not particularly powerful, even when we compared projects that were direct continuations of work already in progress with projects that had little bearing on past work.

What is more important is the coordination of NSHD projects with other NDO efforts in order to achieve more extensive neighborhood revitalization. As stated earlier, none of the NSHD projects was of sufficient individual scope to bring about major changes in NDO communities. In addition, each project was made more difficult by other neighborhood conditions that were not directly addressed in the project. Both these factors serve to underscore that success in revitalizing neighborhoods requires long-term, complementary project efforts.

Even though NSHD projects seem for the most part to be integrated parts of related continuing work, and NDOs, moreover, appear generally to have an overall strategy or focus, it is also important that NDOs have a realistic action plan to meet their broad goals. In our study it was not possible to observe whether or not action plans existed. And given the fickleness of NDO funding, setting out a specific extended plan may itself not be realistic. Ideally, NDOs might be encouraged to develop at least mid-range plans that describe how specific projects are to contribute to long-term objectives, and then be offered extended-term commitments by funders, conditional on good performance at each step.

Summary of NDO Performance

Looking across the multiple measures of NDO performance, we find a significant record of accomplishment. Most projects have at least moved into the implementation stages, and few will be abandoned. Substantial shares of intended concrete outputs are being delivered, especially in housing and community facilities projects but in some aspects of commercial and economic development as well.

Leveraging accomplishments are particularly impressive. The typical three-to-one leveraging of NSHD grants from other funding sources rates well in comparison with the work of other actors in other programs. Total funds raised almost exactly meet expectations, and at a considerable level per project. And private-sector financing constitutes an important share in many projects, despite harsh conditions in the lending market. NDOs also involve community residents in major self-help efforts within their projects.

Of special note, NDOs clearly and consistently performed what might well be considered their fundamental task: delivering the benefits of development to the low- and moderate-income residents of their own communities. By deliberately targeting project benefits, they were able to serve people often largely excluded from the fruits of investment. And the results are being produced in some of America's most troubled neighborhoods.

While these outcomes are very positive, they have important limitations. For one thing, the projects are of modest scale in relation to neighborhood problems and so far show only limited spin-off effects. More promising is the combining of a given NDO's multiple projects over time within a reasonably coherent strategy, although the need to "grab opportunities" complicates strategy pursuit.

Equally important, some NDOs and projects are not performing well. These and other NDOs have significant needs for growth in their capacity to do development work. The remaining chapters of this book examine how to generate broader and more consistent NDO success and growth.

4

Factors in Project Success

A central purpose of the research underlying this book is to determine the factors that affect how successfully NDOs' neighborhood development projects are carried out. Ultimately, we are concerned with the potential to improve NDOs' levels of success and to expand the scope of their effective future work. Careful analysis of factors in success indicates what specific conditions are needed for good performance. Such information is essential for shaping efforts by public and private concerns, as well by the NDOs themselves, to better equip community organizations to perform their work.

Not surprisingly, our study identified a lengthy, diverse list of factors that influenced the level of success of the thirty sample projects we visited and the ninety-nine projects in the entire study population. The impacts of some of these characteristics of NDOs, their projects, and their environments are narrowly specific to individual project situations. But a substantial number of the factors have effects that can be seen across the NDOs we studied and can reasonably be expected to occur in a broader population of NDOs as well.

This chapter examines factors that strongly influence project performance in a substantial number of cases.[1] Identification of these factors can assist in structuring efforts to build NDOs' capacity for project work, in selecting projects that fit NDOs' capabilities and conditions, and in arranging for outside support and assistance that NDOs require. The factors in NDO success are

---

1. In a few cases we focus on factors that have exceptionally powerful impacts in a smaller number of instances.

divided into six categories, each of which is discussed separately in this chapter.

- Internal characteristics, including NDOs' staffing, management, board participation, and experience.
- NDOs' relationships with their communities and with outsiders, in the public as well as private sectors, who play a role in or exert an influence on their work.
- The economic and political environments in which NDOs operate but which they do not control.
- Characteristics of neighborhood development projects themselves that influence the success of NDOs in carrying them out.
- Notable combinations of characteristics across categories, particularly combinations that had strong effects on some very successful and some very unsuccessful projects.
- Characteristics of Neighborhood Self-Help Development grants.

In each category, key factors are identified, those aspects of the factors that most influence project results are described, and the ways the factors produce their impacts are indicated.

This chapter focuses on the success or failure of specific neighborhood development projects. This approach necessarily pays less attention to characteristics that may help determine the overall survival and growth of neighborhood organizations, especially those NDOs doing substantial nondevelopment (commonly, advocacy and human-services) work. The approach may also deemphasize to some extent certain factors that contribute to selection and pursuit of a successful long-term neighborhood revitalization strategy. Nevertheless, characteristics often overlap. NDOs that include development projects on their work agendas must conduct them well in order to prosper. And an effective multiproject revitalization strategy must consist of individual projects that are well chosen, planned, and executed. Therefore, factors in project success are generally factors in broader success as well. Where there are clear differences between narrow and broad factors in success in a particular category, special note is made of them. In addition, because there are NDOs in our study at nearly every stage of organizational development, we had a good opportunity to observe the effects of longer-term factors, although each NDO was studied over only a modest time period.

Our conclusions about factors in success are drawn from three sources. First, the narrative case-study reports of our visits to sample NDOs discuss in detail the way various conditions contribute to project success or failure. From these reports we identified factors that have large and/or frequent impacts on project progress. The other two sources are more formal statistical analyses. As seen in chapters 2 and 3, we both measured how well each project succeeded and quantified a variety of characteristics of NDOs and of their interactions with outside actors and forces.[2] We then tested to see which of these characteristics affected project outcomes—using data for the full study population where feasible and for the sample for characteristics that could only be measured by on-site observation.

The primary measure of project outcome or "success" in the statistical analyses in this chapter is the share of originally planned work (a series of tasks) that has actually been accomplished.[3] This percentage complete index (described in chapter 3) ranges from 0 to 100 and is referred to under the column heading "Percentage of an NDO's Project Work That Is Complete" in numerous tables in this chapter. Unless otherwise noted, the numbers cited in the tables are the proportion of NDOs with given characteristics that completed greater and lesser shares, as specified in the tables, of their intended work.

Each table indicates whether the results are based on the entire study population or on the study sample. For tables based on the sample, the results of a Chi-Square test are reported, showing when the sample observations are sufficient to indicate with a high degree of reliability that a particular NDO characteristic significantly influences project outcomes.[4] Wherever possible, statistical and narrative analyses are combined, in order to give both systematic evidence about what determines success (this has often been lacking in case studies) and a concrete sense of NDO functioning.

Internal Characteristics

Each NDO accumulates a set of capabilities for carrying out development projects within its own organization, by attracting skilled participants, by

2. Many of these "quantifications" were actually qualitative measurements; for example, we rated staff experience with development as substantial, little, or none.

3. This figure is adjusted for the share of the intended work period that has elapsed, as described in chapter 3. The measure is the result of dividing percentage complete by percentage of project period elapsed, as indicated by final project deadlines in the NSHD grant instrument, measured at the last time for which we had data about the organization's progress. Some projects were entirely completed and their grant period over. None was assigned a value over 100 percent for either numerator or denominator. Percentage complete takes into account both preparation tasks (project planning, lining up needed funds and properties, and so forth) and project implementation (such as construction and marketing).

4. Those tables based on all ninety-nine NDOs with NSHD projects contain all available information, and observed relationships stand on their own without statistical testing. One could view the entire NSHD population as a sample drawn from a larger population of NDOs and apply a Chi-Square test, but that is not the view taken here (given especially the NSHD selection process).

carrying out previous projects and programs, by establishing effective internal structures and arrangements, and by learning from trained outsiders. Four of these internal characteristics were found to be especially critical to the level of success of NSHD projects.

One such key characteristic is the skill of an NDO's executive director in a wide variety of activities giving direction to and gathering resources for project work. A second major characteristic is the presence on the project's staff, in a position of major responsibility, of at least one person with experience in and knowledge about development projects, especially the specific type of project being undertaken. A third primary characteristic is a working understanding of issues of project financial feasibility and marketability. And fourth is a track record of accomplishments in development and in related neighborhood work that attracts outside support and helps provide other necessary skills and experience.

Other internal characteristics also had significant impacts on project success in NDOs in our study, although these effects were apparently less profound or frequent. These characteristics included assembling a complete and harmonious staff team; preparing effective proposals and reports and properly taking care of other "homework" duties; getting productive participation from the organization's board of directors; effectively dividing project responsibilities and managing that division; and providing accurate financial accounting of expenditures while making these expenditures only according to funder rules. In specific cases, these characteristics can be as critical as the first group of four.

It should be noted at the outset that one must look carefully at internal NDO characteristics—and their relationship to the demands of projects' circumstances—to discover what determines success. Crude potential indicators of NDO capability bear little actual relationship to project outcomes. Neither an organization's age; nor origin as a development, advocacy, or social service group; nor scale as measured by number of staff, size of budget, and number of current development projects appears systematically to affect an NDO's abilities to complete its intended work. Rather than reproducing the data for all these measured "nonrelationships" here, we can simply provide an illustration by testing the potential link between NDO budgets and the amount of their planned work completed. As table 31 suggests, NDOs with large total budgets are no more likely to carry out development projects successfully than are others. The data in each column in the table indicate the proportion of NDOs of different budget sizes that achieved a given level of success. The numbers show, for example, that a larger proportion of NDOs with budgets under $100,000 (65 percent) completed over half their project work than did NDOs with budgets over $250,000 (61 percent). Thus shorthand indicators

TABLE 31

NDO Budget Size and Project Success

	Percentage of an NDO's Project Work That is Complete	
Size of Annual Budget ($)[a]	0%–50%	Greater Than 50%
Less than 100,000	.35	.65
100,000–250,000	.29	.71
More than 250,000	.39	.61

NOTE: Based on all ninety-nine NDOs with NSHD projects.

a. In fourteen cases we do not have accurate budget information.

will clearly not suffice for policy and program design. The specific ways in which the principal internal capabilities affect NDO project success are described in the pages following.

A Broadly Talented Executive Director

Our analysis showed that NDOs rarely perform well in projects without strong leadership and direction by their executive directors, in a wide variety of project-oriented and broader institutional activities. This finding is unsurprising in itself. But it is worthwhile to examine the executive director's specific functions. To begin with, as detailed in chapter 2, many NDOs are of modest size; and the executive director may be the only staff member with a good understanding of the development process and of all the aspects of a particular project's operations. Clearly, in such instances, if the executive director lacks the perspective and skills to plan a project, to assemble the necessary people and other resources, and to manage project implementation—while meeting NDO needs for support gathering and leadership not specific to the development project—those critical functions will not be performed. Even in some organizations with much more than minimum staffing, other staff members lacked a comprehensive conception of project needs beyond their own narrow responsibilities. In a testament to executive directors' energy and abilities, NDOs in which the director's role was very dominant performed as well as those in which more high-level staff help was available.

In NDOs where other staffers did have broader project responsibilities, we still consistently found executive directors' talents in a large number of areas to be critical to success. These areas included:

- Providing strong, dynamic leadership in forming project ideas; shaping them into manageable work; and then stimulating action by staff, board, and sources of support. This often meant generating energy

TABLE 32

EXECUTIVE DIRECTOR EXPERIENCE WITH THE DEVELOPMENT PROCESS AND SUCCESS
IN LEVERAGING

| | Ratio of Actual (Non-NSHD) Funds Obtained to Planned | |
Development Experience of Project Director	0–.50	Greater Than .50
None	.45	.55
Some or substantial experience	.24	.76

NOTE: Based on sample of thirty NDOs; Chi-Square test significant at .05 level.

and momentum in the face of tremendous obstacles—both major initial ones and new difficulties at each project step.

- Effectively raising funds; nearly always taking the primary role in contacts with outsiders, in identifying opportunities, and often in other aspects as well. This effectiveness depended substantially on the director's dedication, credibility in delivering on promises, political savvy, and nonabrasiveness even in difficult situations. It was important that outsiders come to characterize the executive director in those ways for them to be willing to provide support. Effective fundraising also required that the executive director have at least some familiarity with development work. Executive directors with no experience in this area were systematically less able to meet their objectives in raising non-NSHD funds (see table 32).
- Generating trust in and support for NDO project work by the NDO's board of directors and the community, again frequently through recognition of the executive director's hard work and dedication over a considerable period, as well as through deliberate sharing of information and control.
- Recognizing what technical skills are needed to plan and carry out project tasks; hiring appropriately skilled other staff and bringing in technical assistance when needed; and being eager to learn from such experts. The executive director need not *be* a technically skilled development person but needs to understand the role and importance of those capabilities.
- Having some sense of and experience in overall management—such as in the outlining of tasks, dividing of responsibilities, and fulfilling of needs for oversight and cooperation.

These capabilities are important both in accomplishing specific projects and in other aspects of NDO work. In addition, executive directors need broader talents to help provide for basic institutional functioning[5] in areas such as developing NDO goals, identifying opportunities, and ensuring continued community control of NDO direction.

Numerous NDO executive directors were equipped with the talents listed here, while others did not have the full array. In fact, executive directors so consistently rated highly that we were unable to make a simple statistical test of the importance of their overall skills. The worth of specific talents was best demonstrated by their impacts when they were individually present or absent. Perhaps the examples easiest to observe are a small number of instances in which an NDO's leadership passed to a more appropriately skilled director. New directors broke serious logjams, establishing credibility with funders by making explicit promises and then delivering on them or by improving strained relations with key city staff. In a few organizations, projects floundered, principally because of executive directors' inadequacies in providing momentum and direction and in recognizing what technical resources and tasks were required. Meanwhile others progressed smoothly, despite very limited internal technical abilities, precisely because of such attention and skill. A weak executive director, for example, without devélopment expertise, mistakenly counted solely on political contacts to move his project forward; by way of contrast, a strong one, also without appreciable development skills, assembled board, staff, and outside technical assistants, who collectively had the abilities necessary for successful project work. The effective director used his skill with people to offset a lack of development experience, just as the weaker director had; but the strong director focused these skills on correctly meeting recognized needs of development projects.

Key Staff Member with Development Skills

A technically well-equipped director for development projects proved of enormous value to NDOs that had such a staff person in charge of their NSHD work. The best project directors were knowledgeable and experienced in conceptualizing a project; in assessing its financial feasibility, market potential, and capital needs; in identifying an appropriate financial structure and funding sources; in outlining the steps to completion; in supervising "bricks-and-mortar" components of the project; in managing the efforts of other staff, crews, contractors, and technical consultants; and in responding to crises with ingenuity. Table 33 demonstrates the extreme importance to project success of having a prominent staffer—in the person of either the executive director or a separate staff member—with at least some development expertise and

---

5. See Mayer, with Blake 1981, p. 15, for further details on these broader areas.

TABLE 33

KEY STAFF DEVELOPMENT SKILLS AND PROJECT SUCCESS

Presence of In-House Development Expertise	Percentage of an NDO's Project Work That is Complete	
	0%–50%	Greater Than 50%
No expert	.63	.37
Key staffer with some or substantial expertise	.30	.70

NOTE: Based on sample of thirty NDOs; Chi-Square test significant at .05 level.

experience. Seventy percent of the NDOs with at least some key staff expertise in development had completed more than half of their intended project work, while only 37 percent of NDOs without that expertise had done so. Among NDOs with a project director other than the executive director, the importance to performance of the key staffer having at least some development experience is even more sharply illustrated (see table 34).

Knowledgeable top staff were similarly critical to success in securing funds to finance project work. NDOs where neither the executive director nor a separate project director had any real development expertise were about twice as likely to fall far short of fundraising expectations as were organizations that had these skills on staff (see table 35).

Furthermore, technically skilled staff substantially increased the ability of NDOs to obtain high levels of non-NSHD funds. Consider, for example, the leveraging level of two non-NSHD dollars raised for each NSHD grant dollar. Organizations with at least one technically skilled staffer were roughly three times as likely to do that much leveraging as organizations without such a staff member.

NDOs that had a staffer with substantial expertise did not fare better in meeting expectations (either in project progress or in fundraising) than those

TABLE 34

EXPERTISE OF SEPARATE PROJECT DIRECTORS AND PROJECT SUCCESS

Development Experience of Project Director (Other Than Executive Director)	Percentage of an NDO's Project Work That is Complete	
	0%–50%	Greater Than 50%
No experience	.85	.15
Some or substantial experience	.27	.73

NOTE: Based on sample of thirty NDOs; Chi-Square test significant at .05 level.

TABLE 35

KEY STAFF DEVELOPMENT SKILLS AND SUCCESS IN LEVERAGING FUNDS

Presence of In-House Development Expertise	*Ratio of Actual (Non-NSHD) Funds Obtained to Planned*	
	0–.50	*Greater Than .50*
No expert	.57	.43
Key staffer with some or substantial expertise	.27	.73

NOTE: Based on sample of thirty NDOs; Chi-Square test significant at .05 level.

with some but lesser expertise. A host of external factors and the level of difficulty of projects selected apparently offset the effect of expertise, demonstrating that staff skill alone—even at a high level—cannot guarantee success. It may be that organizations with substantial staff expertise tended to overestimate or overstate their likely project accomplishments. NDOs with strong in-house development skills would do well to pay additional attention to using them to establish more accurate performance goals, while still generating the more ambitious projects they have undertaken.

Project directors who had experience with the same kind of project as the NSHD work were much more effective than others of equal talent. But a substantial number of NDOs began NSHD project work without anyone on staff—or at least anyone assigned to oversee the project—who was thoroughly familiar with the process for completing the type of work being undertaken. This created serious problems for project planning especially—specifically, in accurately laying out the tasks to be carried out, arranging for their proper execution, allowing for contingencies, and anticipating problems. Examples of specific negative impacts included failing to act to meet city code or zoning requirements, resulting in extensive delays; neglecting to establish rehabilitation budgets for specific buildings, resulting in repeated internal disagreements over expenditures; not knowing how to shepherd funding applications through federal agencies efficiently, so that funding was lost or delayed; and waiting too long to line up technical aid for special architectural, marketing, or leasing functions. Lack of basic understanding by staff of the development process also often meant a serious shortage of early attention to financial feasibility issues, as is discussed separately in the next section.

In general, organizations with a development-experienced project director moved far more swiftly through the delineation-of-project-tasks phase, allowing them to concentrate on the many externally imposed problems typically facing their projects. Others not so well-equipped had to feel their way through the definition of project work and stumble over sometimes self-imposed delays, extra costs, and other difficulties.[6]

Developing increased talent and expertise in positions of major project responsibility proved valuable even after a project had begun. As noted in chapter 2, a number of NDOs either fired their original project directors or created and filled new positions for people with special skills after their NSHD projects experienced early troubles. Several of these changes substantially improved project progress. Executive directors might find it good practice to carefully review staff performance and consider making staff changes in midstream. At the same time, it should be noted that many good project directors gained their experience through past NDO project work or in NSHD work itself, so that patience and support of staff are necessary as well.[7]

Skills in the Financial Economics of Projects: Feasibility Analysis, Alternative Financing Approaches, Market Analysis, and Marketing

As indicated earlier, many NDOs lacked internal expertise in financial analysis and business planning. These shortcomings resulted in substantial costs of several types to NDOs in carrying out development work. About half of the organizations with limited skills in these areas clearly suffered some significant project problem as a result of them, and others seem to lack important capabilities for work they hope to take on in the future.

The financial/marketing skills were especially important for commercial and economic development projects, and to some extent for housing projects involving resale. Grouping NDOs by whether they had internal expertise in this area throughout their project, we see in table 36 a close link between such skills and project performance for commercial and economic development projects.[8] However, no similarly sharp differences show up in combined housing, community development, and energy projects (see table 37).

An important problem for several organizations was failure to recognize the need to assess financial feasibility during the early stages of project consideration. Some NDOs spent substantial money and effort taking other project steps without making good preliminary analyses of whether the projects would, for example, result in commercial rents beyond prevailing rates or home resale costs beyond the reach of neighborhood residents. Other projects

---

6. NDOs with more-experienced development staff also sometimes made wiser project selections at the outset, thereby avoiding numerous problems.

7. See discussion of capacity building in chapter 5.

8. However, expected cell sizes are too small for satisfactory statistical tests.

TABLE 36

FINANCIAL/MARKETING SKILLS AND PROJECT SUCCESS: COM
ECONOMIC DEVELOPMENT PROJECTS

Presence of Substantial Skills	Percentage of an ND Project Work That is Comp	
	0%–50%	Greater Than
No (for part or all of project)	.68	.32
Yes	0.00	1.00

NOTE: Based on sample of thirty NDOs; because of small cell sizes, Chi-Square test not appropriate.

were chosen for further work with less than full understanding of their risk-iness, or even of their infeasibility, in the event that the NDOs' most optimistic expectation about financing did not materialize. Furthermore, economic development ventures were sometimes pursued with little early attention to where goods or services could be marketed.

NDOs' lack of basic in-house skills in these areas contributed heavily both to failure to recognize needs for analysis and to a host of related project problems. Inability of such NDOs to draw conveniently on their internal resources in dealing with financial/marketing matters made it difficult for them to do the "quick-and-dirty" assessments that can help shape the choice of a project, to respond promptly to changing financing conditions by quickly recognizing and pursuing feasible alternatives, or to educate their boards of directors about what could realistically be accomplished. Further problems may well arise later when inadequately analyzed projects prove unable to financially sustain continued operations once the "construction phase" is complete.

TABLE 37

FINANCIAL/MARKETING SKILLS AND PROJECT SUCCESS: HOUSING, COMMUNITY DEVELOPMENT, AND ENERGY PROJECTS

Presence of Substantial Skills	Percentage of an NDO's Project Work That is Complete	
	0%–50%	Greater Than 50%
No (for part or all of project)	.38	.62
Yes	.41	.59

NOTE: Based on sample of thirty NDOs; Chi-Square test not significant at any reasonable level.

the crucial financial skills and
le technical assistance did suc-
ckages and make them work.[9]
s area, technical assistance, if it
ovided a reasonable short-term

ng problems also arose through
ject work. In various cases, for
ıadvertently left out of a buy-
me was overrehabilitated for its
;es being simultaneously repaired
rim costs; or new businesses were
ow start-ups or temporary market

downturns. Such basıc pıⱱⱼⱼⱼⱼ ⱼnerally avoided by NDOs with at least modest project experience.

Reductions in federal funding, high interest rates, the complexities of tax-incentive schemes for investment, and NDOs' increased efforts toward partial self-sufficiency all will likely intensify NDOs' need for financial-planning and market-analysis skills in successful projects in the future. Our observations indicate that NDOs should first actively seek outside expertise of this type and then internalize it.

A Competent, Dedicated Staff Team

Assembling a team of staff people who collectively have the necessary skills and energy to perform the range of project tasks, and who work together harmoniously, is another important contributor to project success. In the most general sense, the intense dedication of staff people with shared goals was a key factor in success—allowing NDOs to work through repeated technical problems, to keep prodding reluctant sources for assistance or cooperation, to maintain community support for delayed efforts, and to compensate for funding shortfalls with long hours and hard work. Both NDO participants and our site observers consistently noted the importance of committed teamwork, although it did not fall neatly into any of our categories of hypotheses. Conflicts between staff that interrupted this cooperation, sometimes mirroring disagreements in the community over NDO direction, had significant negative consequences for a few NDOs. Such problems need to be recognized and resolved quickly.

---

9. Many other NDOs of course had success with more simply financed projects with well-assured markets.

TABLE 38

CONSTRUCTION SUPERVISORS AND TIMELINESS OF PROJECT COMPLETION

Site Supervisor Other Than Project Director	*Whether Finished Projects Were Completed on Time*	
	Yes	*No*
Yes, well-skilled	.49	.51
Yes, not skilled	.23	.77
No	.31	.69

NOTE: Based on sample of thirty NDOs; because of small cell sizes, Chi-Square test not appropriate.

A staff team offers more specific benefits as well. One is that several staff members can combine their skills to substitute for a single broadly skilled project director when such a director is not present on staff, provided the right team is assembled by an executive director who recognizes individuals' limitations. We observed successful examples of several types of teamwork: project directors handling "production" specifics while executive directors dealt with funding, local politics, and other outside business; financial and project planning by a trained planner coupled with construction design and management by an experienced site supervisor; and carefully arranged support for an inexperienced project director from other staff with project management, reporting and accounting, and other related skills. We also observed examples of combinations that do not work, often because the skills were more duplicative than complementary: for example, two levels of staff each with construction skills or with project-conceptualizing and community-organizing skills, without anyone to monitor project finances. These drawbacks in staff makeup contributed to cost overruns for early work that later left major project tasks undone.

In addition, we observed the sometimes overlooked significance of including on staff someone competent in site supervision, cost estimation, and other basic project-implementation tasks.[10] The presence of these skills proved important—for example, in accomplishing the number of house repairs (or other direct activities) that were promised and anticipated, although these skills could not substitute for the leadership of a strong executive director or project director in broadly determining success. Table 38 suggests that competent site supervisors were especially helpful in completing work within projected time schedules.

---

10. An example of such a staff person is a production foreman in an adobe-producing economic development project.

Skills in construction cost estimating and supervision were also critical to issues of longer-run project viability. Staff skilled in these areas helped to determine, for instance, whether improved buildings could be rented out at rates that covered costs, given limited tenant incomes; whether construction-company ventures could be self-sustaining and ultimately profitable; and whether the size of net proceeds from the resale of rehabilitated homes met expectations, so that continuing work could be funded from those sales. These skills were naturally especially vital for NDOs that were doing much of their own construction/rehabilitation work but were also important—in initial cost estimating and later oversight—for those using contractors more heavily. Technical assistance often was a valuable supplement in this area (although overall not an effective substitute). Private firms with construction expertise might consider loaning skilled people to work with NDO staff, as a way of contributing to NDO efforts.

Finally, effective staff teamwork is essential even in cases where the project director has a multiplicity of skills. The ability to share responsibilities in an organized way appeared to be a major precondition for NDOs to expand and diversify their efforts. Otherwise the overloading of work on key individuals limited growth.

Doing Your Homework

As indicated in chapter 2, NDOs for the most part were relatively well-skilled in doing "homework" tasks—principally, systematic efforts to obtain and keep funder support, which are not unique to development projects. The variations among NDOs in skill and attention revealed several areas in which homework was a key to success.

- Working at establishing good funding contacts and then actively maintaining them. Some executive directors were enormously good at this, and their effectiveness was directly reflected, in numerous cases, in their ability to fund projects and compensate for losses in federal funds or for rising interest rates.
- Making clear, oral presentations and writing good proposals, even in the absence of great technical expertise. Funders took positive note of NDOs whose staffs could state clearly and simply how money would be used, what projects could be expected to produce, and how much money was needed, and who responded well to requests for further information when initial financial analyses were incomplete.
- Knowing the processes for seeking money or other resources and asking questions as necessary. Several NDOs found opportunities oth-

ers overlooked, or circumvented slow procedures by understanding how application and decision-making procedures work.

- Following correct processes for using money. A very few NDOs exposed themselves to serious trouble by failing to observe rules for clearing expenditures or allocating funds (see discussion of financial reporting later in this chapter for more detail).
- Showing good general management, in terms of such things as personnel administration, internal communication, and being serious about meeting commitments once they were made. Some funders were specifically responsive to NDOs that they perceived as good managers, even if this image was not precisely defined.
- Doing agreed-upon written reporting of progress and keeping supporters up to date on project status. Giving timely explanations of project problems was important in retaining support through inevitable periods of delay and difficulty.

For homework to be done well, it was critical that staff, especially the executive director, treat these tasks as necessary and important. A small number of NDOs regarded homework as secondary in importance and were proven wrong. The immediate impacts often took the form of a delay while such steps were redone properly. In the longer term, key funding support may have been lost. Some young organizations (and others) received helpful technical assistance in making presentations and reports and in general management; but the most important technical advice may simply be to encourage an NDO to take its homework seriously.

Staff Overload and Division of Responsibility

Three aspects of the allocation of project work among staff members proved to have strong impacts on project conduct. The first was overload of a key staff member, either the executive director or project director,[11] to the point that not all responsibilities could be handled well. The most significant short-term effects of overload were a reduction in the quality of management supervision over project details and less effective and less prompt responses to project problems. For example, a project director heavily burdened by housing management responsibilities in a troubled building was unable to provide the supervision and problem-solving energy needed for making major building improvements. More than one overworked executive director left an inexperienced project director too much on his or her own, with the result that the project director floundered and in some cases was ultimately fired.

---

11. These were frequently the same person, which often accounted for staff overload.

TABLE 39

PROJECT DIRECTOR DESIGNATION AND PROJECT SUCCESS

Project Director Designation	Percentage of an NDO's Project Work That is Complete	
	0%–50%	*Greater Than 50%*
Executive director is project director	.29	.71
Separate project director is designated	.30	.70
Separate project director is designated but leaves (voluntarily or involuntarily; replaced or not) or arrives well after project start	.53	.47.

NOTE: Based on sample of thirty NDOs; Chi-Square test not significant at any reasonable level for first two rows of table alone; cell sizes small in third row.

Executive directors doing their own project management had difficulties if, for example, problems in obtaining funding commitments arose on multiple fronts simultaneously. Indeed, the one outcome to which staff size per se contributed was obtaining a high level of funding from non-NSHD sources; having others to help made that effort more feasible. Projects that were finished under circumstances of staff overload were especially likely to be finished behind schedule.

Overload appears, however, to be most problematic in hurting NDOs' abilities to generate new project ideas and proposals in a timely way while implementing others already under way, and in hampering executive directors' abilities to deal with organizational needs not directly related to development projects. Indeed, our tabulations do not show current overload alone as a statistically significant determinant of success in NSHD projects. Adding to the core of key staff is thus an especially important element of long-term success.

Another aspect of division of responsibility that has had impacts on performance was the decision by executive directors to manage projects themselves or to turn over project direction to others. Our statistical analyses showed that the mere presence on staff of a separate project director did not significantly affect success (see table 39). However, delegating substantial responsibility to the project director was associated with lower likelihood of good project progress. Investigating further, we found that the problem was not in the extent of delegation of responsibility but in who was given it. Difficulties arose where project direction was passed on too completely to inexperienced people, to unqualified people who were later fired, and so forth (table 39).[12] If a talented project director was not available, projects fared better when executive directors—even ones with little development experience themselves—retained heavy responsibility for them.

Still, hiring or training good project directors, although difficult, has more long-term potential than shifting responsiblities back to executive directors, both because of overload problems and because a number of these executive directors who turned over project management have little development expertise themselves.

Probably the sharpest lesson regarding division of work was the importance of ensuring that someone has clear responsibility for each task. While costly mistakes were infrequent, several of the worst errors involved expenditure overruns or mishandling of critical homework tasks because no one understood them to be under his or her domain. Weaknesses in tracking project progress and in responding to problems, for example, arose largely out of failure clearly to assign oversight work, rather than from lack of specific skills.[13]

Quality of Financial Recordkeeping

For the bulk of NDOs, whose bookkeeping was reasonably adequate, modest variations in skill and attention to detail were not critical to project success or failure. However, three NDOs we visited exhibited significant shortcomings in keeping track of expenditures, in assigning expenses to the proper accounts, and/or in spending from a given funding source only on approved activities. In two cases these deficiencies resulted, along with other factors,[14] in freezes on expenditures of key project (and nonproject) funds and in one case in more permanent funding losses. The lack of well-organized records made the sorting-out process lengthy, consuming much NDO energy needed for other tasks; and at least one NDO's credibility was hurt, although no illegalities or misdeeds were found. Severe ineptitude in bookkeeping could have disastrous consequences for projects, and in general, weak financial recordkeeping of a lesser degree reduced project success (see table 40).

---

12. The evidence is only suggestive because the number of such situations is insufficient for full statistical testing.

13. While such problems sometimes arose in connection with use of NDO spin-offs or subsidiaries, we found no evidence that spin-off arrangements were systematically responsible for the difficulties. (The small number of sample observations available showed newly created spin-offs outperforming other NDOs and existing spin-offs performing less well.)

14. Interactions between accounting shortcomings and other factors are discussed later in the chapter under "Special Combinations of Characteristics."

TABLE 40

FINANCIAL RECORDKEEPING AND PROJECT SUCCESS

Quality of Financial Recordkeeping and Reporting	Percentage of an NDO's Project Work That is Complete	
	0%–50%	Greater Than 50%
Weak	.80	.20
Adequate	.20	.80
Strong	.37	.63

NOTE: Based on sample of thirty NDOs; Chi-Square test significant at .05 level.

Clearly, NDOs need to devote adequate attention and resources to maintaining correct financial records, and they must also be wary of intermingling funds even when tight finances might make the practice attractive.

In addition, NDOs' limited capability to generate reports for themselves on their near-term financial position—based on projected revenues, commitments in hand, and continuing expenses—may have long-term consequences. Often financial projections were prepared on an ad hoc basis when funding problems became obvious, rather than being produced systematically as planning tools. Such a practice could prove particularly costly as NDOs try to respond to cutbacks in public-sector funding—costly not only in time spent in producing the reports and in collecting missing information but also in damages caused by late recognition of difficulties or the inability to re-create important information.

Cooperative Participation by the Board of Directors

Having seen that NDO boards play active roles in their affairs (chapter 2), we wanted to know if that participation actually affects project performance. In fact, we found that boards of directors were important influences on the success of NSHD projects in more than half of the NDOs we studied. The great majority of these were positive contributions in a small number of specific categories.

One key board function was in acting as representatives of community support for NDOs' projects as the NDOs dealt with city government. Specifically, board members pressed city officials to cooperate with and fund NDO projects. In a number of cases, the board's demonstration of active community interest clearly influenced close decisions—for example, maintaining city support for a long-delayed housing project while the city council changed political makeup or smoothing frictions between NDO staff and city hall. Participation by board members in meetings with foundation and corporate funders, and the credibility of board members in their local communities, helped encourage private-sector support as well. In a few cases, individual board members were the primary links to critically important outside funding sources, making extended contacts themselves or creating opportunities for other staff and board contacts. Such board participants included a city councilmember and a board chairperson with wide business and foundation contacts.

The contributions of boards of directors in helping limited NDO staff to carry heavy work loads were also important to project success in numerous instances. Working boards, for example, identified houses for possible purchase and repair and located potential resale customers. They also volunteered their labor in rehabilitation efforts, including a case in which board members' work enabled an NDO showpiece home to be finished, thus preserving a major funder's support. And another board's business committee worked closely with staff as they learned together how to develop a project pro forma and marketing plan.

Board members also provided critical technical skills. While these instances were few in number, reflecting the overall limits of board expertise, they were highly significant. Some board members brought high-level technical skills in project packaging, architecture, and so forth, that replaced missing staff skills. Board members' participation in some cases contributed greatly to the credibility of project proposals with outsiders. Board members with construction-contracting experience, for example, helped guide (or substitute for) NDO staff in early estimating, bidding, and contracting processes. Although this work was sometimes imperfect in timing or precision, it was a major benefit, especially to several of the younger, least experienced organizations.

Much discussion has occurred among neighborhood activists about how best to structure an NDO board in terms of the mix of neighborhood residents, local businesspeople, and outsiders with expertise, contacts, and money. Our analysis found no systematic link between board composition and project success, probably because the variety of potential board contributions and NDO needs means that no single structure is consistently most effective (see table 41). Even the most likely hypotheses about board composition—such as that a board with prominent outsiders would help increase leveraging of non-NSHD funds—did not prove systematically true.

What contributed most to success was a board that worked eagerly and harmoniously with staff on shared objectives and included some members with specific skills and contacts. Disagreements between board and staff, or within boards themselves, dramatically reduced the potential for these kinds of assistance in the few cases where disagreements arose. Conflicts also caused

TABLE 41

Board Composition and Project Success

Board Composition	Percentage of an NDO's Project Work That is Complete	
	0%–50%	Greater Than 50%
Neighborhood residents and businesspeople	.36	.64
At least some substantial participation by prominent outsiders	.31	.69

Note: Based on sample of thirty NDOs; Chi-Square test not significant at any reasonable level.

significant drains on overall organizational energy. The most pointed evidence of the costs of disharmony lies in the contrast in outcomes for two NDOs whose staffs came under fire by local government: in one NDO a broadly based, unified board came strongly to the staff's support and thus protected some elements of the NDO's local funding; in the other NDO, disunity between board and staff allowed a debilitating attack on the organization that led to total loss of funds. Disagreements arose less frequently when boards were well-attuned to the development process generally, when they agreed on the merits of doing development work, and when they understood its limitations. Some past history in development, and active efforts by staff to include board members in training and decision making, were thus important.

The current-project-oriented analysis here neglects the importance of an active board in shaping a work agenda that serves the community and that gains its support. An interesting finding was that boards of several organizations with successful and substantial project records operate largely as rubber stamps in terms of policy functions, although that is the exception overall. Such NDOs seem protected by the credibility of key staff with long-standing connections and a strong record of work in their neighborhoods, and by the NDOs' demonstrated successes. We do not know if these organizations will pay a long-term price in losing touch with their communities or in being less able to respond to potential adversity. We did find, however, despite the exceptions, that a board that actively participates in formulating policies and programs and in selecting and implementing projects generally contributes to, rather than interferes with, successful project work. The likelihood of project success was greater for organizations in which the board played at least a modest policymaking role than for those in which the board's role was essentially ceremonial. And for projects in which the board played a still more active role, success was even more frequent (see table 42).

TABLE 42

BOARD ROLE AND PROJECT SUCCESS

Role of Board of Directors	Percentage of an NDO's Project Work That is Complete	
	0%–50%	*Greater Than 50%*
Ceremonial	.51	.49
Modest policymaking	.38	.62
More extensive policymaking and/or other active roles	.25	.75

NOTE: Based on sample of thirty NDOs; Chi-Square test significant at .10 level.

Track Record

A solid track record of past performance was enormously important for NDO project success—as mentioned early in the chapter, it was one of the four chief internal factors in successful NDO performance. Of specific value was a track record in development projects; NDOs with substantial experience with human-service and other programs (including but not limited to development) were not more likely to accomplish intended project work than others less generally experienced (see table 43). But NDOs that focused their activities in the development area outperformed other NDOs in NSHD project work (see table 44). Apparently the skills, tasks, and outside contacts involved in development are sufficiently different that, while other kinds of program experience no doubt help prepare organizations for development projects, much more is gained from work that has a specific developmental focus. As further evidence, NDOs with some substantial past development work (two to five projects) were significantly more likely to perform NSHD work successfully than those with little or no development history (see table 45).[15]

TABLE 43

GENERAL PROGRAM EXPERIENCE AND PROJECT SUCCESS

Extent of NDO Experience with All Kinds of Nonadvocacy Programs	Percentage of an NDO's Project Work That is Complete	
	0%–50%	*Greater Than 50%*
None or a little	.31	.69
Substantial	.45	.55

NOTE: Based on sample of thirty NDOs; Chi-Square test not significant at any reasonable level.

---

15. We return later in this section to discussion of weak performance by those NDOs with experience with more than five other projects, as shown in tables 45 and 46.

TABLE 44

PRIMARY FOCUS OF NDO WORK AND PROJECT SUCCESS

	Percentage of an NDO's Project Work That is Complete	
NDO Focus	0%–50%	Greater Than 50%
Development	.26	.74
Social services, advocacy, or a mixture	.49	.51

NOTE: Based on sample of thirty NDOs; Chi-Square test significant at .05 level.

Of course, a good track record in development is itself the product of other capabilities and external circumstances, so that one must be careful in attributing project impacts to past experience. But we were able to identify several important influences of track records themselves. The clearest impact of a strong track record is on an NDO's ability to obtain funds and gain other cooperation such as the turning over of publicly owned land and buildings or offerings of technical assistance. NDOs with more positive and extensive experience in carrying out development projects were consistently better able to collect needed resources for their NSHD work. While in a few instances the true level of experience was masked, sources of support generally were able to acquire a good sense of NDO development history and, indeed, looked for evidence of past success. NDOs often returned to funders who had supported their past efforts and who therefore had specific knowledge of at least that work. Providers of grants wanted some demonstrable assurance that grant objectives would be reached; and lenders sought assurance, on the basis of past successes, that loans would be repaid.

Past project experience was furthermore important for giving NDO participants an appreciation of the development process. When at least some

TABLE 45

LEVEL OF DEVELOPMENT EXPERIENCE AND PROJECT SUCCESS

	Percentage of an NDO's Project Work That is Complete	
Number of Past and Current Development Projects (Other Than NSHD)	0%–50%	Greater Than 50%
0–1	.53	.47
2–5	.29	.71
More than 5	.53	.47

NOTE: Based on all ninety-nine NDOs with NSHD projects.

current staff member had been involved in an NDO's previous development effort(s), the serious problems in basic project planning described earlier in this chapter were much less likely to occur.[16] Experience gave a fundamental understanding of what goes into a project, of how long it might take, and of the costs that should be taken into account.

In addition, a development track record was central to community support. Previous projects not only helped to serve as the foundation for past support, but, as suggested in discussing boards of directors, they gave community members a reasonable set of expectations about what development could produce. In some NDOs without that experience, community members anticipated greater results from available funds than could be realistically produced, because funding levels sounded high and many people had little knowledge of what development costs. Resulting disappointments generated some harmful distrust.

A past track record is also a prime factor in producing a range of internal NDO capacities discussed in this chapter, including broadly skilled development staff and good general management, as well as positive relationships with a variety of outsiders. Track record may well be a useful indicator of the presence of other capabilities, if key staff and board members have remained with the organization (so that the gains from past experience still reside with the NDO).

The type of experience that mattered in NDO success varied for different kinds of track-record impacts. To encourage aid from funding sources and other cooperators, NDOs got substantial mileage just from having some type of successful development experience. Indeed for some NDOs, accomplishing the first steps of the project for which they sought further support formed a valuable track record—for example, winning an NSHD grant or pinning down a Section 8 housing assistance reservation. And in a few instances, a minimal development record coupled with good programmatic work in other fields sufficed. We found direct evidence that NDOs that had completed modest numbers of development projects of some kind were regularly in a better position to leverage their NSHD funds than those with less experience. Table 46 links development experience to NDOs' likelihood of actually obtaining the non-NSHD funds they planned to raise. As the table shows, organizations with two to five past projects were significantly more likely to reach fund-raising expectations than those with less of a track record.

The impact of some kind of development experience on successful leveraging of other funds was most systematic in seeking public monies. As

---

16. Of course, experienced staff may be recruited from elsewhere, rather than trained in an NDO's projects.

TABLE 46

DEVELOPMENT EXPERIENCE AND SUCCESS IN LEVERAGING FUNDS

Number of Past and Current Development Projects (Other Than NSHD)	Ratio of Actual (Non-NSHD) Funds Obtained to Planned	
	0–.50	Greater Than .50
0–1	.38	.62
2–5	.20	.80
More than 5	.50	.50

NOTE: Based on all ninety-nine NDOs with NSHD projects.

table 47 indicates, NDOs with substantial records in development, regardless of specific project type, were more likely to obtain the public funds they anticipated than were those with little or no record. Private financing does not respond in a comparable way. Modest development experience, regardless of specific project type or an NDO's role in it, also served well to introduce community members to the realities of the development process.

Experience specifically with the same kind of project as their NSHD work was of some additional help to NDOs in leveraging funds. In general, goals for obtaining non-NSHD monies were more often reached by NDOs with some such similar experience (see table 48).[17]

But past experience with the same project type was most particularly useful for purposes other than leveraging. In teaching NDO staff the steps in undertaking a development project, the appropriate cost considerations, and other elements of planning and implementation expertise, experience with similar projects was far more valuable than general development experience. For example, commercial revitalization projects could not automatically build

TABLE 47

DEVELOPMENT EXPERIENCE AND SUCCESS IN LEVERAGING PUBLIC FUNDS

Extent of Past Development Experience	Ratio of Actual (Non-NSHD) Public Funds Obtained to Planned	
	0–.50	Greater Than .50
None or little	.47	.53
Substantial	.15	.85

NOTE: Based on sample of thirty NDOs; Chi-Square test significant at .05 level.

---

17. The table somewhat overstates this impact because housing groups doing rehabilitation projects were most likely to have done the same work before, and such projects went more smoothly than others, regardless of NDO characteristics.

TABLE 48

EXPERIENCE WITH SAME PROJECT TYPES AS NSHD AND SUCCESS IN LEVERAGING
FUNDS

Level of Experience with Same Type of Project as NSHD	Ratio of Actual (Non-NSHD) Funds Obtained to Planned	
	0–.50	*Greater Than .50*
None (or none with at least part of multipart project)	.62	.38
Some or substantial	.29	.71

NOTE: Based on sample of thirty NDOs; Chi-Square test significant at .05 level.

easily on housing experience, because the process of attracting businesses differed from the process of attracting residents, the budget line items were new, and so forth. And more narrowly, within the single area of housing rehabilitation, for example, a rehabilitation loan project held new surprises that a grant program had not identified. It was also important that an NDO have experience in the same role it was currently undertaking—for example, as developer in a single-family housing rehabilitation project rather than as the outreach and monitoring arm of a basically city-run program. While any development experience certainly helped, NDOs with a history in same-project types and roles outperformed others.[18]

The importance of track-record impacts on performance has several implications. Given those findings, young NDOs might want to carefully select modest early projects that they can carry out quickly and well, and then publicize them, to establish the beginnings of a track record that attracts further funding. More-experienced groups should move cautiously when they take on new project types and roles, seeking outside advice and expertise. It is worth noting that NDOs with the largest number of development projects behind them did not do well in meeting NSHD project expectations (tables 45 and 46). This may have been because many such NDOs took on relatively difficult projects that differed from their past work. They may not have assembled all the needed skills and resources, banking too heavily on past performance. In general, funders might want to direct support to new projects that are reasonably consistent with NDO experience levels and also encourage

---

18. This observation depends heavily on site-visit information, along with limited statistical analysis. Statistical analysis should control for project type here because of its importance in overall outcome; but few NDOs doing housing projects lack experience of this type, and few doing economic or commercial development have experience in such development.

TABLE 49

DEVELOPMENT EXPERIENCE AND OBTAINING OF NON-NSHD FUNDS: SAMPLE DATA

Extent of Past Development Experience	*Ratio of Total (Non-NSHD) Funds to NSHD Funds*		
	0–2	*2.01–5*	*Greater Than 5*
None or a little	.72	.28	0
Substantial	.33	.38	.29

NOTE: Based on sample of thirty NDOs; Chi-Square test significant at .05 level.

(and support) NDOs that seek expert outside assistance and counsel when taking on new forms of development work.

A further note on the accomplishments of NDOs with substantial development experience is appropriate. While the most experienced organizations were not particularly good at meeting expectations, experience did have its benefits. NDOs with extensive development histories put together larger, often more complex, financial packages to complement their NSHD grants, therefore getting more mileage out of the same NSHD program funds. Data on the ratio of total funds obtained for NSHD projects to the size of NSHD grants demonstrate this well.[19] Those NDOs in the study sample with substantial experience were significantly more likely to match NSHD dollars with at least two, and often five, dollars generated from other sources (see table 49). The results in table 50 for the entire study population—the level of experience for which is more difficult to assess—support this finding, although less sharply than does the sample alone.

TABLE 50

DEVELOPMENT EXPERIENCE AND OBTAINING OF NON-NSHD FUNDS: POPULATION DATA

Number of Past and Current Development Projects (Other Than NSHD)	*Ratio of Total (Non-NSHD) Funds to NSHD Funds*		
	0–2	*2.01–5*	*Greater Than 5*
0–1	.54	.31	.15
2–3	.39	.33	.28
More than 4	.20	.37	.43

NOTE: Based on all ninety-nine NDOs with NSHD projects.

---

19. This ratio is to be distinguished from the ratio of actual to expected total funds in previous tables on leveraging in this book.

The leveraging performance of experienced NDOs means that the scale of successful program impacts can, after all, be increased by funding those NDOs with substantial track records and by helping additional NDOs to build that level of experience, even though full expectations may not have been met in the past. Notably, the findings about substantial track records closely parallel the impacts of having substantial development expertise on staff (discussed earlier in this chapter). Ideally, skilled, experienced NDOs and their supporters could seek to take advantage of positive performance in assembling larger, more complex projects, while avoiding the overambition that seems to have characterized earlier work.

NDO Relationships with Their Communities and with Outsiders

NDOs depend heavily on the participation, support, and cooperation of other people in their work. Given NDOs' goals and limitations, the involvement of community members and good access to capital, technical assistance, and political support and cooperation are fundamental NDO needs. Obviously, then, establishing, maintaining, and making productive use of links to the community and to sources of funding and technical assistance are key NDO skills. The existence of certain established relationships, or their generation in the course of project work, proved critical to successful project conduct.

Three types of relationships were exceptionally important in NDO work. The first was strong support from the NDO's own community. Community members provided dedicated voluntary and paid labor of many types. More important, community members' satisfaction with NDO directions and their participation in shaping them were central to the NDO's credibility with all outside actors and to its ability to generate new projects and maintain staff and board commitment.

The second critical link was a good working relationship with city hall. Resources and powers (such as zoning and disposition of land) within local government control were of great significance to NDO projects, and were increasingly so as other avenues of public funding declined. Local governments often have definite ideas about and attitudes toward NDO activity. Our study showed that the amount of cooperation resulting from such views determined the basic feasibility of many projects.

The third relationship of note was access to competent technical assistance in fields where NDO expertise was lacking. Many types of technical skill were factors in project success, and bringing in outside assistance to fill gaps was a major way for NDOs to obtain needed technical competence.

TABLE 51

LEVERAGING FUNDS AND PROJECT SUCCESS

Ratio of Actual (Non-NSHD) Funds Obtained to Planned	Percentage of an NDO's Project Work That is Complete		
	0%–50%	51%–94%	95% or Greater
0–.50	.61	.17	.22
Greater than .50	.21	.36	.43

NOTE: Based on all ninety-nine NDOs with NSHD projects.

In addition, several other aspects of relations to outsiders contributed to project success, particularly to the ability to obtain specific types of needed funds. Gaining project money in general is of course tremendously important to successful implementation of development plans. NDOs that secured at least a substantial portion of the non-NSHD funds they had anticipated were, as could be expected, much more likely to have carried out the bulk of their planned project tasks (see table 51). Certain kinds of links to funders were especially valuable in making an adequate project funding package easier to assemble.

The nature and importance of each of these crucial relationships is outlined next.

Community Support and Involvement

Most of the NDOs have strong community support, as discussed in chapter 2. The perception by foundations, local government, and other potential supporters that such support existed was consistently critical in NDOs' ability to obtain funds, according to statements made to us by both funders and NDO staff and boards. The relationship of community support to funding was especially well highlighted in six sample cases. In three of these, the pressure of community residents' telephoning local officials to express their support and attending meetings of local government was crucial, at specific decision-making points, to obtaining the release of long-delayed project resources or to retaining support for projects needing more time and money. In the other three cases, the visible and vocal support of community people opened doors closed to other NDOs and garnered support where it had previously been denied. Participation by the board of directors and broader community participation in such efforts frequently complemented each other.

Community support was also critical to giving NDOs the credibility, confidence, and energy to assemble projects in the first place. For example, many organizations' projects involved, at the early planning stages, convincing neighborhood property owners to sell buildings to the NDOs, encouraging neighborhood businesspeople to move into planned commercial space and help in its development, or getting tenants to agree to rehabilitation work while they were in residence. Success in these steps often depended on an NDO's reputation as a viable community-supported organization. In addition, NDO staffs sought appreciation, encouragement, and fulfillment for their long hours of work at low pay—which unified community support could provide. They also needed a background environment of communitywide shared objectives, in order to avoid running into damaging disputes at every step in project work and facing constant risks of community opposition when they generated new project proposals for outside funding. As mentioned in the earlier discussion of the board of directors, community support played a key role in defending against external attacks on NDO activity or in preventing their occurrence.

Direct community participation in NDO development projects also contributed to success, as was partially discussed earlier in this book in terms of self-help performance. Sweat-equity labor by project beneficiaries played important roles in keeping costs affordable in several cases. Community volunteers helped to finish or sustain projects where the lack of funds would otherwise have meant failure; volunteer technical assistance in the housing rehabilitation process was a key factor at the early stages of other efforts by inexperienced NDOs; and block watches protected against vandalism and arson and were notably effective in several neighborhoods—including, in one instance, providing quick warning when a serious fire broke out nearby. In other cases, residents' roles in advocacy and lawsuits furthermore helped to jar loose slumlord properties that had long been unavailable for rehabilitation. In more than a third of the projects we visited and studied closely, direct participation by residents in project work made a singular difference.

The importance of positive resident involvement was underscored by situations where it was needed but had not yet been developed in a project. For example, in a multifamily housing project where resident participation was sought to improve management and conserve energy, bad previous (non-NDO) management had soured tenant attitudes. NSHD project impacts were therefore blunted by lack of active cooperation. More generally, building resident participation in neighborhoods where other institutions have rarely encouraged it is an important but difficult NDO task.

While community support and participation made many identifiable contributions to success, those contributions do apparently have real limits. Statistical analysis shows no systematic positive effect of community support, measured by a single rating, on the likelihood of project completion. The finding may in part reflect difficulties in measurement, especially when so many of the NDOs have quite good community relations. In addition, much of the impact of neighborhood support occurred at early stages of project development, often before NSHD grants were awarded. Still, it is clear that although community support is a necessary and critical ingredient in NDO efforts, it is by no means sufficient to assure success. Many capabilities, relations, and external conditions shape the project outcomes of even the most strongly supported organizations; and each NDO has to address those other factors as well.

Relations with Local Government

The extent of support for NDO work by city government made major differences in the outcomes of a very substantial share of NDO projects. NDOs able to build and maintain good relations with city hall gained important cooperation of several kinds. City governments control large amounts of funds upon which NSHD projects (and often the NDO's other operations) heavily depended. This was especially true for the many younger organizations whose budgets were built around CDBG and CETA funding. In some cases where strong city-NDO bonds were forged, the city provided nearly full financing for large-scale projects on very favorable terms (grants plus cheap, deferred-payment loans) from these CDBG, CETA, or other locally controlled sources.

Other critical project resources, especially buildings and land, are also controlled by local governments. City cooperation in expeditiously granting or selling vacant buildings for rehabilitation or providing scarce land for new projects was a prime determinant of the speed of project progress in several instances. City departments can also smooth NDOs'. project progress with timely advice and detailed technical assistance. Or they can lie back, as several did, letting NDOs make mistakes, for example, in loan processing or subdivision clearance procedures, resulting in costly delays for the NDOs. And local political leaders can affect funding from noncity sources as well. In two cases, dissatisfaction expressed by city officials with NDOs' behavior led to funding cutoffs by other sources.

The importance of good working relations with the city is perhaps best illustrated by examples of projects that were well under way but were then stopped cold. Two of the three such projects in our sample were halted by serious battles that developed between the NDOs and city hall over other matters, leading to a breakdown of formerly positive or largely neutral relations. In the process, funding central to project feasibility was halted for long time periods (perhaps permanently), and NDO time and energy were diverted to responding to city attacks and rectifying management procedures on which the cities focused their fire. By way of contrast, at least two other

TABLE 52

RELATIONS WITH LOCAL GOVERNMENT AND PROJECT SUCCESS

NDO Relations with Local Government	Percentage of an NDO's Project Work That is Complete	
	0%–50%	*Greater Than 50%*
Good relations with elected officials and staff	.18	.82
Good relations with *either* elected officials *or* staff	.60	.40
Poor relations with both elected officials and staff	1.0	0.0

NOTE: Based on sample of thirty NDOs; Chi-Square test is significant at .05 level. The table may somewhat overstate the impact of local government relations over the long term, because our measure of the quality of relations in some cases drew directly on experience during the NSHD project.

projects in the study sample were proceeding slowly and/or suffering similar management problems but nonetheless received continuing, strong city support and assistance, because of good ongoing relations between the NDO staff, board of directors, and community and city officials. In addition, the future progress of two more other projects that have limited accomplishments to date rests on whether or not the NDOs' local political linkages will be adequate to obtain city-held property. Clearly, cooperation from the city government has been and is a major factor in whether many of the less successful NDO projects move forward.

Frequently, city support on all fronts is a major ingredient in the progress of the most successful projects. In at least eight sample cases where projects proceeded especially well, cities and NDOs treated each other largely as partners in the development process. Local governments saw the neighborhood organizations as effective implementers of city goals and programs and cooperated on a continuous basis to bring about project success—providing funds and property, technical assistance, and links to further resources.

The overall importance of city support is vividly illustrated in table 52. Over 80 percent of the NDOs with good cooperation from elected city officials and city staff had completed more than half of the work on their projects. The smaller number of organizations with poor or mixed relations with local government had in a large majority of cases made little progress. Tabulations (not presented here) relating city support to successful NDO fundraising show a very similar pattern.

Notably, cooperation from city staff did not follow automatically from having the support of elected officials. Support from elected representatives was necessary, and often sufficient, to gain funding; but needed advice and cooperation from staff sources had to be cultivated separately. One organization, for instance, gained substantial city funding for a housing rehabilitation project. But it was not until the NDO's new executive director developed improved relations with the city's community development department that city staffers undertook a crucial study that led to the recasting of the project to make it fit residents' incomes. In half the NDOs that had city council support but not staff support, city funds were obtained but staff resistance seriously hindered implementation. As table 52 emphasizes, developing good relationships with both elected officials and staff was critical to success, and it apparently requires a two-pronged effort.

The importance of positive relations with local government produces a major dilemma for neighborhood organizations. Strong advocacy actions— for example, protests against uncorrected housing conditions—can seriously injure NDO-city relations, as can active campaigning in elections, if the NDO's side loses. And poor relations make projects much harder to conduct. But NDOs we visited sometimes see such advocacy and campaign activities as critical to improving neighborhood conditions. In addition, since an NDO is often the leading institution in its neighborhood, frequently no one else in the community is prepared to take on political tasks. The decline of direct federal funding of NDOs and the resultant increasing importance of local support intensifies the dilemma and narrows the options of NDO leaders who see multiple lines of action as needed components of neighborhood revitalization. Discussion of policy issues raised by this dilemma is returned to in chapter 6.

Access to Competent Technical Assistance

Large numbers of NDOs obtained technical assistance to fill gaps in their own expertise, as detailed earlier. The outside technical skills made significant contributions to effective project work for roughly two-thirds of the organizations (not including use of architects and construction contractors in their usual roles). Recognizing the need for technical assistance and having access to people who are capable of providing it were key factors in project success. About one-third of the NDOs had noticeable project problems in areas where technical assistance was lacking or inadequate to supplement internal skills.[20]

In addition to cases where needed assistance was clearly missing, technical aid sometimes lacked timeliness or necessary quality. Some NDOs were

---

20. The number includes some overlap with those who, in other areas, received valuable technical assistance.

slow to recognize the need for help—for example, because they had substantial experience in other types of projects and did not realize the special needs of a new one. Potential technical-assistance sources were sometimes initially unwilling to provide counsel, ocassionally because an NDO needed to improve its overall relations with city hall before city agencies would help or because the NDO and project initially lacked credibility with the private sector. In other instances, assistance sources were simply too busy, too expensive, or located too far away to be regularly available as needed. Or they might be available locally but lack the specific expertise to supplement NDOs' knowledge and common sense.

The potential benefit of technical assistance was especially visible in cases where it was added after projects were well under way. Examples include a newly created construction company that failed to progress until an experienced construction entrepreneur-contractor was brought in as a continuing advisor, and a commercial project that was far along in construction but lacked any real marketing and leasing strategy until outside advice was obtained.

Technical assistance was most valuable under several conditions. Clear recognition and consensus by lead staff that aid was needed, followed by a precise delineation of what assistance was to be sought, were important prerequisites. Selection of aid providers worked best when NDOs could make their own choices, not determined by funders. At least equally important was the presence of a project director who devoted his or her primary attention to the specific project and also was eager to use and learn from technical assistance, so that at least day-to-day project responsibility could pass quickly to NDO staff.

Technical aid was most commonly important in four areas (in order of significance): project planning, proposal writing, financial packaging and feasibility analysis, and help with funder contacts and relations.[21] While these four categories of essential aid partly overlap the types of aid that, as we saw in chapter 2, are the types NDOs most commonly received, they by no means neatly match.

As discussed earlier under internal characteristics, a number of NDOs lacked the experience to identify the basic steps in development of a project and the specific tasks of implementation. Project-planning assistance was often necessary in order to make progress while NDO staff learned the ropes, and, fortunately, this kind of assistance was frequently obtainable. For example, one NDO, which was taking on much more complete project responsibility

---

21. Funder contacts would rate still higher if we included the activities of board members in that area in this count, rather than as a nontechnical board function. Contractors and architects playing their conventional roles are not included here.

for housing rehabilitation than its partnership with city hall had formerly demanded (or allowed), received ongoing, detailed technical advice in the form of lists of specific tasks to undertake. Later, staff themselves were able to perform the task-defining function.

Aid in proposal writing was often deemed vital in obtaining NSHD grants and other funds, especially for a few organizations with virtually no in-house capacity in this area, but for others who wanted improvement as well. Within the broad category of funder contact, technical-assistance sources frequently provided valuable access to private-sector funders in particular—in the form of introductions, favorable recommendations, and advice on who to talk to and how. These types of assistance also seemed reasonably well available and utilized.

The importance of assistance in financial analysis stems directly from the observed lack of such capabilities on NDO staffs. If outsiders did not provide the missing skills, NDOs faced difficulties in responding to changing financing alternatives, as well as unpleasant surprises in trying to pay for and market their project outputs. Regrettably, NDOs used this type of assistance rather infrequently, because they either failed to recognize their need or could not find competent sources of aid. As one approach to this problem, private businesses interested in supporting NDO efforts might well consider creating or expanding programs of lending employees with expertise in financial planning/packaging fields.

Aid of these four basic types was especially useful for younger, less skilled NDOs who might otherwise have been stymied in the early projects. But the technical-assistance route holds some risks. In rare cases, NDOs utilized aid in getting projects started, but were then left to carry out projects they could not handle. More commonly, technical assistance helped NDOs make substantial project progress but was less satisfactory than strong in-house expertise of the same kind in moving projects to full completion. Assistance in both project planning and proposal writing showed this pattern. With proposal writing, NDOs needing and receiving outside technical assistance had no greater likelihood than other NDOs of accomplishing less than half their intended work (see table 53). But they were less likely to meet at least 95 percent of their expectations. Quite possibly, technical assistance was not as readily available for certain follow-up and detail activities as were expert in-house staff in some NDOs, thus leading in the former instance, to less than complete success.[22] Also common was the danger that NDO long-

---

22. Cell sizes are too small in table 53 for a proper test of significance.

TABLE 53

PROPOSAL-WRITING TECHNICAL ASSISTANCE AND PROJECT SUCCESS

	Percentage of an NDO's Project Work That is Complete		
Source of Proposal-Writing Skills	*0%–50%*	*51%–94%*	*95% or Greater*
Weak in-house, technical assistance obtained	.40	.47	.14
Strong in-house	.42	.15	.42

NOTE: Based on sample of thirty NDOs; because of small cell sizes, Chi-Square test not appropriate.

term internal growth would suffer unless determined efforts were made to learn the skills from outside experts during project work.[23]

Certain specialized technical aid served NDOs of diverse levels of sophistication well. For instance, experienced outsiders guided the tax syndication of several projects that were otherwise handled well internally by strong NDOs. Other specialized aid was valuable in accounting,[24] marketing, and leasing in nonhousing projects particularly; and in cost estimating and construction oversight, for less experienced organizations predominantly.

The most important technical assistance often came from nonprofit organizations, typically those organizations specializing in serving NDOs, who were thus more familiar with and sensitive to NDOs' particular needs. Such technical groups also sometimes received grants to support NDO work and could thus offer it at limited cost.

In fact, much technical assistance being offered by various providers is really of little help to NDOs, because it is either insensitive to their needs or insufficiently expert to genuinely fill gaps in NDO capability. To get good technical assistance, NDOs frequently depended on linkages of long-term mutual respect with providers who had worked with them before. The importance of technical aid and the value of these relationships in assuring its quality make finding competent advisors and working with them well key factors in project success.

NDOs whose projects had proceeded to construction stages were divided about evenly between those acting as their own general contractors and those using outsiders. This choice had no systematic impacts on project success,[25]

---

23. Capacity-building issues are discussed separately in chapter 5.

24. This applies not so much for specific projects as for general capabilities.

25. The choice is essentially a long-run one. At the moment of a given project, NDOs either do or do not have construction capabilities.

TABLE 54

CONTRACTORS, NEIGHBORHOOD CREWS, AND PROJECT SUCCESS

	Percentage of an NDO's Project Work That is Complete	
Who Does Construction Work on Project	0%–50%	Greater Than 50%
Contractors	.39	.61
NDOs' own crews from neighborhood	.30	.70

NOTE: Based on sample of thirty NDOs; Chi-Square test not significant at any reasonable level.

as table 54 indicates, although it may well have affected the number of neighborhood jobs resulting. Some NDO supervisors and crews were excellent; others made errors in cost estimating or were slow and less efficient. Virtually the same could be said of hired contractors. The outsiders did seem to work out better when NDOs had more specific leverage with them—for example, a contractor who does a great deal of other work for an NDO's public and private project partners.

Outside architects were more clearly of value to NDOs. Sometimes they were absolutely necessary for complex plans and at other times helpful in producing better specifications and cost estimates. A major ingredient for success in using architects was their location. NDOs repeatedly had problems getting out of-town architects to be responsive and in several cases ended up replacing or supplementing them with local counterparts.

Overall, adequate technical assistance and skill transfer from providers to NDO staff remain keys to NDO productivity and growth. This is particularly apparent for NDOs in our study, who are not limited to the few most sophisticated community-based developers but reflect, in their broad use of outside technical aid, the substantial needs typical NDOs have for additional skills.

Key Links to Private Actors

NDOs in our study are not newcomers to tapping resources and cooperation from the private sector. The private sector served many important functions in NSHD projects—projects that were in planning in early 1980 and often far earlier, well before Reagan administration initiatives to promote private over public action.

A number of projects involved private coventurers, who shared ownership, financing, and implementation responsibilities in varying combinations

TABLE 55

Private Financing Shares and Overall Leveraging Ratios

Proportion of Project Financing from Private Sources	Ratio of Total (Non-NSHD) Funds to NSHD Funds		
	0–2	*2.01–5*	*Greater Than 5*
Less than .1	.48	.15	.38
.1–.5	.27	.47	.27
Greater than .5	.07	.64	.29

NOTE: Based on all ninety-nine NDOs with NSHD projects.

with the NDOs and without whom some projects might not have proceeded. Others had private investors as participants in syndicated tax shelters; in such instances, syndication proceeds were crucial in generating enough equity to attract lenders and keep project costs affordable to their ultimate beneficiaries. Loans from private for-profit institutions were the primary source of permanent financing for a large share of all projects (see chapter 3). Private financing was important in generating high levels of leveraging of NSHD funds. As shown in table 55, those NDOs whose project financing included a substantial proportion of private funds generally had higher leveraging ratios (ratios of total funds to NSHD funds) than did others.

As detailed earlier, private individuals and firms participated regularly in NDO projects as technical advisors and as architect and contractor members of development teams. Local businesspeople were central to planning commercial revitalization efforts. And foundations and corporations were important providers of grants. Such funds were especially valuable because they often came in the form of general support, allowing projects to be identified and planned before project monies arrived and keeping projects (and NDOs) alive when they ran into difficulties. In several instances private foundations had close links with NDOs, providing continuing counsel and financial support and access to technical expertise and other aid.

The shortage of NDO links to the downtown business community (noted in chapter 2) were often costly, making it much harder not only to find tenants for commercial and industrial space but to borrow vital business expertise, to develop markets for services, and to tap additional financing resources. NDOs sought to facilitate these connections by adding people from outside their neighborhood to the board of directors. Having one good contact and using him or her to gain access to others in the private sector was often effective.

Finding the Risk Takers

Several kinds of resources needed to make projects progress have proven particularly difficult but important for NDOs to acquire. Establishing working relations with funders and other actors who provide these resources was a significant aspect of NDO links to outsiders. (These ties of course overlap with relations such as those with city government and the private sector, discussed earlier.)

One critical actor was an institution willing to make the first real commitment to a project while other key commitments were yet to be captured. The commitment might be money grants or loans, land or buildings, firm intentions to buy or lease space after rehabilitation or construction, or willingness to purchase the service or product of a new venture. This actor had to risk putting something forward on a project when there was no guarantee the work would garner the other resources necessary to move ahead. The role of risk taker was most often played (generally with funds or real estate) by the NSHD grant itself, a public agency with some experience with the NDO, or the privately funded Local Initiatives Support Corporation in instances where the NDO early established ties with this still-young organization. Such early commitments from these sources were sometimes explicitly stated preconditions for bank loans and for similar project participation. At other times the commitments served as implicit catalysts in gaining assistance from actors who preferred to contribute to nearly finished packages. Several projects languished, partly because no one would take that first plunge. Tenants for nonresidential projects were the toughest commitments to obtain early, with NDOs' inability to assure rental rates and completion dates contributing to the always difficult problem of attracting business to troubled neighborhoods. In the future, problems might be eased by fashioning more types of definite but conditional commitments that funders might select—in other words, commitments that are firm but still conditioned on others' participation.

Another type of resource difficult to obtain were funds that enabled staff and technical assistants to compile detailed project plans and packages—resources that were harder to assemble when delays and various other complications stretched out the planning period. Again, such funds involve risk to the supporting institutions because the plans they support may not be implemented. NDOs' track records served at times to establish needed confidence, and long-established relations with funders also helped to gain this key support. Local governments and foundations joined the NSHD program in fulfilling this need.[26]

---

26. NSHD grants provide substantial funding for this purpose by program design.

Adequate working capital was also hard to secure—to cover the early needs of struggling new enterprises; to support construction-period work in housing projects; and to take timely advantage of opportunities to purchase real estate. No one set of actors stands out as offering such funding. NDOs with outside relationships that had produced supplies of general operating funds—principally from foundations, local governments, and CSA (before its demise)—were best equipped to cover their capital needs from general accounts. But others had to scramble.

Continuing Relationships with Funders

A large number of NDOs were receiving at least some funding for their NSHD projects from sources that funded them previously and with whom they have continuing good relations. Creating and maintaining these lasting links to funders was an important element in pinning down dollars and therefore, also, in project success. Many NDOs were able to take advantage of such relations because they purposely cultivated them—initially seeking out responsive individuals in funding agencies and institutions, pursuing continuing contacts, delivering on previously funded promises, and gaining an understanding of the funders' interests. These methods of building relations of course are tied tightly to such internal NDO characteristics as skills of the executive director, doing homework, and track record.

The payoffs from continuing funder links were substantial. For example, several sample NDOs were awarded primary project funding from state housing finance agencies with whom they had worked successfully on previous projects. In general, NDOs with positive ongoing relations with state and federal government were better at leveraging NSHD dollars. Other NDOs relied on the continued close support of major foundations for funds and in making other contacts. NDOs attempting projects that deviated from their usual major line of work were especially fortunate if their past funding sources had the program flexibility to support new initiatives, while others in that position struggled to develop a new line of contacts. One NDO cleverly financed its new line of commercial work as part of a funding package for its traditional housing efforts and thus avoided this problem. NDOs that had their historic lines to funders interrupted—for example, by fights with city hall—found themselves in extremely difficult funding circumstances.

Conditions of NDO Environments

Powerful external forces beyond the control of neighborhood organizations had major impacts on the outcomes of many NDO projects. Especially noteworthy were the negative effects of changing national conditions that occurred after the projects were proposed: reductions in the availability of project funds from the federal government, rising interest rates, and the general decline in the national economy. These conditions combined were leading factors in preventing two projects we visited from getting off the ground.[27] They also were important causes of other projects falling short of goals or having their long-run viability threatened. In analyzing the impacts of internal capabilities and relationships with outsiders on project success, we found repeatedly that external factors could overwhelm other potential determinants of progress. The deteriorating national environment for NDOs' work exacerbated the effects of the continually distressing neighborhood circumstances under which most NDOs operate.

NDOs were by no means always optimally skilled and equipped to deal with external difficulties. But to a substantial extent they suffered the same types of setbacks that other project developers would and did in comparable national and local environments. An important difference is that NDOs are, by their own design and objectives, much more often serving neighborhoods and people whose situations leave projects only a narrow margin of feasibility at best, requiring more public support and allowing less room for deteriorating private-sector conditions.

The impacts of major external forces and a few less critical but still significant environmental conditions are detailed in the pages following.

Cutbacks in Federal Funding

Freezes, reductions, and elimination of federal program funds that NDOs had anticipated, and in some cases had begun using in their NSHD projects, caused important difficulties for a substantial share of the organizations whose financial plans included major federal funding. At least eight of the thirty projects in the study sample were blocked or curtailed by the impacts of federal cutbacks. The reason the damages were not still more widespread was that although project planning largely preceded many of the federal fund reductions, the majority of projects were designed to rely more on state and local monies, private funds, or in some cases federal funds already committed

---

27. These were two of only three of our thirty sample projects that have not made some significant progress at least in packaging, if not implementation (though others are stymied after partial completion of work for these and other reasons).

(including NSHD grants themselves) than on federal funds from affected programs.[28]

Cutbacks in EDA, CETA, and Section 8 funding were the principal sources of federal funding problems for sample NDOs.[29] Two projects in commercial and economic development were made infeasible by the loss of anticipated EDA deep subsidies, coupled with high private-market interest rates. A housing rehabilitation project has been held up and seriously threatened by the absence of expected Section 8 substantial rehabilitation monies. The deep-subsidy public programs—like EDA grants and Section 8—that are required to carry out development work in seriously troubled neighborhoods and to serve low-income people are not generally replaceable. CETA cutbacks, often occurring midstream in project implementation, affected many NDOs and in several cases sharply cut their outputs below expectations; and the higher costs of using non-CETA labor lowered the number of housing units and other outputs that could be provided with other funds. Valuable training opportunities were also lost. Cutbacks in EDA, Section 8, and CETA programs furthermore raised longer-term problems for several projects where construction was complete—specifically, in attracting commercial tenants to stores when there were no funds for tenant-tailored improvements, in covering future housing operating expenses, in meeting higher mortgage costs created by use of unsubsidized labor once CETA was withdrawn, and for similar needs. The frequent and multifaceted impacts of CETA and Section 8 losses especially are reconfirmed by Cohen and Kohler's survey, which modestly postdated the completion of our site visits.[30]

The importance of federal funding in making housing construction and rehabilitation projects affordable to neighborhood residents, and therefore viable in terms of NDO objectives, was well demonstrated in numerous successful projects that secured various combinations of Section 312, Section 8, and CETA funding before cutbacks fully took effect. Many NDOs are seeking to make further housing projects feasible by using tax syndications to sell the benefits of newly accelerated rental housing depreciation to private partners. But our own findings, as well as those of Cohen and Kohler, are that syndication alone is inadequate to reach low-income people with these projects. Federal subsidies, or good substitutes for them, are required as well.

---

28. For purposes of this discussion, CDBG funding is considered local money. Total CDBG funding has at any rate not been greatly reduced, although some cuts were made and a smaller share now goes to urban areas.

29. Again, the closer examination that sample projects received made us better able to pinpoint key funding problems for them than for the entire study population.

30. See Cohen and Kohler 1983. Their survey of NSHD grantees and other NDOs took place later in 1982 than our spring site visits.

TABLE 56

PRIMARY PLANNED PUBLIC FUNDING SOURCE AND SUCCESS IN LEVERAGING FUNDS

Primary Planned Source of Public Funds	Ratio of Actual (Non-NSHD) Funds Obtained to Planned	
	0–.94	.95 or Greater
CETA	.58	.42
EDA	.50	.50
All other federal[a]	.53	.47
City	.30	.70
CDBG	.29	.71
State	.44	.56
No non-NSHD public funds	.40	.60

NOTE: Based on all ninety-nine NDOs with NSHD projects.

a. HUD Section 312, Section 235, Section 202, and UDAG; CSA; and Farmers Home Administration funds.

A broader look at the experience of all ninety-nine NDOs in our study confirms the impact of federal cutbacks. We examined the extent to which NDOs met their expectations for project funding other than from NSHD, based on the source from which they originally expected to obtain their largest single bundle of money (see table 56). NDOs expecting to use primarily CETA, EDA, or other federal money (Section 312, CSA, Section 235, Small Business Administration [SBA], Section 202, UDAG, Farmers Home Administration) fared worse in reaching funding objectives than did those anticipating city (including CDBG) or state—in other words nonfederal public—funds. And we found that NDOs were less able to meet expectations for funding from specific federal program sources, primary sources or not, than they were from state and local sources. A further tabulation (not presented here) indicated that NDOs that expected the federal government to be their largest funding source reached planned funding levels least often when all public and private sources of principal funding were considered.

Of course funding alone does not ensure project success, and the relationship between anticipating federal funding and accomplishing a project was not neatly systematic. But development projects cost money, and it is apparent that reduced funds for federal programs made it far harder for NDOs to assemble the resources they felt they needed in order to meet intended objectives.

More extensive and deeper funding cuts are still ahead for NDOs, involving decreased aid from sources of both project and general support monies that have been critical to their successful work to date. As stated earlier, many NSHD projects secured commitments before cutbacks took effect, and some NDOs have continued to work with Section 8 and other project monies that were already in the pipeline but are now coming to a halt. NSHD grants, which, as discussed later in this chapter, played a key role in both project planning and implementation, have themselves been eliminated.

Losses in general funds for basic staffing—to allow new projects to be organized and to operate those previously developed—are already afflicting NDOs more seriously now and will cause still greater difficulty in the near future. Losses in NSHD, CSA, VISTA, CETA, and similar funds mean staff reductions, excessive time spent on fundraising, and inevitable declines in program progress.[31] Our research focused on many projects already well into the planning stages, in significant part with federal support—support whose loss in terms of staffing will clearly be missed.

This trend of federal cutbacks, which is external to and beyond NDO influence, starkly reverses the patterns of the 1970s, during which the creation and growth of CDBG and CETA programs contributed greatly to NDO development. It remains to be fully seen how well NDOs can adapt to these pressures. Many organizations are actively seeking private funding substitutes. But studies of the problem invariably conclude that private contributions cannot possibly fill the gap.[32] NDOs also continue to take on potential income-generating ventures; however, past and current experience suggests that real profits are hard for NDOs to gain, at least in NDOs serving their own neighborhoods and residents. The syndication profits that some have earned, and others anticipate, will dry up for lower-income housing as lack of other subsidies rules out many such projects.

What is certain from our observations and those of others is that NDO projects serving the most deteriorated neighborhoods and the neediest citizens will be extremely adversely affected by reduced federal funding. The unique role that NDOs serve in targeting the benefits of development where others do not is clearly threatened.

Rising Private-Market Interest Rates and an Economy in Recession

The great majority of NSHD projects involved the rehabilitation or construction of buildings. The sharp rise in and continued high levels of interest rates for private construction hurt the many NDOs whose project plans (made prior to the interest-rate increases) included obtaining private loans for themselves or their "clients." Like their purely private developer counterparts,

---

31. Confirmed again by Cohen and Kohler 1983.
32. See, for example, Salamon and Abramson, 1983a; and Rosenbaum and Smith 1981.

NDOs have suffered from the increased costs of doing construction with borrowed money, from the higher mortgage costs that must be met if they rent out structures for whose purchase and rehabilitation they have borrowed funds, and from the difficulties that potential purchasers of properties developed by NDOs encounter in affording private financing. At least eleven sample NDOs faced significant problems of these types, comprising most of the projects not protected by public-only or largely public funding or by advance commitments of private funds at better-than-market rates. In the population of all grantees, nineteen of the forty-four NDOs that anticipated using any private-lender financing obtained less than 50 percent of their intended levels of funding, including eleven that obtained no money from that source. This was the worst performance, by those standards, in reaching planned funding goals from any private or public funding source category except EDA. NDOs' internal weaknesses and the nature of their neighborhoods no doubt dashed some expectations of private financing. But the unavailability of conventional loans, or NDOs' inability to use loan funds available only at high market rates, surely helped make private-loan funding goals nearly the least well reached.

The problems caused by high interest rates merit further discussion here. As indicated earlier, for two sample NDOs, high interest rates combined with loss of federal funds to make their projects infeasible. Dampened demand for commercial and industrial space, due to the slack economy, also contributed to these projects' failure. Several sample NDOs were conducting projects to buy, rehabilitate, and resell houses to individual homeowners. High interest rates prevented many of the resales, forcing the NDOs to become housing managers and precluding the planned reuse of sale proceeds for further project work. Notably, an NDO that got a firm commitment for lower-interest financing for resale in advance of project start-up had a much more favorable experience. Rising uncertainties about employment and falling incomes also were perceived to hurt home sales. Other projects were slowed by NDOs' having to look only for properties with assumable loans, limiting themselves to repairing buildings that public fund allocations could finance, or waiting while state governments deferred trying to sell tax-exempt bonds in the troubled bond market.

In addition to the eleven sample projects with direct interest-rate difficulties, others suffered important indirect effects. Most NDO economic development projects involved the creation of construction companies or of producers of building materials. High interest rates and the effect of the recession on people's finances and outlooks lowered potential demand for these companies' services, limiting their growth and threatening their viability in some cases.

TABLE 57

PRIMARY PLANNED FUNDING SOURCE AND PROJECT SUCCESS

Primary Planned Sources of Funds (Public or Private)	*Percentage of an NDO's Project Work That is Complete*	
	0%–50%	*Greater Than 50%*
Private lending	.58	.42
Foundations or religious	0	1.0
Program income	0	1.0
Various private	0	1.0
City[a]	.40	.60
CDBG	.20	.80
State	.20	.80
EDA	.75	.25
CETA	.17	.83
All other public	.27	.73

NOTE: Based on all ninety-nine NDOs with NSHD projects.

a. Often CDBG funds were placed in this category by NDOs and HUD.

Several broader observations regarding the effect of high interest rates on NDOs deserve attention beyond the impacts of such rates on individual projects. First, those NDOs that most diligently pursued private-sector leveraging, as encouraged by public-sector actors and others, were naturally among those hit hardest by the worsened financing situation. NDOs that had anticipated private lending as their primary funding source did less well in completing project work than any other NDOs, except those that planned for long-frozen EDA funds to be the largest source of their money (see table 57). While other factors may help explain the relatively poor outcomes of these projects, certainly the lack of private long-term financing available (if at all) at anything like the costs anticipated in 1979 and early 1980, when many NSHD projects were planned, was a significant contributor.

Second, sharply higher interest rates mean greater needs for other sources of "cheap money," public and private, to make projects feasible in low-income neighborhoods. NDOs cannot easily turn to private financing to absorb public cutbacks in periods of very high interest rates. They need, at a minimum, to couple significant grants and low-interest loans with the private, market-rate funds.

Third, past studies have shown that NDOs have difficulty attracting private lenders to their projects and neighborhoods even in periods of lower rates, when they might better afford to use them. We found in this study, as previous Urban Institute research had shown, that the Community Reinvestment Act helped to encourage lender cooperation in a number of cases. But

TABLE 58

Race, Ethnicity, and Public Versus Private Funding

Race or Ethnicity of NDO Neighborhood	Ratio of Public Funding to All Funding (NSHD Projects)		
	0–.5	*.51–.9*	*Greater Than .9*
White	.29	.50	.21
Black	.07	.33	.59
Hispanic	.08	.08	.85
Asian	0.00	.33	.67
Mixed	.22	.44	.33

Note: Based on all ninety-nine NDOs with NSHD projects.

even when interest rates become more affordable, NDOs will still likely have to struggle to bring private loan capital to their communities.

These last difficulties may well be particularly acute for NDOs operating in racial and ethnic minority neighborhoods, based on NSHD experience. NDOs located in black, Hispanic, and Asian communities were far more likely to obtain predominantly public funds for their projects—as opposed to those from private lenders or other private sources—than were NDOs in white or mixed neighborhoods (see table 58). Some 85 percent of predominantly Hispanic and nearly 60 percent of predominantly black NDOs used virtually all public monies, compared with just over 20 percent of predominantly white NDOs.

While this outcome could be of the NDOs' own choosing or result from other factors, it is likely that at least some of the contrast results from a mixture of lender reluctance to loan in minority areas, relative lack of private-sector contacts by minority groups (with both lenders and other private sources), and relatively unattractive economic circumstances in the neighborhoods of minority NDOs, even relative to other NDO communities. In any of these cases, private loans will be especially difficult for minority NDOs to pursue even should national conditions improve.

Neighborhood Conditions

Most NDOs in our study operate in neighborhoods characterized by many low-income residents, serious crime and other social problems, dilapidated buildings, and struggling local economies. Rarely, we found, are other actors engaged in similar development efforts in these neighborhoods. Although difficult conditions may make NDO staff, board, and community members that much more determined to make projects succeed, the direct effects of such environments most often make projects much harder to complete successfully. Using a crude assessment of the intensity of community problems, we found significantly less likelihood of project success for the over one-third of our sample organizations whose neighborhoods were deemed at least as troubled as any other in their respective cities.

A clear illustration of the impact of neighborhood conditions is that low incomes and declining populations may drastically limit attempts at commercial revitalization. One NDO, for example, has adequate low-cost funds[33] to renovate space for numerous stores and offices, but it remains to be seen whether the neighborhood—with limited purchasing power of its own and a negative reputation with outsiders—will either attract commercial tenants or adequately sustain them. Other NDOs had difficulty lining up the advance commitments from commercial tenants that were required by funding sources before they would grant financing for construction or repair. Similarly, low incomes, often coupled with high proportions of elderly residents, have joined with broader economic factors to limit demand for homeownership in NDO repair-and-resale programs. On the other hand, NDO neighborhoods do generate ready demand for decently repaired NDO rental housing if rents can be kept low, precisely because of predominantly poor-quality housing and low incomes.

Vandalism, theft of materials, and arson have been costly to NDO projects, especially because project funds often leave little leeway for unanticipated costs. Crime also clearly discouraged some businesses from agreeing to locate in NDO project buildings. NDO neighborhoods' reputations for high crime rates sometimes had negative effects on the willingness of businesses and customers to come into the areas, beyond what actual statistics would suggest, and several organizations sought with limited success to alter such perceptions.

A further impact of neighborhood economic and social problems for a few NDOs was in credibility. Some potential sources of technical assistance or funding considered NDO neighborhoods such unpromising places for development, based on community conditions and reputation, that they were slow to give NDO projects a hearing or to provide at least the minimal resources that would allow the projects to be developed with other primary funds.

The typical NDO neighborhood's impact on availability of buildings and land for NDO projects was somewhat more mixed. In some places, numerous boarded-up buildings were available at nominal cost from the public or private sector, making projects less costly (but representing obstacles to long-run

---

33. These refer to grants and deferred payment loans.

neighborhood revitalization). Even where buildings were severely run-down, they could be profitable to operate and hence hard to obtain, as evidenced by the legal action required by two NDOs attempting to buy structures with serious code violations. Easier-to-get sites were often hard to take advantage of—for example, an urban garden hillside site too steep and landslide-ridden for other uses or a commercial site probably not yet ripe for development. Several NDOs operated in neighborhoods on the upswing, where displacement was a key problem, and had some difficulty finding buildings to buy at prices that made their projects affordable to residents.

Overall, the fact that NDOs take on work under very trying conditions substantially lowers the likelihood of project success, regardless of the NDOs' competence. This fact must be duly considered by NDOs in selecting projects and by outsiders in assessing NDO efficiency and then determining levels of assistance to be provided based on NDO performance. Outsiders whose policies are unrealistically demanding because they neglect or minimize neighborhood impacts in reviewing NDO work implicitly threaten to write off NDOs' neighborhoods as unredeemable or their goals of serving people of limited means in those neighborhoods as infeasible.

Weather and Strikes

An exceptionally cold winter slowed many NSHD construction and rehabilitation projects, raising costs as well as creating delays in completion relative to expectations. In a couple of cases, strikes had similar effects. Observers judging the efficiency of NDOs must recognize this coincidental impact, and some NDOs need to allow room for such unexpected events in their project planning and budget.

Changes in Local Government

As discussed earlier, a cooperative relationship with city political officials and key staff is an important element in NDO success and one that an NDO can actively pursue. But local government can and often does change in ways beyond NDO control, and these changes can certainly influence project success. For eight of our sample of thirty NDOs, changes occurred during their NSHD project work.[34] In half of those cases, the changes apparently had a marked impact on provision of key project resources by cities.

---

34. The NDOs so affected fall heavily into project-type categories that are oversampled, so that the eight of thirty modestly overrepresents the expected studywide share.

One case involved election of a city council and mayor less sympathetic to neighborhood concerns and organizations than their predecessors, which was later a factor in project funding cutoffs to an NDO heavily dependent on local funds. In another case, an official's desire for support in an upcoming election helped obtain long-delayed release of a city-owned building for NDO renovation. In still other instances, changeovers in staffing of community development departments helped produce heightened levels of cooperation with support for NDOs. Change in local government itself, regardless of its direction, sometimes inhibited project progress, as NDOs courted newly elected officials or waited for reorganized agencies to deliver aid under revised programs. Finally, two of the most delayed projects were frustrated largely by political or bureaucratic delays in local governments' turning over of key properties—delays generated by factors beyond NDO control.

In sum, maintaining good relations with city hall was a continuing process and one by no means dependent only on NDO skill and effectiveness. This fact raises questions about the appropriateness of making public funds available to NDOs solely from local sources.

NDO Response to Environmental Conditions

Although NDOs, at least in the short term, have little influence over the external forces just discussed, they can become more effective in responding to them. NDOs' abilities to respond have certainly influenced their NSHD projects' current and potential levels of success.

Examples of effective and ineffective NDO responses have been cited often in this book in other contexts. An NDO doing commercial revitalization in a troubled neighborhood, for example, has drawn local businesspeople into the project process early on, as a way of encouraging their own future tenancy and of determining what might attract others; the NDO is also hard at work on neighborhood security and image problems. Several NDOs organized community support to protect their buildings from damage and theft; some proved adept at shifting and combining funding sources in the face of federal cutbacks and rising interest rates, while others did not; one moved cannily through the local political structure to capture a land parcel quickly, while another's lack of attention to bureaucratic procedures created a delay that lost it the chance to purchase houses central to its project at good prices.

Within limits, then, the responsiveness of NDOs—built on skill in project planning or financial analysis, community support, and other factors discussed in this chapter—was a factor in success as well.

TABLE 59

SAMPLE PROJECT TYPE AND PROJECT SUCCESS

	Percentage of an NDO's Project Work That is Complete	
Project Type (Sample Projects)	0%–50%	Greater Than 50%
Housing rehabilitation, housing construction, community development, and energy	.27	.73
Commercial revitalization and economic development	.57	.43

NOTE: Based on sample of thirty NDOs; Chi-Square test significant at .05 level.

Projects Themselves as Factors in Success

There is no inherent reason to expect that NDOs will have the same level of success with differing projects. In fact, we found that project characteristics mattered greatly—in interactions with the internal capabilities, outside relations, and environmental conditions with which NDOs came to them. Project types, their complexity, and the quality of their original conceptions all had powerful impacts on the likelihood of success.

Project Type

To examine the impacts of types of projects on project success, we will look first at the projects we visited, those for which we have the most precise knowledge of project components and outcomes. NSHD sample projects in housing rehabilitation and construction and community development were systematically more successful than those in economic development and commercial revitalization.[35] Ten of the fifteen projects coming closest to producing initially expected results were in housing and community development. Only six of the other fifteen projects falling shorter of expectations were in these categories. Among those latter fifteen, four are part housing and part economic development or part housing and part commercial revitalization. Across those four, the housing components are less likely than the others not to be proceeding as anticipated. Table 59 shows the substantial difference in likelihood

---

35. Our sample also contained a single energy project. Note that projects that were of mixed categories were assigned, for sampling purposes, to their predominant type, except that those with both a housing rehabilitation or community-development component and another component were in all cases assigned to the other categories (outside of housing and community development), which had far fewer total members in the population.

TABLE 60

NSHD PROJECT TYPE AND PROJECT SUCCESS

Project Type (All Projects)	Percentage of an NDO's Project Work That is Complete		
	0%–50%	51%–94%	95% or Greater
Housing rehabilitation, housing construction, community development, and energy	.32	.30	.38
Commercial revitalization and economic development	.46	.32	.22

NOTE: Based on all ninety-nine NDOs with NSHD projects.

of completing planned tasks between housing, community development, and energy projects on the one hand and predominantly commercial and economic development efforts on the other. Nearly three-fourths of the former group are well along, but less than half of the latter are.[36]

Looking at projects by type for the full population of ninety-nine NDOs (where our ability to measure percentage of overall work complete is somewhat more restricted), we see a comparable if not quite so sharp distinction (see table 60).

These differences in NDO accomplishments are made clearest by examining again actual outputs compared with planned outputs for the variety of types of projects. Table 61 (which, for convenience, repeats findings from

TABLE 61

RATIO OF ACTUAL TO PLANNED OUTPUTS, BY OUTPUT TYPE, FOR COMPLETED PROJECTS

Output Type	Mean Ratio of Actual to Planned Outputs
Weatherized housing units	.97
Housing units rehabilitated	.83
Housing units newly constructed	.54
Businesses assisted	.37
Commercial square footage rehabilitated	.46
Commercial square footage newly constructed	.09
Economic development jobs created—permanent	.39

NOTE: Based on all ninety-nine NDOs with NSHD projects.

36. Weights are applied to the sample observations, so that the percentages in table 59 do not precisely correspond to the raw numbers in the paragraph.

chapter 3) focuses on relative accomplishments among projects that are complete. As noted earlier, housing rehabilitation and energy (weatherization) work show much greater accomplishments, measured as the ratio of actual to planned results, than do other types of projects; and housing construction work ranks third. Community development projects generally involve single, discrete outputs (for example, an urban park) and are not well measured in this way; but they also generally fared well (not shown in table). The various outputs intended to be produced in commercial and economic development projects were much further away from being realized. As also noted in chapter 3, comparable ratios of now-expected to originally planned outputs, for unfinished projects, show a similar pattern, although of course they are less certain. Overall, project type often dominated other determinants of success. Because of the power of project type to determine outcomes, it was necessary at times to analyze the impacts of other factors on performance separately for the two broad categories of projects, in order to isolate those factors' effects.

There are several logical reasons for the importance of project type, some more subject to change than others. The central reason is that housing projects have ample ready markets, if they are kept affordable by subsidies, hard work, cheap buildings, and so on. NDOs' neighborhoods are full of ill-housed people, many paying high housing costs, who are eager to move into higher-quality units at affordable rents or carrying costs. The situation is different for projects of other types. Commercial revitalization projects generally, and some economic development efforts, depend on attracting private businesses to troubled neighborhoods from which other businesses have departed. Even if good-quality space is provided at favorable rents, the enterprises may well feel that other neighborhood disadvantages (discussed earlier in this chapter) outweigh that attraction. Retailers of goods and services may feel that lower-income residents will not provide an adequate market by themselves; that troubled neighborhoods, often with negative reputations, will not attract other customers and clients; and that the absence of other stores and related activities nearby will limit business. Nonretail enterprises may worry about the willingness of present employees to travel to these same areas, the costs of security, and so forth. Neighborhood effects are, in sum, especially powerful in nonhousing projects.

These effects were definite problems for the NDOs we studied, as evidenced by their difficulty in lining up tenants. The problems are not easily solved, especially by narrow, project-specific measures. Several organizations are, in their broader strategies, intelligently addressing the neighborhood conditions that are at the root of the problems.

Similarly, NDOs' own new enterprises, producing various goods and services, are more dependent for success on the existence of strong markets than they are on creating good buildings for them to work from. Initial savings from lower space costs, even coupled with grants for start-up capital needs and labor subsidies, often do not give the new enterprises enough of a "price" advantage to assure them a place in critical markets. Markets may, for example, depend also on neighborhood economics, on word-of-mouth advertising in communities outside NDO neighborhoods, or on links to key individuals and institutions. The modest scale of NDOs' own ventures, and the greater control the organizations have over their own (rather than others') investment decisions, did make these efforts more successful than projects designed to attract other business during a sharp recession.

Unfortunately, NDOs had relatively little experience and expertise in dealing with various kinds of market concerns, as indicated in our discussion of internal skills. Staff members underestimated the likely difficulties of, and knew little about, attracting tenants and/or markets for nonhousing projects; they provided inadequate technical assistance in this area and were not well-informed about how to find such expert advice. This set of circumstances is more under the control of NDOs and their supporters than are market conditions themselves and might be corrected.

Other reasons why economic and commercial development projects fared less well are more peculiar to the timing of our study. For one thing, federal funding cutbacks and freezes took effect earliest for EDA monies, and several economic and commercial development projects depended in whole or in part on these monies. The massive reductions in federal housing subsidy programs affected a smaller share of housing projects, both because the cutbacks came later and funding commitments had been obtained long in advance, and because many of the numerous housing rehabilitation efforts for homeowners in our sample were not dependent on federal subsidies. (New construction, which was more dependent on federal money, fared worse than rehabilitation.) The deep recession hurt commercial and economic development projects especially. The types of enterprises that these projects sought to attract were already struggling because of the strained economy, and markets for new NDO enterprises were difficult to locate in the face of declining demand. As mentioned earlier, rising interest rates that troubled some housing projects also choked off much demand for the work of NDOs' own most common economic development enterprises—their own construction companies.

The permanent market differences between commercial and economic development projects and other projects, plus time-specific forces, combined to make the former types of projects less able to attract financing. Commercial and economic development efforts were generally less able to meet fundraising expectations and to leverage NSHD dollars than were projects in housing, energy, and community development. The worst problems were experienced by NDOs planning major private financing, suggesting that the perception of potential funders that markets were inadequate was key.

All this of course does not mean that NDOs should be discouraged from taking on nonhousing work. Economic and commercial development projects are central parts of comprehensive neighborhood revitalization efforts. It does mean that market issues will have to be given due concern in project planning, that greater expertise to address these issues will have to be generated internally and from the outside, that new sources of financial support for these projects will have to be developed, and that arrangements to provide and ensure viable markets might become a major part of the aid outsiders can provide. It also means that NDO efforts toward self-sufficiency, which often focus on presumed opportunities to earn profits in nonhousing projects and are now being widely encouraged in the face of public funding cutbacks, are not going to be quick or easy solutions to financial problems.

Project Complexity

Some NDOs took on projects that had larger numbers of more complicated tasks than others. Not unexpectedly, these complexities made project success more difficult, challenging even the more experienced and sophisticated NDOs that often took on the tougher efforts (as we saw in the earlier discussion of track records and staffing).

Three dimensions of complexity were apparent. First, some projects involved obtaining funding and other participation from a large number of sources, without many commitments initially in place. This obviously created an increased chance that one or more key project components would fall through, and it heightened the problem of finding participants who would take the initial plunge that might bring in others. The difficulties of such projects were especially acute for NDOs with overextended staffs, in which one or two key staffers were left with many tasks to juggle in lining up support. In contrast, some projects used mainly NSHD funds and one other early commitment of financing (say, CDBG monies). These projects were able to make substantial progress at least in the "construction" phases, even in NDOs without exceptional skills.

Other projects were made more difficult by their large and diverse scope. For example, one well-run NDO included in its NSHD project major commercial construction, commercial rehabilitation, technical assistance and loan funds to local businesses, creation of a security program, and establishment of a credit union—all in the context of a large housing project in the same immediate area. It accomplished many but not all parts of this program, as did others with somewhat less ambitious but still multipart efforts. Projects

TABLE 62

MIXED PROJECT TYPES AND PROJECT SUCCESS

Project Mix	Percentage of an NDO's Project Work That is Complete		
	0%–50%	*51%–94%*	*95% or Greater*
Projects of a single major type	.33	.29	.38
Mixture of two or more major types	.58	.42	0.00

NOTE: Based on all ninety-nine NDOs with NSHD projects.

involving a mix of two or more major types of work consistently had less likelihood of success than those of any single type (see table 62).

Projects also varied in the difficulty of their nitty-gritty work. Some buildings, for example, were far more difficult to repair, and some were rehabilitated to higher standards than others, creating greater chance of construction mistakes, cost overruns, and marketing problems. Difficulties also arose in sometimes using inexperienced construction managers and site supervisors, as well as crews with many trainees. Projects to rehabilitate a very small number of houses could usually progress well by one means or another, while larger-scale efforts were somewhat more often trapped by funding shortages or other problems. An ultimately successful new-housing construction project was seriously delayed (and nearly derailed) by slow HUD processing. In this instance, clearance took longer in part because of project complexities unfamiliar to HUD: cooperative ownership, solar water heat, and an expanded community facility and garden.

From a narrow perspective, these straightforward findings might suggest that outsiders should support mainly modest, simple NDO projects, as well as projects that already have commitments lined up and are perhaps even under way, as were some NSHD efforts. Clearly, however, larger and more complex projects often serve important functions in neighborhoods, addressing problems that small, narrowly defined projects cannot. Furthermore, undertaking such projects is a significant aspect of the growth in NDOs' abilities to generate future revitalization. And our evidence shows that the chances for success can be substantial even for more ambitious efforts.

A broader and more productive viewpoint parallels the lessons of track-record building. NDOs should take pains to select, and supporters to encourage, those projects whose complexity matches NDOs' evolving capabilities and resources. Attempting of more complex projects should be encouraged, but in line with rising NDO capacity to perform. Supporters should also work to ensure that when more difficult work is undertaken, the level of difficulty is recognized and supported by technical, financial, and other means.

Project Selection

Certain projects were more successful than others because, from the time of their conception, they were better suited to neighborhood environments and overall NDO programs. Some addressed well an obvious but previously unmet neighborhood need. For example, two housing cooperative projects, in gentrifying areas that lacked any other provision to protect lower-income residents, fit this description well. The clear need for these projects and their unique appropriateness for dealing with that need meant ready markets, strong community support, and city cooperation beyond what politics alone would have provided. Other NDO work missed the mark in these terms, including a project to make very low-income and elderly renters into homeowners and another to build industrial space for rent in a city with much new vacant space already available in superior locations.

Some projects, mentioned elsewhere in this book, were well conceived in terms of specific resource opportunities or their relation to other NDO work. A good example of the use of available resources was a terraced urban garden on a steep hillside not otherwise usable, in an overcrowded neighborhood where space is at a high premium. Another previously cited project was an NDO's financing of its first commercial construction as part of a large mortgage for a combined housing and commercial building, which the NDO obtained on the basis of its housing record. On the other hand, a project to involve tenants in energy conservation was seriously hurt by its connection to other NDO work; tenants were displeased by poor management and repair of the building (owned but not managed by the NDO) and could not see cooperating in an effort that seemed peripheral to their real problems. (That response might have been anticipated and basic housing improvements initiated first.)

Overall, projects benefited when careful thought was given to their relation to neighborhood conditions, available resources, and overall NDO strategies. Sometimes risky projects that do not fit neatly with other conditions may still be very appropriate to select. For example, one NDO undertook commercial revitalization in a location with serious problems—actual and reputed—that made success uncertain. But the history of the location as the center of its community provided a possibility that success there would serve as a showpiece, with the potential to generate much other change in the neighborhood. What matters is that both the risks and potential were explicitly recognized in advance, an informed choice was made to proceed, and work was done to offset some difficulties. Less satisfactory are projects that encounter problems because their "fit" was not well considered.

Special Combinations of Characteristics

Some characteristics of NDOs' internal capabilities, relations with outsiders, environments, and projects were clearly more important to project success in combination with other specific characteristics than they were alone. While certain combinations were mentioned earlier in the chapter, three deserve brief further attention because they were significant in explaining the progress of a number of the most successful projects we observed and the difficulties of many of the least successful.

Fighting City Hall with Gaps in Your Defenses

Two of the three previously cited sample projects that were effectively halted after making significant progress were stopped because of disagreements with local governments. As noted, angry local officials suspended funds that were central to project financing. However, those cutoffs occurred, and were lasting, not because of political disagreements alone but in large part because NDOs' lack of attention to proper management left them vulnerable.

In one instance, an NDO leader was visibly active in a local election on the losing side. At the same time, the NDO had sloppy bookkeeping practices and violated the letter of restrictions on how money from the city was to be spent. When the displeased election winner sought to chasten the NDO, ample ammunition was available to use to hold up funding and to demand extensive audits. Political and agency supporters of the NDO were unable to argue for release of funds in the face of suspicions of wrongdoing that could not be neatly erased. Similarly, another NDO challenged the direction of city action on a neighborhood project separate from NSHD work. At the same time, NDO staff were somewhat lax in observing loan clearance and follow-up procedures on the NSHD project and related efforts using city funds. When the city looked for leverage with the NDO to control its actions in the non-NSHD dispute, officials found excellent grounds on which to base a funding freeze, which might have been avoided.

Taken separately, poor relations with city hall or inadequate homework and accounting were not necessarily sufficient to produce these serious results. An NDO with equally deficient recordkeeping as that of the organizations just cited but with good outside relations received instead a short funding freeze and the offer of technical assistance to shape up management. And

NDOs with touchy advocacy relations with local government but not easily apparent procedural shortcomings escaped damaging attack.[37]

The lesson is clear for NDOs: Make sure that basic paperwork procedures, especially those having to do with finances, are demonstrably in order if you are involved in a struggle with local government (or elsewhere in the community). These are sensitive matters at any time and leave a neighborhood organization deeply vulnerable if they are not carefully tended.

Assembling a Strong Project Team

Some of the most successful projects were carried out by a closely cooperating team, consisting of many actors—not only NDO staffs but also members of NDO boards, sources of technical assistance, coventurers, and so forth—that we have discussed separately as contributors to success. NDOs took on tough projects in difficult situations with limited internal resources. Bringing together an array of participants able to meet specific project needs significantly increased the chances of a smooth undertaking. Some NDOS without great internal development expertise paid particular attention to developing this coordination and effectively raised their project capability.

Two prime examples illustrate this concept. In one, an executive director with little development experience and a small staff assembled staff, board members, outside experts, local government, and private businesspeople to oversee and implement a successful residential hotel rehabilitation. A private hotel owner was persuaded to allow his vacant building to be renovated and to invest some of his own funds. Board members helped convince a city development agency to supply cheap financing. It helped also that the city already viewed the NDO as a cooperating partner with shared goals. Board members and city officials with development expertise joined the NDO director on an advisory committee to oversee project development. They and the hotel owner helped identify a competent project architect and a contractor, both of whom were eager to cooperate because they had done business in the past with the city and the private owner and hoped to do more in the future. An NDO staffer and local crew did some of the rehabilitation finish work (cabinetry, painting) at the hotel at a savings in cost. And a dedicated former NDO staffer with extensive experience with neighborhood residents accepted the difficult task of resident management upon completion of hotel improvements.

In another example, an NDO with a longer track record but still limited internal development expertise similarly filled the necessary roles in a mul-

---

37. Of course, not every city government responds to challenges in the same way.

tifamily housing rehabilitation project. The executive director had maintained long-time harmonious relations with city hall—which provided buildings at low prices, as well as critical funding. A project director with some financial and construction background was hired and worked with two ongoing sources of technical assistance that specialized in aiding community organizations. A construction and development company the NDO was working with on other projects coventured this effort and did part of the rehabilitation. However, expert housing management skills were not added to the team, and this, plus the lack of prior direct involvement by building residents, made conversion to a cooperative a less successful project task. Where key team members were missing, performance fell off.

In these and other cases, recognition, usually by executive directors, of the roles that need to be played and the possibilities of filling them from multiple sources of cooperation helped significantly to determine the extent of success. Of course, past efforts to build an active board, good relationships with various outsiders, and a united and complementary staff were critical in making team assembly feasible.

Limited Ability to Respond to Funding Cutbacks or Other Losses

NDOs that both lost major project funds they had counted on and were inexpert in financial analysis had an especially difficult time getting their projects back on track and were prominent among NDOs that made little progress. Some organizations with limited skill in assessing feasibility attempted projects that depended heavily on deep subsidies—perhaps more heavily than they were fully aware of—making it harder to develop substitute financing when cutbacks occurred.

Others lacked the expertise to quickly identify, understand, and analyze the feasibility of alternative funding packages or to generate innovative combinations of funds, which might have rescued their projects. If NDOs had technical assistance in these areas, it was sometimes too slow or it came too late to substitute well for internal skill and ingenuity. As noted previously, changing external funding conditions and possibilities heighten the value of staff financial and economic expertise.

Holdups in city transfer of needed project properties also contributed to an important share of the most severe project shortcomings, but especially when combined with internal weaknesses in staffing and management. One NDO's inattention to detail triggered the loss of a property, and another's lack of real estate expertise and good basic management until late in the project made it much more difficult to pry loose a needed site.

Overall, in an environment where resources of all kinds are increasingly difficult to obtain, strong internal capabilities are needed to offset the problems and to avoid compounding them.

Value of NSHD Grants

While this study is not an evaluation of the NSHD program, it is instructive to look at the role of NSHD grants in the projects we tracked. The grants were designed to support the later stages of planning and packaging of development projects that were already reasonably well-defined or to provide a portion of the funds for actual project implementation, or both. Additional funds were to be obtained in each case from other sources, along with nonmoney resources, including, especially, the participation of neighborhood residents and businesspeople. The NSHD program also provided— at least until it began to be phased out—for access to certain kinds of technical assistance and "brokering" aid in finding additional needed funds. We can learn about effective structuring of assistance to NDOs by examining NDOs' experience with the NSHD program and by studying the value of well-designed aid.

NSHD grants averaged about $114,000; were most heavily concentrated in the $100,000 to $135,000 range; rarely were larger than $150,000; and in no case substantially exceeded $200,000. For some NDOs, the NSHD grants were important, among other reasons, simply because they comprised a significant share of total project resources. For one-third of the projects, NSHD grants provided one-third or more of total money resources; for two-thirds of the projects, NSHD money comprised one-sixth or more of the total. (For complete details, see the discussion of leveraging ratios in chapter 3.)

How was NSHD money used? Our information is fairly rough, because reported categories are broad and were interpreted differently by different NDOs.[38] Staff salaries and construction costs were most often the largest categories (sometimes overlapping for NDOs that had their own construction crews). Other major categories were property acquisition, equipment purchases—particularly in starting up new economic development ventures, writedown of home resale costs in appropriate projects, and purchase of consultant services—especially for projects still heavily in the financial packaging and architectural design stages at the time their grants were awarded. Grantees

---

38. Also, we have complete information only for planned, not actual, use of funds; actual use differed in some cases where NDOs requested changes formally and perhaps in some cases where they did not.

were, upon request, sometimes given permission to reallocate NSHD funds. This proved valuable to NDOs in a series of circumstances: for example, when other expected funds for some critical purpose were lost or when some aspect of a project was made infeasible by external circumstances but another could be salvaged and even expanded.

NSHD grants were of substantial value in leveraging additional funds, from two points of view. In selecting grantees and working with them at early stages, NSHD program operators insisted that NDOs show firm commitments or at least real potential to garner other funds. The result was that every dollar provided under the NSHD program was in fact combined with about three other dollars for the median NDO. And, as was mentioned previously, leveraging expectations were frequently met.

More important, close observation suggests that in many cases NSHD funds were explicitly of value in the effort to obtain other monies, rather than merely being added on to project funding already in place. In a number of cases, access to other funds was clearly conditioned on obtaining the NSHD money. In one instance, a savings and loan offered attractive interest rates on loans for home purchase and resale, provided an NSHD grant was obtained to cover administrative and some rehabilitation costs. In another, a city loan to help capitalize a new venture was available only if NSHD grant money could be secured to make the start-up appear feasible. In still another, the need to meet an NSHD application deadline led to the granting of conditional commitments of resources by public and private funders who had previously delayed taking action. In a related situation, NSHD money was necessary to pay staff expenses in order to make use of a state-sponsored rehabilitation loan pool.

NSHD monies, once actually granted, also gave important credibility to young NDOs seeking funds and other assistance. Several NDOs in our sample benefited from being recognized as winners of a national competition, especially as they continued to seek funds and cooperation from city hall and technical assistance from the private sector. And technical assistance provided by NSHD program staff in identifying and making contact with potential funders proved useful as well.

Even for projects where NSHD money clearly provided the principal cash financing for planning and implementation, substantial leveraging nonetheless often occurred. In one, much of project cost was met by volunteer labor, "scrounged" and donated materials, and a grant of land. Another NDO is generating income from the sale of products by a newly created venture, and a third is reselling homes, which will leave a pool of funds for future work.

More broadly speaking, the NSHD program played an appreciable role as a willing early risk taker in the financing of NDO projects—a role whose

importance was discussed in detail earlier. Yet by sticking firmly to its leveraging goals and standards, the program avoided becoming the stand-alone
financing mode for inadequately funded projects. One project represents this
balance especially well: an NSHD grant was given for further packaging and
fundraising efforts and potentially for part of implementation costs, in a case
where the NDO had a good performance record but where financing appeared
hard to obtain after expected federal funds were withdrawn. A dollar limit
was placed on NSHD grant spending until a financial package could be
obtained, and the remainder of the grant was to be withdrawn if the package
was not ultimately developed.

Even where other funds were not conditioned on NSHD grants, the
NSHD money was often critical to financial feasibility. Primarily, NSHD
funds could make the difference in rendering the products of NDO efforts
affordable to neighborhood residents. By paying for part of the costs of
construction/rehabilitation (and its oversight) with grant funds, NDOs were
much better able to offer rents and resale prices that local people could afford.
This contributed substantially to NDOs' excellent record of targeting benefits
within their neighborhoods.

NSHD grants were of further worth in keeping alive projects that suffered
long delays in securing other commitments. In at least three sample cases,
NSHD funds were essentially *the* source of support for core staff as the NDO
wrestled with problems in gaining property and funding commitments—problems largely not of the NDOs' own making. Without NSHD funds for project
preparation, the projects would likely have been canceled; but at least two
and perhaps all three will now succeed. The fact that NSHD grants were
project-specific, but available in advance of the construction stage and not
restricted to bricks-and-mortar uses, preserved these projects and helped smooth
the way for other projects as well.

Another significant contribution of NSHD grants was in allowing NDOs
to pursue new directions in terms of the kinds of projects they attempted.
The NSHD program made awards based on either "proven record"—experience with a similar project—or "demonstrable capacity"—experience with
relevant other work plus capabilities apparent in applications. The latter category allowed a number of NDOs to pursue lines of work they had long
sought to make part of their overall revitalization effort but, until the NSHD
grant, had lacked the opportunity to undertake. It also permitted support of
NDOs with very modest development experience of any type. These project
departures are discussed further under track-record capacity building in the
next chapter. It should be noted here that NDOs that were awarded grants
under the "demonstrable capacity" standard performed nearly as well as
those under "proven record." The support for opening new lines of work

was largely a success, probably because careful attention was given to identifying capacity and to keeping project scale and scope in line with level of experience.

Finally, many NDOs reported that the technical assistance accompanying NSHD grants was of real value to them. Financial management and record-keeping assistance from the Support Center was viewed as helpful because it was well focused on the needs of nonprofit development organizations. Management needs assessments, funded by small portions of the NSHD grants themselves, identified areas for improvement of internal capacity in a way that at least several NDOs found nonthreatening and of practical use. Repeatedly, NDOs expressed regret that, as the NSHD program was phased out, they lost further program-related opportunities—for technical assistance, brokering aid, and travel to Washington, D.C., to meet and learn from leaders of other NDOs facing similar problems.

In general, although a few NSHD grants simply funded part of the expanded work of experienced NDOs in well-established patterns, most made special contributions to NDO projects and future prospects. Careful focus on funding well-defined projects kept the success rate high, but without limiting the program's leveraging and capacity-building impacts.

5

Capacity Building: Progress and Future Needs

Building increased capabilities to do neighborhood development work is, or should be, an important goal for most NDOs. Many organizations recognize that they lack specific internal skills as well as certain links to outsiders that could help them carry out projects more effectively, or that the capabilities and contacts they do possess could be strengthened. We observed in our study that many NDOs, limited in size and development experience, also fell short in some of the capabilities identified in the research as key factors in project success.

In order for NDOs both to play an expanded role in revitalizing their neighborhoods and to confront the massive difficulties that revitalization entails, they must increase their capacity to do larger numbers of and more complex projects. The NSHD program took serious note of this need and made capacity building an explicit program goal, equal in importance to that of generating successful projects. The program also encouraged applications from NDOs that were below those at the highest rung of past achievement and, because of the number of grants it awarded, was able to assist many organizations in the intermediate range of initial capability. By taking some risks on project outcomes, the program raised the likely level of capacity building and thus the possible impact of the program on long-term NDO work. While this study is not an NSHD program evaluation, it is useful to interpret the level of capacity building that occurred in light of the program's conscious choices about the NDOs to be funded, NDOs that thereby became the subjects of our study.[1]

We examined in detail the growth in NDO capacity during the course of NSHD projects. Because of the close examination required, this analysis was based entirely on the experience of the thirty NDOs we visited; the NDOs cited in this chapter as being involved in various kinds of capacity building are from that group only. As indicated earlier in this book, we visited most NDOs in our study sample twice. A primary purpose for doing this was so that we could better observe institutional growth directly. We also asked NDO staff, boards of directors, and outside project actors to describe increased capabilities that either preceded our first visits or were, as often happened, not readily visible during the short periods we were at the site. Again, as in our earlier examination of the determinants of performance, our focus was on projects rather than on general organizational growth: what capacity for future projects was being built as a result of (or at least in some connection to) work on NSHD projects? As with the earlier discussed factors in success, however, the elements of capacity building that are relevant to projects often overlap those involved in broader organizational growth.

We found a host of powerful capacity-building impacts. The experience of carrying out projects, the successes they produced, the hiring of additional staff and outside expertise, and the establishing of new ties with (and through) outside project participants all contributed to major improvements in NDOs' abilities to do development work. Four broad areas of growth stand out. Increased staff expertise in the entire development process was one important element, especially in basic project planning. A second was expansion of NDOs' track records of successful development projects, creating greater credibility and support, particularly for the many organizations in the study with limited past experience. The third and fourth major elements of capacity building were improvement of and expansion of relationships both with community members and with funding sources, most often as a result of delivering promised project results. In addition, we observed more modest growth in the strengths of NDO boards of directors and spin-off organizations, in planning and proposal writing, in management capabilities of various kinds, and in relations with sources of technical assistance and other outsiders.

---

1. Capacity building might have been still greater had the administration of the NSHD program not been interrupted by the program's cancellation. As noted earlier, management needs assessments indicating areas for improvement were canceled for many NDOs; and HUD monitoring and technical-assistance efforts, including "brokering" (linking NDOs with funders and sources of technical aid), were cut back as the number of staff assigned these functions was reduced.

Each of these components of capacity building is described separately in this chapter, grouped into elements of internal capacity building and improved links to outsiders. In sum these components represent a notable addition to the abilities of the nation's NDOs to revitalize urban neighborhoods. Still, there are important elements of capability that study NDOs commonly need yet to strengthen. These needs for future capacity building are described in this chapter as well, within the discussion of components of increased capability.

It is important to remember that capacity building has many possibly short-lived components. Recent capability gains may be lost if, for example, newly experienced staff are laid off because of funding cutbacks, or if an absence of reasonably "cheap" project funds stymies efforts to continue NDOs' records of service to neighborhood residents. Reduced federal funding during and immediately after the completion of NSHD projects, cited in chapter 4, has already had a significant impact in these terms. Work on individual projects that are well-chosen and aided as necessary by outside advice may do much to strengthen NDOs; but continuity of financial support is a necessary complement to individual project efforts in any serious capacity-building strategy.

This chapter's findings have several implications for policy and program design. The substantial level of capacity building we observed indicates that well-supported project experience has great value for NDOs' growth; that continuing aid to NDOs can have great cumulative value; and that NDOs have good potential for improved and expanded performance, beyond that recorded in chapter 3 as a result of continued project work. But we also noted capabilities that were not developed, and learned something of why capacity building occurred in certain cases and not others. That understanding has implications for what various actors can do to further the process of building NDO capability, a topic pursued in chapter 6.

Building Internal Capabilities

A number of broadly defined components of internal capacity may be strengthened through the experience of project work: skills of NDO staff and board members, working relationships and management arrangements among them, methods of planning and project development that NDO staff and board members have established, and NDOs' overall records of accomplishment. Building capacity in terms of these components may well involve the help of outsiders, but the capabilities focused on in this section ultimately reside within the NDO itself. The ways in which specific internal capabilities grew during the projects we observed are described in the paragraphs following.

Staff Skills

Increasing the skills of key staff[2] in various aspects of neighborhood development project work was a prime capacity-building result of NDO efforts. Because most staffs were initially of modest size and/or development experience, and because many projects involved new lines of work and areas of responsibility, there was considerable need to enhance staff capability. Half of the NDOs added significantly to their staff capabilities as a consequence of their projects, and others added at least modestly to their internal skill levels. The bulk of the skills building occurred as a result of project experience for staff members, rather than through the hiring of fully trained newcomers.

Most often, the primary learning was done by executive directors, in organizations in which they already played dominant roles (at least in development programs) and in which they had a broad array of project responsibilities. In these situations, other staff were not involved extensively in learning-by-doing at major points in the projects, because other people simply were not assigned to the projects, except in narrow roles. Many of these NDOs either could not afford to hire or could not find a project director who might have shared both the learning experience and the project burdens.

For a substantial minority of the NDOs where staff capacity building occurred, however, project-director-level staff benefited markedly. Inexperienced or moderately experienced people were given major responsibilities for projects. With proper support, they gained much increased knowledge about the development process and the specifics of implementing the type of project they directed. A few NDOs hired people with more real estate and finance knowledge than had existed in their pre-NSHD staffs; such staff took on the role of project director or performed other major tasks, such as housing management or loan underwriting, where they supplemented the work of executive directors who remained in the project director role. These kinds of development of key staff beyond the executive director are particularly important. As stated earlier in this book, we found that an important source of project problems originated in the passing of project responsibility from executive directors to underqualified project directors. We also found in previous research that the longer-term growth of NDOs is heavily dependent on gen-

2. Additional elements of capacity building related to staff skills are contained under "Getting to the Beginning," later in this chapter.

erating in-house development expertise beyond the executive director.[3] The findings of the current study, that work overloads for executive directors are often a problem in a broad range of NDO activities beyond NSHD projects, reinforce our previous findings on long-term growth.

It should be noted that much potential for staff capacity building was, or may be, lost in one way or another. Departures by key staff after they have had a chance to learn from project experience were a primary source of loss. Of the fourteen NDOs showing major staff capacity building during their NSHD projects, two have already lost key people, including in one case the executive director. Two more NDOs may lose their executive directors in the next year or so. Five other NDOs have suffered real declines in staff capacity since the start of their NSHD projects, as the result of staff departures due to funding-level declines and to employees pursuing alternative opportunities outside the NDO, as well as in response to internal problems. As indicated in chapter 4's discussion of factors in success, a number of NDOs put staff in prominent positions in NSHD projects—both old loyalists and new employees—who did unsatisfactory work and had to be fired, instead of successfully learning from the experience. Moreover, some potentially competent staff were not adequately directed to focus attention on careful project planning, homework, and feasibility analysis as required. And in a few projects, progress was stymied too early to offer much learning experience.

Overall, then, some critical needs for assembling competent principal staff remain. For many organizations, important learning during the NSHD project was limited to the executive director, and good project directors were not found, trained, or retained. Yet the experience of this and other studies makes clear that increasing the numbers of staff with expertise in development who can take on major responsibility is essential to expanding the scope and scale of NDO efforts. There is still significant work to be done in recruiting, in giving experience to, and in finding resources to maintain a solid core of development staff at the project-director level. Means must also be found to develop new leadership capable of taking over executive directors' roles as the directors, eventually, move on.

What specific types of skills and knowledge have NDO staffs added? Primary is growth in project planning: the ability to prepare a comprehensive and well-ordered outline of project steps and to know what is required to implement them. Because so many NDOs and staffers were taking on new projects and roles with their NSHD grants, they learned much, by trial and error or outside advice, about the basic process of undertaking a development

---

3. Mayer, with Blake 1981, p. 16.

project. For staff of inexperienced NDOs, learning the particular tasks that the development projects generally required—in assessing their viability, in obtaining government clearances, in assembling resources, or in making agreements with contractors and others—was important capacity-building experience in itself. The staffs of many more-experienced NDOs learned about new needs for projects of types they had not done before—for example, the steps in finding tenants for commercial developments when past experience was only in housing. They also learned when and where to seek technical assistance with project-specific problems. Together, about one-third of the organizations of all degrees of experience showed notable gains in being able to "put together the pieces" of development project undertakings.

Capacity-building results were more mixed in the areas of financial feasibility and market analysis and marketing. Several organizations showed very substantial progress—moving from not knowing the basics of how to find or "run the numbers" to being able to assess alternative cost, revenue, and finance options. Others seemed only partially to realize the importance of such analysis, even after encountering associated problems, and continued to be heavily dependent on outsiders for the work itself. They remained unable to do their own "quick-and-dirty" assessments of project possibilities and to efficiently consider alternative funding approaches as conditions and opportunities changed.

Given the large number of organizations with initial weaknesses, the need for expanding skills in the financial feasibility and market-analysis area remains large. As noted in chapter 4's discussion of success factors, such developments as high interest rates, declining public funds, increased NDO pursuit of self-sufficiency opportunities that have emerged as a result of recent tax revisions, and emphasis on partnerships with the private sector all place a premium on skills of this type. NDOs do not have an easy time recruiting experts with such skills. The organizations will have to concentrate on taking full advantage of the skills of outside providers of technical assistance, not just to accomplish specific projects but to help train existing NDO staff by involving them with the experts as project work proceeds. A precondition to that active training stage for some NDOs is a better understanding of the role these skills play and of the NDOs' needs for them. Technical-assistance providers that work hand in hand with NDOs in putting projects together, and funding sources as well, might try to increase NDO sensitivity in this area.

Important capacity building took place for many NDOs in learning the basics of rehabilitation and construction processes. Staff members learned by experience to estimate costs with greater precision, to manage construction crews and contractors, to identify buildings that can be rehabilitated, and the like. Retaining skilled construction supervisors through periods of slowed project funding may be a problem in the future (as it has been in the past for some older NDOs). And a good number of NDOs still need a proper balance of entrepreneurial and bricks-and-mortar skills, either combined in a single person or divided between two complementary staffers.

Many NDO staff also gained a more realistic understanding of the conduct of development projects. The most common lesson involved better knowledge of the time, costs, typical difficulties, and needs to allow for contingencies. This lesson has been impressed upon NDOs from their actual experience—for example, owing to contingencies, the substantial majority of all NSHD projects will finish behind schedule. Other lessons in realism included increased appreciation of the importance of the national and local economy in project feasibility and of politics—frequently over other considerations—in gaining public-sector financial support. Executive directors, especially, learned the need to be flexible and to adapt in the face of recurring surprises.

In terms of the specifics of how staff capacity building occurred, as already indicated, skill upgrading more often took the form of learning by nonexperts than of hiring already fully equipped technical staff. Numerous people were hired primarily to take charge of or to work on NSHD projects specifically, but only a handful of those with broad responsibilities were highly skilled in major aspects of development when they were hired. And many project directors already held an NDO staff position at the time NSHD grants were received.

Technical assistance was frequently valuable in improving staff expertise. This function of technical assistance as a transmitter of knowledge for future internal use was notable in about a quarter of the NDOs. Outsiders were especially helpful either in teaching a broad range of skills in defining, planning, and packaging a project or in transmitting a specific highly technical skill, particularly in the complexities of financing. Board members and other neighborhood volunteers taught construction and rehabilitation specifics. In both sets of cases, the transfer of capability was more effective when capacity building was defined from the outset as a goal of the technical aid. In one of the most successful learning experiences, an accomplished housing project packager and an NDO executive director jointly agreed to treat the entire assistance effort as an explicit training effort.

Staff capacity building also benefited from arrangements for supporting inexperienced members with other staff. For example, an NDO assigned its knowledgeable housing development staffer to help shape the commercial project work of a novice project director.

Still, learning the actual process of carrying out a development project with its many obstacles was the most important source of training. Additional project opportunities and greater resources to retain staff members as they grow in expertise are therefore keys to capacity building.

Track Record

NSHD projects provided major expansions in the track records of the NDOs undertaking them. This extension of NDO experience is as important an element of capacity building as any other we observed. Many NDOs proposed projects that were significant advances or departures from their past work. The NSHD program invested in the associated risks and opportunities in selecting its grantees; and its choices were reflected, in numerous cases, in impressive track-record growth.

The returns to an NDO of an expanded record of development work are multiple. Such experience plays a key role, for example, in training staff and board or in improving relations with funders and community residents. This part of the chapter concentrates on identifying the kinds of advances and departures from past work that NSHD projects provided and some of the major benefits those yielded. Specifics on capacity building that resulted in terms of staff, outside relations, and so forth are treated separately elsewhere in the chapter.

The powerful track-record effects associated with NSHD projects are due, in substantial measure, to the large number of "firsts" involved. Two of the thirty sample NDOs were getting their first development experience (and two others virtually their first), and twelve more were doing projects of a specific type (economic development, energy, and so forth) for the first time.[4] As noted in chapter 2, out of all ninety-nine study NDOs, nearly half were doing projects different from their predominant type of past work. Some of these and others were also playing new and expanded roles in their projects.

Of course, not every NDO had a *successful* first experience to contribute to its track record. But for more than a third of the NDOs, NSHD projects clearly have already been enormously important in generating successful project experiences with some special value, including the kinds of "firsts" just mentioned. Two other projects still in relatively early stages could have similar impacts if they are well implemented, and five have had more modest but

---

4. This overstates the proportion in the population, because nonhousing rehabilitation projects are oversampled and are more often the new types being taken on. The number also includes mixed-type projects, one component of which is new to the NDO and another is not.

still notable benefits. The next few paragraphs look at these track-record gains in more detail.

Three of the four sample NDOs with no or virtually no development experience conducted successful NSHD projects. For each of these organizations, the first effort produced major gains of several kinds: improved staff and board understanding of the development process and its limits, technical training of many kinds, credibility with the community in being able to deliver visible results and with funders as viable development institutions. One group's new housing project took several years from inception, owing largely to delays beyond its control. But from the time outside resources were first sought and committed, the project provided a rallying point for the community and built credibility with other outsiders. As a result of the long, ultimately successful effort, the NDO earned respect for its dedication, perseverance, and growing skill. The experience of battling continuing problems served to raise the project's visibility, and the project's impending completion and occupancy will, along with other projects meanwhile under way or finished, cement the NDO's reputation as an accomplished developer. The other successful newcomers to development gained in particular an understanding of and greater confidence in handling the development process, as detailed elsewhere in this chapter under staff, board, and community-relations capacity building.

Three NDOs with housing and human-service backgrounds successfully broke ground on new types of projects in economic and commercial development. One NDO, for example, had long sought to widen its scope of development action from a highly successful housing program. The NSHD project allowed the NDO to increase staff in the commercial area, gain experience, and integrate the commercial work directly into a major housing development. If the commercial work shows long-term operational success, the NDO will have extended its excellent reputation into a major new line of work while retaining its tight geographic focus.

Several organizations acquired significantly more credibility and expertise as developers by taking on expanded roles in types of projects they had done before. As indicated in chapter 2, these most notably included NDOs that took full charge of development projects for the first time. In another important instance, an NDO that had been seen as an advocacy and service organization doing development on the side successfully carried out a larger and more complex project than it had attempted in the past, gaining it an image as a sophisticated developer in search of real estate investment dollars.

Still other projects provided further types of major track-record benefits. One NDO completed its first residential hotel renovation project to initiate a specific line of work it wishes to pursue, a success that has already led to other opportunities in this field. Other NSHD projects involved complex financing, the successful packaging of which has yielded new credibility with funders and the expertise to pursue wider funding options. And NSHD projects served as showpieces for their NDO developers and for supporters in city hall and elsewhere.

Of course, risk taking in new directions also resulted in project failure in some instances. These nonsuccesses frustrate important NDO goals, especially because many of them occur in new areas of activity. Our observations suggest that such failures need not produce negative and permanent external perceptions of NDOs, especially if outside forces are largely at fault. It is important, however, that NDOs not have contributed to project failures by poor performance on basic planning, homework, and reporting tasks. It is equally important that NDOs recognize when projects are not feasible, that they inform their funders that projects cannot go forward and the reasons why, and that they then move on to revised or different work. Supporters of NDOs seemed to have great patience and respect for good effort even when projects moved slowly or not at all.

Even given the new or expanded undertakings that NSHD grants supported, NDOs in the study still have much to do to establish successful work records. Many commercial revitalization and economic development projects have still to prove that they can attract enough tenants and customers to become sustaining operations over the long run—if only because they are as yet too newly completed. Certainly investors, other funders, and potential clients will want to see some long-term successes of these kinds, which relatively few NDOs can so far point to.[5] Because the bulk of NDOs' NSHD-supported and pre-NSHD projects have been in the housing rehabilitation area, most have yet to establish even a short-term record of accomplishment in other types of development work, and especially in nonhousing revitalization efforts.

Furthermore, the scale of typical NDO projects has been quite modest; and some NDOs still have not.dealt with even those projects' more complex problems. For example, a quarter of all NSHD-supported housing rehabilitation projects planned to upgrade ten units or fewer. In several rehabilitation projects, repair work has been accomplished but difficult financial circumstances remain (in terms of making resale of single-family homes affordable or rental self-sustaining). Gradually, bigger, more diverse, and more complex projects will have to be taken to completion, both to train NDOs in such efforts and to enhance their credibility with outsiders. The needs of NDO neighborhoods are so great that larger-scale activity is essential and may also

---

5. Relatively few NDOs have attempted such projects, compared with housing and human-services work.

help to overcome some impacts of difficult neighborhood environments. But many NDOs have continuing work to do on capacity building in moving toward this type of development.

Nonetheless, the level of success we have seen certainly suggests that, with careful project selection, hard work, attention to capacity building, and necessary support, NDOs can continue to build the expanded track records that NSHD projects clearly helped develop. It is important that other providers of resources encourage NDOs to reach for new types of projects and expanded responsibilities and scale of activity, and then give credit to evolving NDO records of performance in considering further NDO requests for support.

Boards of Directors and Other NDO Structures

The NSHD project experience had a significant impact on the capabilities of boards of directors in roughly a third of the NDOs. Important changes occurred primarily in organizations relatively new to the development field, rather than occurring more across the board, as in the case of growth in staff capabilities. In these NDOs, board members' attitudes toward and participation in development work had not yet been clearly and permanently established. Taking part in the substantial development efforts that NSHD grants supported affected the shape of board members' future involvement in several ways.

Probably the most substantial single impact was in increasing boards' basic understanding of development—in a few cases where development work was entirely new to the NDOs—and in making these NDOs comfortable with that area of work. Although this impact was substantial in only a few instances, the extent of the change and its importance for the organizations made it significant nonetheless. In one NDO, for example, board members were initially wary of incurring project-related debts, were intimidated by the idea of establishing a project budget, and were generally unfamiliar with the development process. By participating actively in each stage of the NDO's housing rehabilitation project, board members gained an understanding of the costs involved and of the value of budgeting for them, of the ways their investment was protected and paid for, and of the other steps in development. This understanding, as board members have already affirmed, is crucial to their willingness to take on additional and larger projects in the future. In another case, a previously advocacy-oriented board was initially divided as to whether the NDO should move into development at all—some members believing, for example, that such work was a sham, earning money for someone else but producing few benefits for the community. The board was also overly optimistic about what could be accomplished with the project money available. However, through a combination of direct hands-on and oversight experience, advice from a trusted executive director, and good technical assistance in board training, the board came to see development as a process over which they could assume control, rather than as something to be suspicious of, and as a vehicle to meet some community needs within realistic limits. Resolving whether to pursue development is essential in order to avoid a paralyzing dispute. While not every community organization should be a developer, each should reach a clear, informed decision on this matter, with sufficient consensus that the debate is not continually renewed as new project opportunities arise.

NDOs must work to educate their boards in the development process at all stages of organizational growth or risk losing active board participation. Some of the more sophisticated and experienced NDOs had not made a practice of doing this, so that staff knowledge about development grew to far outstrip boards' knowledge in this area, leaving boards with relatively little to contribute. Other younger organizations are in danger of following that path, especially because they are pressed for time (keeping board members well-informed is a time-consuming task).

Boards of several NDOs quite new to development also learned by experience much about the basics of purchasing and repairing homes—especially in organizations with limited staff and funding where board members were working members who performed project tasks. A further transition may be required, however, to move board members from operational roles into policymaking roles. As NDOs grow and add staff capability, it generally becomes more important for board members to exert influence on program direction than to assist in day-to-day project tasks; but NDOs do not always recognize or plan for this change. Members of a few boards gained valuable experience in this area by working on advisory subcommittees specifically for the NSHD projects.

Next to gaining basic understanding of development, the most important element of board capacity building was an increased sense of shared participation and strength among NDO actors as a result of dealing with some difficulty or controversy. For example, boards emerged more active and more unified from siding firmly with their staff in a fight with city hall, from resolving a dispute between two principal staff members over the direction of NDO project work, from lobbying a project through extended periods of external delay, or from conducting more conscientious reviews of staff decisions about the disposition of property. But these situations were risky for NDOs too. In one instance, a board and community split deeply in dealing with issues of staff conduct and city relations, exacerbating an already serious threat to the NDO's viability. Continuing attention to building harmony and trust between staff and board is needed to assure that crisis experiences strengthen rather than weaken cooperation. NDOs that have so far assigned relatively minor functions to board members may not have attended to this need, leaving a potential problem, although the NDOs have not yet been tested by crisis situations.

No clear patterns emerged in NDO efforts to increase board capacity by recruiting new members with added skills or those representing other constituencies. Many NDOs had no observable intentions in this regard; as many failed as were successful; and only rarely did the NSHD project affect recruitment. The potentially valuable roles such recruits can serve suggest that this might be an area for further attention.

Other new structuring of NDOs did result directly from NSHD projects, however, as indicated in chapter 2. Most notably, one sample NDO spun off its first development-oriented entity, and four NDOs created separate construction or similar companies they hope will serve to employ neighborhood residents and generate profits to use in other organizational activities. It is still too early to judge the outcomes of these projects, although several were off to a growing, if not yet profitable, start under difficult conditions. We also have yet to see whether the cooperatives that NDOs began will be effective self-managers in the long run.

Getting to the Beginning:
Strategic Planning, Project Development and Selection, Proposal Writing and Packaging

To a more modest extent, NDOs built capabilities in preproject and early-project activities through their NSHD experience. One clear result was improvement in proposal-writing capacity, but only for a half-dozen organizations in the sample. This most often resulted when one key staffer—the executive director or project director—worked closely on the NSHD proposal with technical-assistance people who had cooperated with NDOs often before. Unfortunately, an equal number of other NDOs either lost their most skilled proposal writers because of funding reductions or other upheavals, or failed to internalize the skills of technical consultants who virtually wrote the proposals for them. This is regrettable because, overall, technical assistance in proposal writing proved less successful in obtaining anticipated non-NSHD funds than did in-house expertise in this area (see table 63). A significant amount of capacity building in proposal development has yet to be done, especially to put NDOs in a position to seek funds from new sources with increased competition.

TABLE 63

Technical Assistance in Proposal Writing and Success in Leveraging Funds

Use of Proposal-Writing Technical Assistance	Ratio of Actual (Non-NSHD) Funds Obtained to Planned	
	0–.50	Greater Than .50
Did in house on own	.29	.71
Used technical assistance	.56	.44

Note: Based on sample of thirty NDOs; Chi-square test significant at .10 level.

Another capacity-building result was improved skills in financial packaging. With substantial technical aid, at least three NDOs learned well virtually from scratch to put together the materials for seeking development financing. Another two NDOs clearly gained abilities to assemble more complex financial packages than they had previously dealt with, and a few perhaps gained a sense of confidence in being able to put together a project that looks like an impressive real estate deal to potential funders or investors. But the learning was far less than universal, and numerous groups still do not have this skill in house. Like related financial feasibility and market analysis, packaging skills are of increasing importance in the changing funding environment, making this a significant capacity-building need for the future.

A handful of NDOs learned, usually by painful experience, some vital lessons about project selection. They now know more clearly, for example, that homeowners are far more resistant to rehabilitation loans than they are to grants and that tenants who are unhappy with basic building conditions are not likely to cooperate in energy conservation projects. How well NDOs translate such experience for use in other and different projects remains to be seen, but NDO resourcefulness and common sense hold good promise.

A few NDOs developed improved, broader plans to revitalize their neighborhoods, at least in part as a result of their NSHD projects. In one instance, an organization designed a more sophisticated development plan for its neighborhood in cooperation with a consultant. The plan contained a more realistic time frame and more feasible project options that greatly enhanced the plan's credibility with potential outside supporters. The understanding of and experience with the development process gained by this NDO's executive director during the NSHD project was instrumental in helping him to contribute to that plan. But such instances were rare. For good reasons and bad, most NDOs' planning proceeds from one target of opportunity to another, as promising possibilities, especially for funding, arise. If NDOs could better rely on continuing funds to support projects they selected, development of revitalization strategies would be a clearer capacity-building need—and one to which they might well happily respond. Even in the absence of such commitment, a sharper picture of how to address overall neighborhood needs would be a desirable goal for many organizations.

Management

Project and general organizational management was an area in which we and NDO participants themselves identified only a modest amount of capacity building during the course of NSHD projects. This may be in part because such growth is especially hard to pinpoint without extensive continuing observation, and in part because some important elements of capability that might have been categorized under management—namely project planning, as well as predicting costs, timing, and likely contingencies—were treated by us under increases in staff skills (see "Staff Skills," this chapter). Given our primary focus on individual projects, much of the content of management improvement may fall under that heading. NDOs did show improvement in other elements of management, at least in limited numbers. And a substantial set of organizations made advances in financial recordkeeping and reporting.

Several executive directors learned a good deal about what their true staff needs were for specific projects, in terms of both skills and numbers, from their early experience in directing those projects. They then reshaped project staffs to reflect this knowledge. In an extreme case, a home repair project's staff was pared by well over half, largely by eliminating workers who were not doing their intended jobs of personal outreach to and loan packaging for homeowners. The services of a formerly full-time but underutilized rehabilitation specialist were obtained on a part-time, as-needed basis, and a key link was added by hiring a well-qualified loan underwriter.

NDOs also learned some valuable lessons about structuring of management responsibilities, especially in dividing areas of authority. One NDO, recognizing how an unclear division of responsibility between itself and a spin-off enterprise left important work undone, decided to retain tighter cooperative links with spin-offs in the future. Another eliminated the problems generated by having a shared executive directorship between two people who differed in their philosophies about the NDO's NSHD project and its future, by switching to one director and an assistant. Surprisingly few NDOs reported growth in their abilities to manage contractors and consultants, probably because many already felt competent in that area.[6] Developing clear lines of responsibility as NDOs expand and as executive directors share more re-

---

6. See chapter 2.

sponsibilities is an important future necessity. Since NDOs' needs for structure correspond to those of organizations that have preceded them in the growth process, there is likely value in training and technical assistance in this area.

Executive directors in several organizations became more adept at and committed to delegating some day-to-day responsibilities to other key staff, allowing the directors needed opportunities to generate new project ideas and resources. Executive directors also grew in understanding how to support inexperienced staff to whom they had delegated heavy responsibility. Hiring and training people capable of taking on delegated responsibilities—as discussed earlier under staff capacity building—was of course at least as important a component of this growth as learning to delegate. When recognition of the desirability of spreading responsibility was coupled with success in attracting skilled or trainable staff, the results could be excellent. One executive director saw the need for a development operations person and a housing manager, as his own project-packaging work load expanded and NDO-owned housing multiplied. NSHD funds helped hire well-qualified people for what is now a strong staff team. But it is unclear whether executive directors can "learn" to find better project directors—and certainly not without funds. It must be noted that NSHD projects and the further work they generated sometimes more contributed to staff overload than reduced it, as in the case of an executive director who now heads both a parent NDO and its NSHD-financed maintenance and construction company offshoot. The shortage of project-director-level staff remains central.

NDOs had a variety of needs to tighten up their operating procedures, progress reporting, and other means of meeting grant and contract requirements—although most NDOs already performed quite well in these areas. Experience was mixed on whether capacity building needs apparent in the NSHD project were met. For one NDO, the NSHD grant was its first funding with specific schedules and requirements. It seemed to welcome and take advantage of that fact, using it to impose structure on project work. Another reacted to thefts and other problems in its housing management operations by establishing a solid set of procedures to combat them. But at least two NDOs whose lack of attention to operational detail and grant requirements caused them obvious problems seemed oblivious to clear needs for improvement. Blunt calling to task on these matters by outside supporters would be to NDOs' long-term benefit.

Results were also mixed on the development of capabilities and confidence in "general management." While several executive directors reported an improved sense of overall control through experience, other NDOs were losing (or about to lose) that management capability through executive director departures. In some organizations, future growth may have to be accompanied by a tightening of currently very informal management approaches and a greater commitment to coordinating activities by holding regular staff meetings even when key staff are busy with their own work.

The clearest case of substantial management improvement is in the area of financial recordkeeping and control. Only some instances of this capacity building were project related, responding to needs generated by NSHD work and the multiple funding sources connected to it. Others simply overlapped in time with NSHD grants, although in several cases, accounting technical assistance associated with being a grantee had a major role in generating the improved bookkeeping. For over a quarter of the NDOs, such improvements were worthy of some note. The bulk of them were made with substantial advice and cooperation from outside experts—most effectively from those with specific experience with nonprofit organizations.

Such assistance was most useful where NDOs recognized their own accounting needs: to get information about their budget situations more quickly and efficiently, and in forms easier for busy staff and board to use; or to create fiscal controls that would assure against any abuse or perception of abuse. But in fact a few NDOs responded only to crises regarding funders' recordkeeping requirements. This is unfortunate, because times of tight budgets and shifting funding sources make good internal financial management reporting a valuable asset worth developing even when minimum external reporting requirements are already being met. And some NDOs may have weaker basic reporting systems than they are aware of in the absence of crisis. The pressure of recent funding limitations seemed to encourage NDOs to recognize the need to develop regular reporting and projections for their own use.

Building Relationships with Community Members and with Outside Actors

As stated earlier, much of any given NDO's ability to revitalize its neighborhood depends on the support of neighborhood people and institutions and on outside sources of funding, technical assistance, and other forms of cooperation. NDOs simply are not actors of adequate size and scope to take the stage alone. Building relationships with the community and outside actors is thus a critical part of overall capacity growth. The relationship building that resulted from NSHD work is described in detail here for study-sample organizations.

Relations with Community Members

NSHD projects produced significant benefits in building NDOs' credibility and support among community members.[7] Many projects were highly visible and clearly valuable in serving neighborhood needs. They demonstrated the ability and commitment of NDOs to directly serve their members and constituents, who responded with a variety of expressions of appreciation, participation, and support. Again the impacts were strongest when projects studied were the first (or nearly the first) true development efforts the NDOs had undertaken under their own control. Many other NDOs already enjoyed excellent relations with community members, based on the organizations' past productivity and the involvement of the community in shaping and carrying out their programs.

The broad impacts of visible, valuable projects on community support were most noticeable in five of the thirty NDOs we visited. One NDO had previously done maintenance work in residential hotels owned by others but had not done development work with which it could easily be identified. The NDO's residential hotel rehabilitation and management labeled it clearly as a first-rate housing provider in the community and earned it, among other things, the cooperation of many of the hotel's residents, who regarded the improved building with pride. The NDO that built an urban garden, mentioned earlier in this book, had previously worked mainly to spin off many independent human-service programs. But it built and retained operation of the garden itself. The garden gave many community residents rare opportunities to enjoy social interactions and the outdoors as well as to raise needed food. Located in a highly visible, well-publicized location, the garden represented community permanence, in sharp contrast to the encroachment by freeways and other intrusions that had characterized recent development. The project thus cemented a bond between the NDO and a broad cross section of community residents that had been forming since earlier days of protest activity.

In addition to the actual cases of strong positive impacts on relations with the community, several other NSHD projects have the potential for such impacts, in that they so clearly and visibly are designed to respond to vital community needs and interests. The problem is that these projects have made limited obvious progress to date. Vacant lots and buildings, even with well-advertised good intentions and plans, arouse some interest and cooperation;

---

7. Note that growth in direct involvement of community members in project work was treated separately as self-help in chapter 3. Also, capacity building in community relations closely overlaps that in board of directors' participation, treated separately in the previous section of this chapter.

but naturally in most instances visible results have been central to broad community awareness of NDO work, beyond that of boards of directors and other active volunteers. The great majority of NSHD projects will show some valuable outputs by the time work halts, which should contribute further to attaining community support.

Building community trust in NDOs' work was another element of improved relations with their communities that was an outgrowth of NSHD projects, with visible results especially for four organizations. In one neighborhood, residents suspected that the city would attach conditions to its funding support of an NDO's planned commercial project, so that the project would no longer serve identified community needs. They feared that the NDO would cave in to city pressures, as they felt other institutions ostensibly serving them had done in the past. The NDO's willingness to buck the city on money questions, to preserve space for a community center, and to fund a community-favored design raised its credibility and maintained local support and participation. In another case, tenants of properties to be rehabilitated feared that large rent increases would result, despite NDO assurances. The proof contained in actual outcomes—better housing without significantly higher rents— led to improved confidence and support.

NDOs were initially disappointed in their ability to build resident participation in the management of housing cooperatives they created, as noted in assessing self-help in chapter 3. Many new residents of the cooperatives continued to play the roles of tenants, which they had long performed, without taking on decision-making and operating responsibilities that in their previous rental housing had fallen to landlords (or to no one). Determined training and encouragement were beginning to have an impact by the time of our second site visit in at least one of these instances, at least for those residents on the cooperative's board; but more work is clearly needed. In each instance, getting tenants to participate took much more time and energy than had been anticipated. Other NDOs were able to build new levels of sweat-equity participation in housing and community development projects in exchange for the direct benefits provided.

A variety of other gains in relations with the community were made in specific situations. For instance, several NDOs forged new links with local businesses as they pursued commercial development projects, and another calmed the racial antagonisms that had initially greeted its color-blind sale of rehabilitated homes. But an equal variety of concerns, jealousies, and misunderstandings yet await NDO efforts—especially because projects produce good jobs, housing, and so forth, but in very limited quantities. These deserve continuing attention. It appears that NDOs' operation of some human-service, recreation, housing, counseling, or similar programs that can reach more people with a given level of funding is a useful adjunct to development work, in order to retain and build broad support.

Fortunately, many NDO leaders remain actively in touch with community concerns and problems, through direct daily contact with neighborhood citizens. For some, though, there is the potential danger of leaving the staff isolated from the community (as the staff were sometimes separated from boards of directors), by focusing on sophisticated development schemes without maintaining adequate contact with and understanding by the community. Overall, with due attention to that danger, NDOs' consistent delivery of results that directly benefit neighborhood residents of itself does much to generate rising community support. Outside aid to keep those results flowing is a critical constraint, along with limitations in NDO skill; but community members recognize those who act in their behalf.

Relations with Funding Sources

Successful NSHD project experiences helped strengthen NDOs' existing relationships with funding sources and established new ones, building credibility that seems likely to lead to continued and expanded support. This was one of the most important components of capacity building we observed: it was significant for some two-fifths of the NDOs,[8] and very pronounced for a good share of these. The impacts we identified were largely in relation to the specific funders who actually participated in financing the NSHD project. Successful projects may attract future support from other funders as well, as discussed in assessing growing track records. But our study did not follow NDOs after their NSHD projects were completed and thus missed most such potential results.

One major aspect of improving links with funding sources was that of tightening connections with key funders with whom NDOs had previously worked. Cementing a continuing relation and building a true cooperative working basis were results for several NDOs, mainly with local and state governments that in these instances provided NDOs with their primary funding. The potentially enormous value of these relationships is underscored by the experience of several NDOs that, because of funding links already developed, could virtually count on support for new projects. Important elements

---

8. This proportion in the sample understates the likely proportion in the entire population of grantees, because these impacts were most common in housing rehabilitation projects, which are deliberately underrepresented in the sample.

in establishing these relationships were explicit NDO efforts to cooperate with agency staffs and to build upon access that political ties initially provided.

In other instances, NDOs built relationships with funders who had agreed to be major sources of NSHD project monies but had no extensive prior development experience with the community organizations. These were "test" situations, at least in some cases, in which NDOs had the opportunity, with good performance and harmonious cooperation on the project, to create a basis for substantial future support. An excellent example of positive results in such a case was a project involving funding by a local development authority. In the NSHD project, although the NDO was the developer, the public authority provided only a loan to the well-to-do private owner of the building to be renovated. The project proceeded well, and the development authority participated in a highly successful project advisory committee that gave development authority staff continuing contact with the NDO. Now in a new project, the development authority will provide funds directly to the community organization for renovation of its own building, for a larger share of the total project costs. The positive experience clearly made the funder willing to take expanded risks. As another example, at least two other NDOs that previously received only in-kind aid from city governments so impressed the city with the value and success of their projects that grant funds were later forthcoming, and access to city-owned land or buildings was made easier.

Still other NDOs established contacts with funders for the first time in the course of an NSHD project, funders whose support played only a secondary role but one that might be expanded upon in future work. For example, a highly experienced housing organization learned the cast of characters and procedures in seeking modest levels of EDA, SBA, and state economic development agency funds for its first major commercial development project, although the project's primary funding came from other housing-related sources. Other NDOs began to build credibility with LISCs in situations where LISCs' funding share was limited.

And even within our study period, several NDOs established reputations and contacts that resulted in funding for post-NSHD projects. For example, an organization's successful housing rehabilitation effort generated a major new foundation grant to expand work supported previously by the city in conjunction with private lenders.

Developing funding links with private lenders remained difficult. One NDO, despite using bank loans in its project, illustrates the difficulty. The organization successfully put together a complex financial package of public and private funds and performed its project well. The banks involved have expressed willingness to be involved in future projects. But they have stated that they would again require protection against risk at the same high level provided in the work just completed—which in that case meant acquiring substantial equity funds from NSHD, other public, and LISC sources.

NDO neighborhoods are often not attractive to private lenders no matter what an NDO's record and approach. Also, many NDOs found private loans too expensive to comprise even part of their package and so have no ties with such lenders to build upon in the future. Continued efforts at making lender contacts are important so that private loans can be obtained if and when interest rates decline adequately. Improving NDO skills in financial analysis and packaging, along with expanding track records, will no doubt contribute to that process. But for many projects, subsidies from elsewhere, in order to create adequate levels of financial feasibility and security, will continue to be essential to securing lender involvement in NDO work.

Factors other than good project performance and cooperative working contacts affected NDOs' building relationships with funders. Some charismatic executive directors were able to maintain and expand upon good relations even when projects were stymied. And, as stated earlier, funders gave NDO staff credit for dedication and ingenuity even when outside forces delayed progress. Board members with special credibility arranged new contacts. Unique circumstances of many types—including election of sympathetic or unsympathetic local governments—intervened.

The net result, however, was markedly improved standing with critical sources of financial support for many NDOs, arising principally from their own good work and their efforts to ensure that funders on current projects were well pleased. Some very experienced NDOs gained little in terms of this element of capacity because they already had excellent relations with their primary sources. Very few suffered deteriorating relationships, in connection with fights with city hall, discussed elsewhere. One potentially more serious consequence is that many of the public funding sources with which NDOs carefully built good links are being eliminated or being given reduced resources. This can produce a dual loss. The most direct loss is in relationships already built. But those relationships also helped NDOs to link up with new funding sources, enabling the NDOs to use smaller pots of money from funders making their first commitments. Thus some potential for growth and adaptation is also lost. Again, giving NDOs the resources to pursue their work can go far in helping them build further access to support based on demonstrated performance.

Relations with Other Actors

In the course of project work, NDOs built links to a variety of people and institutions, besides funders and community members, whose cooperation could be valuable in the future. Principal among these, in our observations, were sources of technical assistance. About a quarter of the organizations found important new sources of aid or strengthened their relationships with people with whom they had already worked—largely in the areas of financial analyses and packaging, syndication, and accounting.

Most of these NDOs were involved in projects other than housing re-habilitation—projects that frequently were tougher and/or more often were new to them, in which technical advice was especially needed and less often previously used. These NDOs were not, however, systematically the least experienced NDOs in terms of total past development work. Some NDOs with longer track records recognized needs for outside counsel and had good contacts to find it. For example, an organization with fairly significant housing experience sought and used heavily on a continuing basis an expert contractor to help it establish a for-profit construction business and to do more substantial rehabilitation than before. The NDO realized from past mistakes it had made in the construction business that such aid was required.

Inexperienced NDOs, on the other hand, may have trouble obtaining technical aid even when they understand their needs. One organization taking on a difficult development project for the first time on its own was initially rebuffed in seeking advice and information from other developers. Apparently the NDO lacked both the credibility to be taken seriously in such a challenging effort and the contacts to obtain advice regardless of project specifics. Only later after the project had obtained funding commitments and otherwise pro-ceeded toward implementation was the NDO able to work through contacts in city government, to LISC, and then to sources of needed expertise in financial analysis and planning. Unfortunately, we could not formulate any systematic description of how NDOs made the technical-assistance contacts that were valuable to them, except to say that recognition of need was a critical first step. Finding expert assistance that will be readily available when it is needed is a continuing capacity-building requirement for some NDOs. The difficulty of that effort is reason enough to pay attention to the long-term building of in-house capacity.

Less common but potentially important links were those developed with possible coventurers in future projects. At least four NDOs specifically at-tracted the interest of private investors and property owners, other nonprofit organizations, and nearby local governments in working jointly with them on ventures similar to those using NSHD grants. The success of the NSHD projects gave the coventurers confidence that cooperating with the NDOs would be beneficial. For example, residential hotel owners in one neighbor-hood saw the opportunity to get good management and maintenance that an NDO provided in its first hotel project, by involving the NDO in the operation of the owners' hotel. In another, landowners are seeing possibilities for doing new development in an area otherwise tightly restrained by growth controls, if they cooperate with an NDO in building housing for people of modest incomes. Given the increased competition for all resources that declining public funding generates, the interest of potential partners who have buildings, land, contacts, and/or cash can be of major value in generating new neighborhood work. Of specific interest are connections with people who can assemble tax syndications of NDO projects as a means of getting needed cash to make projects feasible.

Several NDOs also made new ties with efficient and cooperative contractors and architects they can use again,[9] with the local businesspeople whose assistance is critical in doing commercial revitalization projects, and with a scattering of new, key suppliers and customers of their enterprises.

What NDOs were often unable to create through NSHD work[10] were many new links to their cities' major businesses and business organizations. Some NDOs did obtain project financing from banks or savings and loan associations. But several that sought to add "big business" expertise and contacts to their boards of directors or to generate joint ventures with members of the business establishment were unsuccessful, while others failed to seek or take advantage of participation that was obtainable. Intermediaries—such as foundations, LISC, or nonprofit technical-assistance organizations—that have ties and experience with both NDOs and the business establishment can apparently be helpful in building productive links between them. They were useful in generating a high proportion of the capacity building that did take place in this area. Further expansion of links to the business community might be particularly useful in locating markets for the services and products of NDO enterprises, tenants for commercial or office projects, opportunities in joint ventures, and in-kind technical assistance, in addition to cash support. Access to these potential benefits will clearly be important for the growth of NDO project work in the future and of nonhousing work particularly.

---

9. A few NDOs learned who not to use again.

10. Neither were such ties created through earlier projects or other activities, as chapter 2 notes.

6

Policy and Program Implications for NDOs and Their Supporters

From the outset, the primary purpose of this book has been to answer three questions of policy and program content:

- How much and in what situations should we rely on and support NDOs as vehicles for neighborhood revitalization, based on their performance and potential?
- How can NDOs' concrete accomplishments best be extended and successful projects be assured?
- How can NDOs, as continuing institutions, be strengthened in their capability to do further work?

A fundamental assumption is that both NDOs themselves and a host of outside actors can choose courses of action that increase the effectiveness of NDO effort. The findings of our research suggest that this is indeed the case. This chapter draws together conclusions about what can and should be done to promote successful NDO work.

A Basis for Supporting NDO Work

From a broad policy perspective, one particular implication of the research may be most significant: for many reasons, NDOs are worthy of continued and expanded support in their neighborhood development efforts. The organizations play unique roles, attack broadly recognized national problems and pursue goals extensively shared by society as a whole, and demonstrate strong current performance and longer-term promise. They operate, virtually by definition, in areas where indigenous resources of all kinds are in acutely short supply. These facts provide a clear rationale for a broad range of outside institutions to direct further support to NDOs.

Our research demonstrated that NDOs are good at their work. Despite enormously difficult local and national conditions, the organizations show substantial progress in their NSHD projects throughout the country. Particularly in the housing, energy, and community facilities fields, a high level of success was achieved in meeting well-defined project goals. In the inherently more difficult commercial and economic development fields, an improved national economic climate, together with carefully planned NDO capacity-building efforts, could turn already impressive but still-mixed results into more consistent progress, despite serious neighborhood-level disadvantages. Virtually every NDO in our study made significant progress in pursuing its planned project steps, even where internal and external circumstances ultimately combined to restrict concrete outputs.

Furthermore, NDOs are prominent among the short list of actors who have put into practice the widely touted concept of building public-private partnerships. As private organizations themselves, NDOs clearly have combined resources and cooperation from many government and private institutions and have used them to develop tangible results in the form of housing, jobs, community facilities and businesses, and the like. As chapter 3 detailed, private-sector participation, particularly by lending institutions, has played a substantial role in many NDO projects, despite the fact that NDO neighborhoods have in the past frequently been considered unattractive risks for private investment of all types. NDOs were consistently successful in meeting their goals for securing project funds beyond the NSHD grants, and the typical leveraging levels of three or more other dollars for each dollar granted by the NSHD program ranks as a strong performance relative to the leveraging by other institutions under other programs. In addition, NDOs, alone among developers, have demonstrated that they can draw on the energies of residents themselves in bringing neighborhoods to life.

Perhaps most important, NDOs take on a singular and critically necessary task, that of carrying out development and investment in distressed neighborhoods for the benefit of disadvantaged citizens living and working in those areas. No other actors are seriously competing for that role in any comprehensive way. Much "successful" neighborhood revitalization has, by design or inadvertence, improved local physical and economic conditions—but principally for the benefit of newly arriving, higher-income residents at the expense of the previous lower-income occupants of the neighborhood. NDOs have taken as their explicit objective the serving of people of limited means who already live in their neighborhoods (or who are likely to move there). They do not have to be "bribed" with extensive tax incentives or subsidies to so target their work. And NDOs have met that objective systematically: NSHD program experience repeatedly demonstrates that NDOs have brought improved housing to lower-income people who could not otherwise afford it; have given new jobs and job training to unemployed neighborhood youth; and have provided financial and technical assistance to small businesses in troubled commercial strips.

NDO work thus performs extremely well under the criteria set by national policy debates about the best means for aiding lower-income people. NDOs focus on providing people with good opportunities to help themselves, gathering resources needed to make those efforts feasible, and substantially extending the reach of scarce public funds. By dealing simultaneously with disadvantaged people and troubled localities, NDOs relieve powerful conflicts and tensions between policies that administer to the problems of people and places separately.

Any serious effort to revitalize city neighborhoods and to serve their residents and local businesses should therefore support, draw upon, and build the capabilities of NDOs to do their unique work. The rhetoric, if not necessarily the practice, of representatives of a broad segment of the political and policy spectrum is consistent with this thrust.

Furthermore, NDOs show great potential to improve their performance if they are given reasonable, continuing support. We have seen that NDO capabilities grow substantially even as a result of quite modest experience. Some NDOs have become large and sophisticated; but many more are poised to do so, building on early records of good performance and rapid learning. There is apparent potential for NDOs' individually modest projects to have greater cumulative impact as their work continues. If these gains are not interrupted or reversed by inadequate and inconsistent provision of resources, we can expect to see still greater productivity than that shown in the NSHD program, where many young grantees had much to learn and develop.

There is ample justification for a serious commitment of public and private resources—both funds and other assistance and cooperation—to enable NDOs to expand on positive but often limited track records. As a matter of conscious policy, NDOs could be given a larger role in pursuing the national agenda of aiding those people and neighborhoods that cannot deal with their problems alone. Because it is inherently a national agenda, federal funding should be a major component of assistance to NDOs (whether aid flows directly to neighborhood organizations or through intermediaries). The sharp, uncompensated cuts in federal support for NDO work in the last several years will no doubt destroy many of the fragile recent gains in NDO strength and accomplishment. Effort should thus be made to restore needed assistance from the federal government, both in funds going specifically to NDOs and in broader programs of which NDOs have been substantial users.

Public-sector aid from all levels of government will continue to be crucial to NDO success. The central lesson in NDO use of private-sector resources, in the NSHD program and in numerous other cases, is that public money must be available to complement private funds. Otherwise, private participation is much less likely to be forthcoming; and, even more important, only with public aid can NDOs continue to serve their lower-income constituents with economically feasible development projects. At the same time, private-sector assistance and cooperation should be increased, both to offset losses of government aid and to support expanded total NDO programming efforts.

Whatever the level of support, it must be provided in a form and targeted to uses that best promote NDO success and growth. Similarly, NDOs must learn to tailor their own actions so as to make optimal use of available opportunities. Assistance will never be sufficient to allow it to be used inefficiently. This study has produced many lessons about how to provide and use resources well. The rest of this chapter highlights these lessons for specific action.

NDO Roles in Improving Performance

NDOs can do much on their own initiative to help produce successful development projects and to, at the same time, raise their capabilities. Unequivocally, NDOs need outside assistance in substantial amounts to operate and to grow. But they can direct their energies in many ways to use well those resources and those of their own neighborhoods.

The specific findings in previous chapters about how to gain strong project performance and build successful, permanent institutions have many implications for NDO practice. In broadest terms, NDOs need to pay serious attention to developing and using the internal capabilities and external relations that our study's research indicates are pivotal in project success. Developing such capacities requires experience and time, with NDOs undertaking projects and educating themselves while they are doing the work. But that is only part of it. In focusing its project and capacity-building efforts, each organization can take advantage of lessons already learned by many other NDOs.

"Recognition" is a key to such focused efforts in two ways. NDOs must first recognize that developing certain identifiable capabilities and performing their work in certain ways are critical to their potential success—critical enough to deserve substantial time and attention. Providing that attention is enormously difficult, given the unending pressures of work and shortages of staff and funding. That means that NDOs must, as much as possible, incorporate as accepted parts of their ordinary business the tasks we can identify as critical to success and to capacity building. Commitment by NDO leadership, and especially the executive director, to the capacity-building process, based on a genuine understanding of its value, is a minimum requirement for integrating growth and learning into everyday work.

NDOs must also recognize what specific elements of capability are of primary importance and how these might be effectively developed and used. It has been the intent of this book, chapters 4 and 5 especially, to help identify those elements. The remainder of this section translates these findings into a summary of recommended actions. Note that many NDOs are already heeding the majority of these lessons well, based on their own experience and intelligence and on sound advice from others.

- One of the most critical needs is for NDOs to build a core of development expertise, specifically at the project director level. Technical expertise on staff is a fundamental and powerful determinant of project success and a capability too rarely fully gained and held by NDOs. Developing such competence among project- or overall-development-director-level staff is essential for NDO growth. Executive directors will no doubt gain development knowledge at the same time. But they need some freedom from primary technical responsibility in order to carry out their other roles in generating ideas and contacts and in management. Other staff must also play prime technical roles if long-run growth is to occur.

  NDOs should anticipate filling the need for expanded technical staff principally by giving well-structured learning-by-doing experience to people with good potential but limited specific experience. That entails transferring real responsibility to project directors, while arranging needed support and training for them. Salary levels and other circumstances, coupled with a limited supply of skilled people, make it unlikely that NDOs will frequently be able to hire already fully equipped technical experts, especially ones sensitive to neighborhood and NDO concerns.

  Even the on-the-job training approach clearly requires that effort be devoted to finding the resources to support technical staff and then to retain them. It also likely involves the eventual grooming of potential replacements for executive directors, by having current directors share some leadership and outside-contact functions with other high-level staff. Such sharing not only provides for the transfer of executive directors' special skills, should they depart, but also gives project technical staff the wider perspective needed to perform their work well and to keep them interested.

- At the same time, delegation of project responsibility must proceed with care. The evidence is clear that executive directors must ensure that staff are given only those levels of responsibility they can reasonably handle or grow into. Thrusting responsibility on unprepared project directors produced worse project results than any other division of work among executive directors and other staff. Project directors and other key staff must, while they learn, be able to rely on executive directors who are available and accessible to guide them, other staff or board members with specific complementary skills, and technical assistance that fills remaining gaps. Where real consideration was given to what project directors did and did not know and how they should be assisted, lead project staff with many different levels of expertise achieved success and personal growth in the course of NSHD work.

  If, in an effort to assemble needed technical skill for a project or projects, an NDO finds that its staff and resources are too thin and recruitment too difficult, then planned work may well be beyond NDO capability. NDO leaders—both staff and board members—need to be prepared to defer projects under such circumstances.

  Executive directors must also review the performance of key staff and replace or reassign them when performance dictates. Competence of newcomers is not easy to judge in advance. But troubled projects can often be rescued even well after their start by better staffing. Patience and support are central in "growing" good project directors, but both we and the NDO actors immediately involved saw instances where replacement was clearly necessary and should not have been avoided for the sake of at-best-temporary harmony.

- Making divisions of responsibility clear is also an important task for executive directors and other lead staff. The most notable project management problems arose when some major activity fell between the areas for which staffers perceived themselves responsible.

  One way to help avoid such problems is to hold regular staff meetings—both for project staff and for entire NDO staff. Under time pressure, even scheduled staff meetings are often allowed to slide. But staff meetings can have substantial value in clarifying project work—especially in identifying continuing problems before they generate emergencies—and in maintaining the morale of staffers who otherwise might feel unnoticed or isolated from NDO work except for their own immediate tasks.

- Provided that responsibilities are clearly divided, NDOs can and should take advantage of assembling balanced staff teams. The key is to bring together staff with different and complementary skills, as already suggested in this book's discussion of support of project directors. Of particular value is a competent construction supervisor who can complement others' financial and management skills, though some construction skills (such as cost estimating) can be acquired from the outside. Like project director selection, staff team development is worthy of candid review once projects are under way. Evidence indicates that NDOs can fill gaps and eliminate redundancies along the way as they evaluate how project implementation is actually proceeding.
- NDOs need to make serious step-by-step project plans when embarking on new projects, giving attention to each of the planning, implementation, and operating stages of their projects. Good project planning is crucial to good performance in general, as well as to developing project directors, to dividing responsibilities, and to using staff teams in particular.

  A clear sense simply of what needs to be done in a project, and in what order, is tremendously valuable, even if at first this is a "best guess." Many NDOs demonstrate that they understand well the value of project plans. But others need to learn to see project plans as tools for focusing initial work, which can be updated as new information and expertise are gained, and not as irrelevant requirements imposed by funders and other outsiders.

  Initially, young NDOs or those launching new types of projects can profitably draw on technical assistance to help make competent project plans. But project planning is a vital in-house skill, and every effort should be made to learn from technical-assistance providers and from project experience, so that NDOs can make more complete and realistic project plans internally.
- It is important for NDOs to continuously plan one or a few projects ahead, even while under current project pressure, for a variety of reasons related to maintaining momentum and support. A specific goal should be to provide enough work-load continuity to hold on to staff expertise once people are recruited and trained. Learning by doing is obviously a far more useful strategy if the knowledge is then retained

within an NDO over the long term. The sharp fluctuation in availability of external resources has of course had major impacts on the ability of NDOs to attain staff continuity.

- NDOs must recognize the importance of examining the economic feasibility of projects early in project development. Feasibility analyses should be done, at least on a rough basis, before time and money are lost on unpromising projects or on approaches to financing and implementation that will not produce successful projects even if fundraising and other goals are met.

  NDOs also need to be able to identify and assess alternative financing schemes that might make initially infeasible projects workable, and they must be able to do this in a timely way that allows them to adjust to changing external circumstances. Recent alterations in the funding environment exacerbate these needs.

  Thus far, many NDOs have exhibited major shortcomings in recognizing the need for and then developing these capabilities. More NDOs should be obtaining staff training, as well as buying technical assistance and then transferring outsiders' skills to staff in these areas. Because flexible, responsive planning requires the ability to quickly review project feasibility and financing options, these skills should be brought in house as rapidly as possible; but until they are, outsiders should be used to help in work that has too often been deferred.

- NDOs also need to better understand the significance of markets and market conditions in determining the feasibility of commercial and economic development projects and some housing projects (especially those involving resale). NDOs can also raise project performance if they understand that unless certain considerations (for example, security, neighborhood reputations) are dealt with, even well-renovated buildings and well-run enterprises may lack tenants and customers. This understanding can be used primarily to identify further tasks tha need attention rather than as a deterrent to undertaking projects— although it may be best to abandon and replace some projects that are particularly unpromising from a market viewpoint, since their likely failure will in any case deny the benefits being sought.

  For some organizations, a required first task is literally that of becoming concerned about markets—learning to look automatically with each project at such practical questions as: Can businesses reasonably be expected to come to our building, given the rents dictated by our costs and the prevailing rents for other space? If not, what can we do about it? For other NDOs, one or more of a series of specific issues need to be addressed: What type of product, service, or space will meet identified needs? How can we make our project known and of interest to customers? What improvements in those aspects of the neighborhood environment over which we have at least some control might affect the market? What improvements in our project financing might make a difference to our clients? What changes are forced on our project plans by the economic recession?

One of the most useful outgrowths of concern for markets might be an effort to work with private businesses as customers. NDOs could approach firms that have an interest in contributing to neighborhood revitalization, in order to encourage them to become customers for NDO businesses that are to be created or expanded—in fields such as office-building maintenance, subcomponent manufacturing, and the like. Attention to getting access to and commitments from potential customer markets in this and other ways will be especially necessary for successful job creation and commercial revitalization, given the decline in deep federal subsidies from CETA and other sources.

- More broadly, NDOs must take seriously the greater difficulties involved in commercial and economic development as compared with subsidized rental-housing rehabilitation or construction. As just indicated, NDOs need to take on these tougher projects with due concern for market potential and financial feasibility—lining up firm tenant or customer commitments in advance if at all possible. But they must also take care to assemble the extra resources—funds and especially staff and technical-assistance providers who have expertise with the specific project type—to match the difficulties. Taking advantage of a first learning experience that extends capabilities into the more difficult types of project categories, perhaps with the assistance of a coventurer or other continuous aid, is an important element of long-term NDO growth.

- Although many NDOs already recognize the significance of doing good homework, others still need to do so. Good homework means following procedures in seeking resources, permits, and so forth; keeping supporters informed about progress and problems through timely progress reports and informal discussions; and doing the detailed spadework of fundraising. It also ideally involves internalizing on staff the skills in proposal writing and in development of funder contacts that might initially come as technical aid. A prime condition for getting and benefiting from good homework is that executive directors must treat it as important and not expect to use political support to erase the need for it.

- It is essential that NDOs develop and maintain sound bookkeeping systems and that they be especially certain that their records are in order when entering into any political battles. Failure in this area can genuinely threaten organizational survival. Basic bookkeeping tasks should be internalized within the NDO if they are not already, and lead staff should become knowledgeable enough to oversee them if there is no senior-level financial manager.

  Key staff should also gain a sense of the potential value of up-to-date management and financial information and projections, especially in the current period of funding cutbacks. Reports beyond simple income, expense, and balance-sheet records could have real use in planning for future fundraising, staffing, and so on, if they are generated systematically. Again, some initial staff training—including an introduction to what is possible and a discussion of how identified needs can be met, led by a knowledgeable accountant—would be useful.

- NDOs have to work hard at keeping their boards of directors well-informed about NDO activities and about the development process, and in general should help them to feel that their input counts. If this activity is allowed to slacken when development work initially becomes more complex, it is very difficult to reenlist board aid when it is needed. An important component of this process is for staff to actively share information and decision making, thus preserving trust and harmony between board and staff that are so important in warding off internal strife and external attack. Many NDOs could also benefit from further effort to recruit board members with specific skills and contacts: people with technical capabilities, members of the business community or those with access to it, and others.

- Because experience is central to gaining many of the specific capabilities already mentioned, NDOs should engage in project work that meets their particular needs for capacity-building experience. Most notably, organizations new to development should take on some quite modest first project as a means of learning the development process. Learning by doing is invaluable in numerous areas such as project planning, estimating project costs and timing, and finding links to funders. And community support and funder interest often come from doing something, even on a quite-limited basis, well.

- NDOs should select projects with a conscious eye to building lines of continuing work that serve major objectives of a neighborhood revitalization strategy. Some NDOs received tremendous boosts to their long-term potential by impressing others and honing their own skills in projects that were particularly visible, reproducible, and/or responsive to widely perceived, unmet needs.

Some additional medium-term planning would be a useful adjunct to the project selection process, to balance NDOs' inherent emphasis on responding to targets of opportunity. But such planning would be more valuable if more medium-term and flexible resources were available from the outside, to make it more likely that plans would become project reality—a factor largely outside NDO control.

- Increased NDO attention to building records of successful long-term project operation, beyond initial ''construction'' stages, is warranted. Care in feasibility analysis, concern with markets, and detailed project planning can contribute to progress in this area. Difficult and changing NDO environments cause many of the problems that can later arise. But conscientious attention at the outset to ensuring the future of projects is an area in which some NDOs could use improvement— especially those NDOs that view requirements for preparing longer-term operating plans as unnecessary impediments.

- NDOs should cut their losses on infeasible or failed projects or projects that continue to drain resources and energy over the long term. Funders and other supporters respect NDOs that recognize and acknowledge problems and that take necessary steps to deal with them, even if this sometimes means that a specific project does not become a success. If the cause of problems is not sloppy work by an NDO itself (or if such weaknesses are corrected), and if supporters are kept well-advised of difficulties, a project failure need not prevent overall NDO progress.

- More generally, NDOs need to expand carefully the scale and variety of development projects they undertake. Growth and diversification should proceed gradually, with attention given to fitting expanded project efforts to the development of other key capacities.

Even in a period of restricted funding possibilities, self-discipline in considering whether to pursue a new opportunity is needed. It is useful to remember that several of the largest and most experienced NDOs had limited NSHD project success, in large part because they took on too much or leaped into new areas for which they were not fully prepared. Other NDOs endeavoring to respond efficiently to funding cutbacks are now discovering harmful gaps in their basic operations, caused partly by inadequate attention to systematic organizational development during earlier periods of growth.

It is critically important that NDOs push ahead to bigger and more difficult projects to meet their neighborhoods' needs, but only as capabilities that give a high likelihood of successful performance are assessed and put into place within the NDO. Unfortunately, we must anticipate continued instability in levels of outside support to NDOs. NDOs will need to intelligently control their own growth processes as much as possible within that context.

- Turning from NDO internal capabilities to relations with others, building and maintaining strong community support remain vital tasks. As in the case of boards of directors, it is essential that NDOs continuously educate and involve the community as they move into initial or more complex development projects. The development process will be unfamiliar to many community residents, who may feel that it is slow, expensive, and uncertain. Without active efforts to involve and inform them, community members may still support NDO work tacitly but may be unavailable for such active roles as supporter and demonstrator in the fund-seeking process, volunteer worker, or program participant. Again, recapturing participation is more difficult than retaining it, so that a process of continuing resident education and participation is preferable even though the time needed to keep contact is being vied for by other pressing tasks.

  Conversely, NDOs must not regard strong community support and the ability to summon it as a replacement for developing project skills. Experience shows that relying solely on the political "muscle" of community support may yield short-run funding but will produce neither long-term NDO success nor concrete project benefits to the community, both of which require many other capabilities as well.

- In all the processes of developing staff skills, good management, project records, and community links, NDOs must realistically assess what technical assistance is needed and then go after it. Again, early recognition by NDOs is important, identifying at the beginning of project development the specific skills in which NDOs are deficient, rather than finding this out later by having to face problems created by the lack of technical aid. NDOs with significant development experience will be able to make this assessment, while others could well use a trusted advisor (often a technical-assistance provider) experienced with nonprofit development to help identify needs. Ultimately, assembling a complete project team from among staff, technical-assistance providers, board members, and other outsiders can serve an NDO well.

  For best use of technical assistance, NDOs must convert broadly defined needs for such aid into well-specified tasks to be performed. And a project director (executive director or other staffer) with reasonable understanding of the development process, though not necessarily of the detailed mechanics of project work, should work closely with the technical-aid provider. There is a great deal of poor-quality technical assistance for sale. Finding good sources and then maintaining continuing links with them is therefore an important NDO task as well.

- NDOs should take aggressive advantage of their use of technical assistance as a learning process, in addition to its more obvious role as an aid to current work. Project planning, proposal writing, financial feasibility and market analysis, making funder contacts, and construction-cost estimating and supervision are prominent areas in which technical assistance can be beneficial. But in each of those areas, NDOs' growth and achievement of the highest levels of performance are, as we have seen, dependent on internalizing the skills among NDO staff. The fact that technical assistance is of uncertain quality makes the internalization process all the more important. One way to ensure that skills are transferred is to make the teaching process an explicit part of the assistance agreement (except when purchasing obviously specialized skills that are not intended to be internalized). Another important element in the skill-transfer process is for the project director to appreciate that a fine learning opportunity exists and should be exploited.

- NDOs can successfully either use their own construction crews or hire outside contractors, though the former may have shortcomings for very large projects. In either case, an adequate level of knowledgeable supervision by NDO staff (or a trusted technical advisor) is what is most needed. To ensure the advantages of creating jobs in the NDO neighborhood while avoiding unmanageable construction complexities, a number of NSHD grantees wisely allocated in advance construction work in part to NDO crews (for demolition, finishing, and so forth) and in part to contractors for more complex skills.

- Many NDOs could usefully pursue a relationship as a genuine partner with city hall in neighborhood developments. This means creating a perception within local government that an NDO can and does accomplish things that meet city goals for delivering desired project results and for enhancing the city's image as a successful program provider. The city might then become a much more eager collaborator in NDO efforts.

Building a track record of success is of course a crucial element in this process of partnership building. But NDOs need also to forge cooperative links not only with elected officials but also with city staff. Sharing NDO plans with city personnel and eliciting their review and suggestions at early stages of a project is particularly valuable in building a relationship that can otherwise sometimes become competitive instead.

The effort to create substantive partnerships with cities—for mutually perceived benefits—offers NDOs at least some possibility of retaining an advocacy stance on vital neighborhood issues while they are also obtaining crucial local public-sector aid. Nevertheless, it is a difficult balancing act to court city hall's resources and also preserve neighborhood goals.

- NDOs have important work to do in expanding their currently limited links to the private business sector as a source of financing, markets, technical assistance, and coventuring. NDOs, which often lack many initial contacts, should actively take advantage of available intermediaries—such as board members, technical-assistance sources, local committees of LISC—to build these relationships. Business and syndicator/coventurer support and cooperation are clearly more important than ever in the current public policy environment of limited public-sector grant funding.

Similarly, NDOs should make aggressive use of the infrequent opportunities to make contacts with private lenders in particular—taking advantage of lender participation in efforts like those of the Neighborhood Reinvestment Corporation; of lender concerns with meeting Community Reinvestment Act requirements; and of lender interest in profitable deposit, financial service, and investment opportunities within NDO operations.

- NDOs should try to make relations with funders continuing and interactive by discussing plans with them, jointly considering alternatives, and keeping them advised on currently funded projects. Such relations might lead not only to continued support but also to a greater ability by NDOs to define their own needs and to obtain money to fulfill them, rather than having to respond to program specifications that are seemingly fixed by funders.

An important tactic, especially with private funders but with public sources as well, is to take advantage of the entrée provided by a supporter's limited participation in a first project. By not only getting such participation but producing good results, providing the funder with ongoing information, and deliberately generating NDO-funder interaction, NDOs can secure more valuable participation—in type and scale—thereafter.

- Turning now to NDOs' relations with their environments, it makes eminent sense for NDOs to seek out opportunities to develop increased self-sufficiency, both for their own independence and security and to respond to funder pressures to show progress in that direction. But NDOs need to recognize the risk and limitations in trying to generate profitable enterprises and real estate deals while serving seriously troubled neighborhoods and low-income residents. Indeed, many "profit-making" efforts by NDOs, and by other actors under better conditions, instead become resource drains.

A useful intermediate goal would be to carefully design and finance some individual development projects that, given accurately defined initial aid, have a solid chance of becoming self-sustaining, given external market conditions beyond NDO control.

- To a limited extent, NDOs may be able to address some of the broader neighborhood environmental conditions that have an impact on their projects. Some elements of image, public attention and interest, security, and the like, are within reach of well-planned NDO action, in relation, say, to a commercial revitalization project. Because of the power of the neighborhood environment to affect project outcomes, NDOs should work hard at helping other actors (neighborhood businesspeople for example) to identify conditions in critical need of attention and should draw on successful experiences in similar neighborhoods to attack them.
- To a great extent, NDOs will not be able to change important external conditions and will have to continue to try to anticipate and respond to neighborhood and broader environmental conditions that they cannot control. NDOs that develop capability in project planning, feasibility analysis, funder and private business contacts, and some related areas will have, among the major benefits of those efforts, the increased ability to predict and react to external conditions as needed.

Indeed, all of the efforts to build NDO capability and performance require enormous ingenuity and adaptability in the face of extremely difficult conditions. Fortunately, ingenuity and adaptability are skills that NDOs are often well equipped with. NDO leaders must assure that these abilities are directed consciously and systematically toward an NDO's growth and success, focusing on the factors that truly matter.

The Roles of Sources of Support

NDO project efforts, capacity building, and, ultimately, broader community impacts require sufficient money and other resources from the outside.

The necessity of resources targeted to these purposes cannot be overemphasized. NDO work does benefit from good national economic conditions when they occur, but those are simply not enough for an NDO to succeed. NDOs carry out their work in neighborhoods and for people who are generally passed by in the process of overall economic growth or are buffeted by the changes it creates. The fact that their neighborhoods have been left out of broader economic progress is a primary trigger to the creation of NDOs.

As argued at the outset of this chapter, the performance and promise of NDOs' development work make them worthy objects of increased support. But sources of funds, technical assistance, cooperation, and other forms of aid have limits on the amount of their resources that can be devoted to working with NDOs—limits made much narrower in recent years by reduced federal funding on many fronts. It is important, therefore, that programs of assistance and cooperation be shaped in ways that serve NDOs well. That means that resources must flow to NDOs that can take good advantage of them, in forms that are well-directed to primary NDO needs, and under conditions that encourage and support NDOs' best efforts and growth. Otherwise, some of the great promise of NDO activity will doubtless be lost. Study findings delineated many elements of an effective, broad-based approach to supporting neighborhood groups doing community development work. Specific ideas for what sources of aid might do to effectively target their funding are presented in the remainder of this section.

- In choosing which NDOs to support, it is important that funders not select them on the basis of such simple criteria as staff size, budget, age, or number of past programs, although those measures are the most readily visible characteristics. The evidence is that these factors in themselves do not predict NDO performance. Many NDOs of modest size, history, and reputation had good project success when given the chance; and other older and larger organizations sometimes performed less well under certain circumstances. In order to effectively allocate their aid, supporters need to look for signals that more closely correspond to identified factors in NDO success.
- Among less apparent but still readily visible criteria, supporters could usefully look for some evidence of understanding on the part of staff of the nature of the development process and a record of performing well at some kind of development-oriented work, in order to predict performance. As a funder has more experience and contact with NDOs, it will want to look for other of the many internal capabilities and relations with outsiders that characterize successful performers.

- NDOs do need real, substantive capabilities in order to take on development projects under difficult circumstances. As we have seen, these include considerable technical skills, elements of effective management, access to key outsiders, and the like. Supporters should be serious about identifying whether such capabilities are present and should pattern their decisions accordingly. Where needed capacity is absent or insufficient, effort should be made to help NDOs develop this capacity. Project support should be kept in line with that development, in order not to swamp the NDOs' own growth and assimilation processes. But help certainly need not be denied, especially since gradually expanding experience, adequately assisted, is central to growth in capacity.
- Money given under certain specific circumstances can be especially useful to NDOs—for example, when a funder acts as the risk taker in the project of an apparently capable NDO. A supporter that provides an early commitment of funds, markets, or other aid around which further resources can be obtained, often contributes greatly to an NDO's ability to pull the multiple pieces of a project together.
- It makes sense, as risk taker or other supporter, to press NDOs to show signs that they are leveraging other resources. For a specific project, this might involve offering a financial commitment that is conditional on an NDO's finding other likely support as well, but making clear that the money will be forthcoming once other funding potential is identified, in order that the NDO can show others that initial support has already been gained. Or money might be provided immediately, but the share that is allowed to be spent could be limited until likely sources of adequate funds are secured. In many cases, of course, good signs of other funding potential will already be visible; and then no conditions need be set, as the successful leveraging of NSHD grants proves.

  The NSHD program demonstrated that supporters who take an early lead in funding, but who require evidence of leveraging potential and grant only one (significant) portion of total project needs, produce good leveraging outcomes. Indeed, such an approach provides a good leveraged funding program model.
- Funders can play an important role by providing funds for the later stages of project planning and for the start of implementation financing. Putting together a development project takes time and money. NDOs rarely have "profits" left over from past development projects to do feasibility studies, get technical assistance in packaging, secure

options for purchase of property, and so forth. And, at least in some cases, the money is needed before major implementation financing that might cover predevelopment costs is available.

Providers of such predevelopment funds, and of other project funds as well, should be flexible in setting requirements for how quickly the funds must be spent. Development projects, regardless of who undertakes them, are often delayed for a host of external reasons that are beyond developer control.

- Funders and other policymakers must recognize that some provision of cheap project money is necessary if NDOs are to continue to serve low- and moderate-income people and to attract businesses, jobs, and investments to troubled neighborhoods. The money may be in the form of grants, loans at preferred rates or with deferred repayments, operating subsidies, or combinations of these and other types of funding; but it must in some way be forthcoming. Obtaining more such funds is currently the key to generating many new NDO development projects, across a wide spectrum of other circumstances. Given special NDO goals in terms of targeting the benefits of their work, cheap money is inherently needed, regardless of the source.

Cheap money, often but not only from the public sector, is crucial in enabling NDOs to use private, market-rate funds (or funds close to market rate) in projects that still serve their own communities. The NSHD experience showed that NDOs could get and use significant levels of the private monies, provided that cheaper money was available to be used in combination with the private funds, in order to lower the overall cost. Continuing high interest rates further tighten this linkage. The private sector—foundations, corporations, religious groups—could give further attention to sharing with government the burden of providing inexpensive finances.

- Efforts should be made to increase private institutional lending in NDO neighborhoods. Larger-scale NDO projects require the reasonable availability of such loans to use with other resources, but these loans have been in short supply. And loans have frequently been coupled with requirements for very high levels of equity capital to secure them against perceived risks—equity that is difficult for NDOs to come by, especially with sharply reduced federal support.

To some extent, lenders can expand credit availability themselves, by examining some individual projects in greater detail, rather than assuming that risks in NDO neighborhoods are too great, and by being willing to take on some expanded risks or at least uncertainties as a contribution to community vitality. NDOs' efforts to more carefully evaluate the economics of their own projects can contribute to lender responsiveness. Other supporters could pay attention to possibilities for providing partial loan guarantees, to assembling loan pools, and to other mechanisms that reduce lender risk. Actors willing to commit themselves to buying NDO products, to renting their space, and so forth, also are valuable in reducing risk by assuring revenues to NDOs. As already indicated, other funders need to provide the cheap monies that make NDO projects feasible when partly financed by market-rate loans. And in some instances, effective regulation of lender behavior, particularly in the context of Community Reinvestment Act provisions, will be appropriate. Unless a combination of such actions is taken, urging NDOs to pursue private monies implies false promise and promotes frustration.

- Funders should seek to provide adequate initial capitalization and/or subsidization of NDO ventures so that projects will have long-term viability. Some NSHD projects where physical improvements or market generation have proceeded well nonetheless were so tightly budgeted or financed initially that the burden of creating stable future operations is significantly increased. Clearly this is a false savings from which both NDOs and their supporters should be weaned.

  Instead, NDOs should be encouraged to present realistic long-term project plans, based on the expanding financing-planning skills noted here as important for them to develop. Funders should then be vitally interested in assuring from the outset that outside support is sufficient to sustain the effort. Since funders can distort NDO planning by their frequent eagerness to support projects by providing the fewest possible number of dollars, funders should take the lead in ensuring that adequate resources are budgeted.

- In some situations, funders should consider providing readily accessible pools of funds to NDOs for land banking and the timely purchase of properties as they become available. Especially in areas where housing markets are tight and displacement may be threatened, but in other situations of opportunity as well, NDOs are disadvantaged by lacking quick-action lines of credit.

- With all the specific types of funding important to NDOs' work, NDOs still need flexible general-support money. Foundations, religious organizations, businesses, and government at all levels must provide resources to allow the adequate staffing, project-generation work, organizing, and longer-term planning that are fundamental to, but not adequately supported by, project-specific funds. Many supporters are more eager to provide project-specific funds so that they can see clearly

associated results. But if an NDO is turning out a good series of
project efforts, it makes sense to meet the NDO's critical need for
basic sustenance, without which no project succeeds.

- Outside sources of aid should be supportive of NDO institution building, not just projects. Such supporters need to encourage NDOs to
  pursue capacity-building goals in the course of project work and general operations. Such goals could be made a part of funding application
  and proposal processes and of the review of ultimate performance, at
  least for some public, foundation, and corporate grants. Funds explicitly for capacity-building purposes could be included within project
  and general-support grants.

  NDOs could be pressured to make assessments of their capacity-
  building needs and plans for meeting them, and given funds for both
  the assessments and follow-up action. Or at a minimum, NDOs could
  be selected for funding at least partly on the basis that their own
  proposed projects seem likely to help upgrade their capabilities as a
  part of project work itself.

  The availability to NDOs of skilled developer-entrepreneur technical
  staff is so critical a part of capacity building that funders should, in
  addition to supporting NDOs themselves, separately fund organizations that offer effective training to key NDO staff.

- Funders should be responsive to requests for money that preserves
  capacity growth that has already occurred. For example, general-
  support money that protects against layoffs of newly trained and experienced project director staff, or timely project funds that help make
  for track-record continuity to ensure community support, might be of
  special value. Key skills such as project planning are so inherently
  learned by experience that it is important to help NDOs avoid having
  to learn them over and over again after losing major staff members.

- It is vital for supporters to take project risks with NDOs that have
  some good capabilities but that lack experience in development or in
  the particular line or scale of proposed work. The evidence from NSHD
  program results is that there are a great number of inexperienced NDOs
  with much potential, and that along many dimensions of capability,
  experience itself is a necessary builder of skills and relationships. The
  NSHD program provided for numerous successful expansions of track
  records by investing in such "firsts." Foundations and corporations
  are in especially good positions to take similar risks, at least with the
  funds they have allocated to grant making (as opposed to funds given,
  in larger amounts perhaps, as loans of assets).

  Notably, some aspects of track records are important primarily for their value in attracting outside resources. Simply by being more willing to work with organizations that have only limited experience with a proposed type of project, therefore, funders can moderate the constraints that lack of experience imposes, and thereby facilitate NDO growth.

- Outside supporters should work with NDOs to see that the specific projects NDOs propose and for which they receive funding match well the capabilities that the organizations have developed to date. Where the match of capacity with proposed project is reasonably close, but where some additional staff support, technical assistance, or other reources are needed, NDOs could be helped to identify those needs and to fill them at the project's outset.

Although some larger, more sophisticated NDOs attempted projects that exceeded their capacities in NSHD work, such organizations clearly are capable of greater efforts than are their inexperienced counterparts. Such expanded efforts are critical if NDOs are to have real impacts on overall neighborhood conditions. Supporters should help NDOs stretch their limits in order that a larger number of more sophisticated organizations can be developed. As NDOs do expand their skills, funders should give them credit for capacity development in reviewing further proposals, and should then be willing to invest in still larger and more complex efforts.

- It would be highly useful for funders to create and/or participate in institutionalized sources of *continuing* support for NDOs that perform well—support that would be flexibly available for various kinds of projects that NDOs may plan over time. That kind of multiyear funding would make it rational for NDOs to formulate concrete, multifaceted neighborhood revitalization strategies and would allow them to pursue component projects of those strategies in a more orderly manner. It might well thus expand their abilities to generate indirect impacts and perhaps broader community revitalization results. Support from the Community Services Administration to advanced community organizations doing development work formerly fit that mold, before funding was reduced and continuity of support made less certain.

- Supporters should help provide for technical assistance to NDOs in key areas of work and should encourage NDOs to use it and learn from it. There should be clear recognition by all parties that use of technical aid implies no shortcoming by the NDO but instead a rational response to needs. Supporters could also be helpful in encouraging NDOs to make training of staff an explicit part of the technical-assistance process.

The private business sector could be especially valuable here, particularly in lending in-kind expertise, but also in putting NDOs in contact with qualified experts they could hire and in urging the experts to provide good service (when they are people who also serve private business, so that leverage exists).

Some technical-assistance resources should also come in the form of cash, however, so that NDOs can choose experts themselves and use the services of people experienced in working with and sensitive to the needs of NDOs specifically. Those specialists are often very useful in, among other things, helping NDOs recognize what further technical help they need, so that they can make good use of other technical-aid sources. Such NDO-oriented technical-aid groups, as exemplified by the Center for Community Change and the Support Center, are also worthy of continued and expanded support on their own.

- The private business sector in particular can and should extend other valuable nonmoney "resources" to the work of NDOs, in addition to in-kind technical assistance. A vitally important element is this regard is willingness to provide markets for NDO (nonresidential) projects—purchasing goods or services from their ventures, renting commercial or industrial space they have renovated, or putting them in touch with other people who will. NDOs and businesspeople could work actively together to identify situations where mutual needs would be met by such arrangements. Perhaps, for example, developers of downtown office buildings could use the services of an NDO office maintenance firm that employs nearby residents. Advance commitments by businesspeople agreeing to be tenants or customers could have significant value in moving NDO projects forward. The provision of markets is both enormously useful to NDO efforts and a means of assistance that can cost businesses little or nothing beyond normal expenses, especially if the businesses also help to ensure that NDOs have other aid needed to become efficient producers.

Private businesses could also give NDOs a "piece of the action" in profitable new ventures—jobs, ownership, profits, markets, and so forth. They might do that as a form of contribution to NDO and neighborhood long-term well-being, or in exchange for a valued service (for example, housing management), and/or to meet requirements imposed by local governments in exchange for city aid and permits. And they might seek coventures of many kinds that combine NDO and private business capabilities.

To bring about some of these relations, private businesses could take more initiative in seeking out links with NDOs—volunteering advice, technical assistance, and possibilities of shared development efforts to explore. That initiative could complement expanded NDO efforts in this same direction.

- City governments specifically should recognize and cooperate with NDOs as partners in neighborhood revitalization, making properties, cash, and regulatory clearances available, and directing city agencies to actively offer technical advice. Especially in growing cities, but in particular instances in almost any city, local government can be very valuable in initiating requirements that NDOs be cut in on other developments that need city aid and approval. In that way, NDOs can gain opportunities to earn money outside their distressed neighborhoods in order to pay for programs within them. At little expense to itself, the city can also be a valued customer for NDOs' work and can guide other customers to them, thus helping NDOs deal with limitations in markets for goods and services they produce.

   Cooperation with NDOs has the potential to be a genuine partnership from local governments' viewpoint in that it is a source of mutual benefits and assistance. We have seen that NDOs can be highly productive in attacking the problems of troubled neighborhoods in ways that other actors cannot; city governments can thus use NDO support as a means to deal with difficult problems already of concern to the city. And it is clearly beneficial to NDO progress to have city cooperation in these multiple forms.

   But NDOs should not have to obtain aid from the public sector only at the local level. Some local governments are resistant to even the best NDO efforts and are slow to respond at all to the problems of lower-income neighborhoods. Moreover, NDOs need some shielding from the dilemma of acting as advocates on critical neighborhood issues that city government must rule upon, while being dependent on city resources for development-project work.

- The enormous costs of federal funding cutbacks to the progress of NDO work should be recognized and responded to. Losses of explicitly NDO-oriented programs and those that NDOs use in their projects have severed funds vital for continuing general operations, for deep subsidies needed to serve low-income people, and for resources to offset neighborhood disadvantages. Crucial NDO growth processes have been interrupted once again, as they were, for example, in the federal housing program moratorium in the early 1970s.

   Many types of lost monies should be restored to NDO use or directly substituted for from federal funds. These losses are too great to be compensated for from other sources. Still, private grant funding should expand to take up some of the slack, especially funding from those institutions and individuals who have benefited greatly from tax reductions.

- In particular, sound federal policy might well include restoring a program with the basic structure of Neighborhood Self-Help Development. Many of that program's provisions proved of special value: its focus on project planning and partial implementation funding; its pressure for leveraging and help in making funding contacts; its calculated risk taking with projects and organizations; its attention to capacity building and aid in planning for it; and its usefulness in making projects targeted more to the poor. Coupled with restored project implementation funds, such a program could continue to contribute to NDO production of concrete results, institutional growth, and formation of partnerships.

  Recognizing the value of such programs, Congress did, in 1983, create the Neighborhood Development Demonstration Program, providing grants to neighborhood groups for purposes similar to NSHD and requiring a local match of grant funds. It is regrettable that the Office of Management and Budget has delayed program initiation on technical grounds—a delay that, it is hoped, will soon be resolved.

- More broadly speaking, the federal govenment should provide funds to NDOs to meet critical needs identified in this book, especially for general support, planning and proposal development, and early risk capital to finance well-thought-out ventures. The funding should include incentives and requirements for NDOs to leverage additional funds from other sources, as well as to build their own capabilities in the process of project work and to use technical assistance as appropriate. The federal resources should flow to NDOs that show strong promise of good performance and future growth based on the success factors identified throughout this book.

  These kinds of federal support create the conditions within which other actors in both the public and private sectors can effectively contribute their resources to NDO work. Other institutions could then carefully examine how their assistance would best complement federal resources.

- People concerned with NDOs in the public and private sectors need to be realistic about NDO development of economic self-sufficiency, even over the long term. There are real limits to the extent that any organization can serve lower-income people and neighborhoods while turning a profit sufficient to support that and further work. Projects can be restructured or relocated to make them feasible and to reap surpluses; but the cost can be great if NDOs are diverted from their unique function.

Supporters would be better advised to focus, as suggested before, on providing enough money and expertise up front so that projects can be expected thereafter to be self-sustaining, perhaps modestly surplus generating, or at least running accurately projected deficits that are justified by perceived benefits.

More generally, policymakers need to remember the difficulty of the community development process for even the best of NDOs (and the best of for-profit developers as well). During our study NDOs were battered not only by the continuing intense problems of their own neighborhoods but also by a major recession, sharply increased interest rates, and deep federal funding cutbacks. Those problems need to be taken fully into account in judging NDOs' progress and the merits of further funding to them.

It must be clearly understood that NDOs need cash support, as well as other resources, to continue serving people of limited means in resource-poor neighborhoods unattractive to many other investors and developers. Although most NDOs have dedicated staffs and boards of directors and supportive communities, magic alone will not allow them to provide good housing to people unable to afford it, to successfully staff their ventures with untrained neighborhood youth, or to do other similar tasks when others cannot. Properly supported NDOs, however, can prove to be excellent vehicles for such work.

In sum, decision makers can take a series of actions to increase the effectiveness of their support for NDOs, based on the findings of this study. In broad terms, these include choosing effective NDOs based on criteria that have been proven to matter, giving cash aid in especially useful forms, influencing the behavior of NDOs to encourage their own growth, expanding the use of other powers and resources to assist in noncash ways, and recognizing the limits on and needs of neighborhood organizations in their performance of difficult but critical work. All these actions need to be taken within a context of adequate total resources to address deeply rooted neighborhood problems.

Where both NDOs and their supporters give careful attention to the specific needs and constraints inherent in NDO development efforts, the great potential for successful neighborhood revitalization work that NDOs have demonstrated can be even more fully realized. This is a joint effort well worth making, if we are at all serious about revitalizing our urban neighborhoods for the benefit of those who live and work within them and if, more broadly, we are serious about fully extending the benefits of the nation's riches to the lower-income residents of our cities.

Appendix A

Neighborhood Development Organizations in the Study

*1. Anacostia Economic Development Corporation, Washington, D.C.
 2. Banana Kelly Community Improvement Association, Bronx, New York
 3. Bayfront Neighborhood Action Team, Erie, Pennsylvania
 4. Bethel Housing, Inc., Chicago, Illinois
*5. Better Homes, Inc., Bristol, Pennsylvania
 6. Better Neighborhoods, Inc., Schenectady, New York
 7. Bickerdike Redevelopment Corporation, Chicago, Illinois
 8. Blue Hills Homes Corporation, Kansas City, Missouri
 9. Brightwood Development Corporation, Springfield, Massachusetts
*10. Burnside Consortium, Portland, Oregon
*11. Carnales, Inc., Austin, Texas
 12. Catholic Charities, Brooklyn, New York
 13. Central West Area Council Corporation, Toledo, Ohio
*14. Cherry Community Organization, Charlotte, North Carolina
 15. Citizens to Bring Back Broadway, Cleveland, Ohio
 16. Clarksville Community Development Corporation, Austin, Texas
 17. Code North, Inc., Memphis, Tennessee
 18. Communities Organized to Improve Life (COIL), Baltimore, Maryland
 19. Community Concern #13, Philadelphia, Pennsylvania
 20. Community Housing Improvement and Planning Association, Salinas, California
 21. Downtown Urban Housing, Inc., Jersey City, New Jersey

22. East Bay Asian Local Development Corporation, Oakland, California
23. Eastside Community Investments, Indianapolis, Indiana
*24. 18th Street Development Corporation, Chicago, Illinois
25. Evanston Community Development Corporation, Evanston, Illinois
26. Ferry Village Improvement Association, South Portland, Maine
27. Fifth Avenue Committee, Inc., Brooklyn, New York
28. Fillmore-Leroy Area Residents, Inc. (FLARE), Buffalo, New York
29. Greater Birmingham Ministries, Birmingham, Alabama
30. Greater Roseland Organization, Chicago, Illinois
31. Harlem Interfaith Counseling Services, New York, New York
32. Housing Opportunities, Inc., Pittsburgh, Pennsylvania
33. Inner City Christian Foundation Non-Profit Housing Corporation, Grand Rapids, Michigan
34. Interfaith Adopt-A-Building, New York, New York
35. Interfaith Council for Action, Ossining, New York
*36. International District Improvements Associations (INTERIM), Seattle, Washington
*37. Inquilinos Boricuas En Accion (IBA), Boston, Massachusetts
38. Ithaca Neighborhood Housing Services, Ithaca, New York
39. Kensington Action Now, Philadelphia, Pennsylvania
*40. Jones Falls Community Corporation, Baltimore, Maryland
41. Latin American Community Enterprise (LACE), Yonkers, New York
42. Maintenance Central, Inc., Detroit, Michigan
43. Manchester Citizens Corporation, Pittsburgh, Pennsylvania
44. Manhattan Valley Development Corporation, New York, New York
45. Metropolitan Community Development Corporation, Louisville, Kentucky
46. Metropolitan Washington Planning & Housing Association, Washington, D.C.
47. Mexican American Unity Council, San Antonio, Texas
48. Near Southeast Side Neighborhood Development Corporation, Fort Worth, Texas
49. Neighborhood Development Corporation of Jamaica Plains, Boston, Massachusetts
50. Neighborhood Housing, Inc., New Haven, Connecticut–Dwight
*51. Neighborhood Housing, Inc., New Haven, Connecticut–Ferry
52. Neighborhood Improvement Company, Minneapolis, Minnesota
53. Neighborhood Resources, Passaic, New Jersey
54. 19th Ward Community Association, Inc., Rochester, New York

*55. Northeast Hawley Development Association, Syracuse, New York
*56. Northeast Neighborhood Improvement Association (NENIA), Flint, Michigan
*57. North Omaha Community Development, Inc., Omaha, Nebraska
*58. North Ward Educational & Cultural Center, Newark, New Jersey
*59. Northwest Action Council, Milwaukee, Wisconsin
 60. Northwest Bronx Community & Clergy Coalition Inc., Bronx, New York
 61. Operation Life Community Development Corporation, Las Vegas, Nevada
 62. Pacific Asian Consortium in Employment Housing & Community Development (PACE), Los Angeles, California
 63. Philadelphia Community Rehab Corporation, Philadelphia, Pennsylvania
*64. Portland West Neighborhood Planning Council, Portland, Maine
*65. Potrero Hill Community Development Corporation, San Francisco, California
*66. Renigades Housing Movement, Inc., New York, New York
 67. Reservoir Hill Community Association, Baltimore, Maryland
 68. River East Economic Revitalization Corporation, Toledo, Ohio
*69. Riverside/Cambridgeport Community Corporation, Cambridge, Massachusetts
*70. St. Clair–Superior Coalition, Cleveland, Ohio
 71. St. Nicholas Neighborhood Preservation & Housing Rehabilitation Corporation, Brooklyn, New York
*72. San Bernardino Community Development Corporation, San Bernardino, California
*73. San Juan Center, Hartford, Connecticut
*74. Santa Barbara Community Housing Corporation, Santa Barbara, California
*75. Savannah Landmark Rehab Project, Inc., Savannah, Georgia
 76. Skid Row Development Corporation, Los Angeles, California
 77. Somerville United Neighborhood (SUN), Somerville, Massachusetts
 78. Southeast Development, Inc., Baltimore, Maryland
 79. Southern Brooklyn Community Organization, Brooklyn, New York
 80. Southside United Housing Development Fund, Brooklyn, New York
 81. Southwest Germantown Community Development Corporation, Philadelphia, Pennsylvania
 82. Stop Wasting Abandoned Property (SWAP), Providence, Rhode Island

83. The East Los Angeles Community Union (TELACU), Los Angeles, California
84. The Martin Luther King Center for Social Change, Atlanta, Georgia
85. The Woodlawn Organization (TWO), Chicago, Illinois
86. Total Action Against Poverty, Inc. (TAD), Roanoke, Virginia
87. Tremont West Development Corporation, Cleveland, Ohio
*88. Tri-City Citizens Union for Progress, Newark, New Jersey
*89. Tucson Barrio Association (TBA), Tucson, Arizona
*90. Upper Albany Community Organization, Hartford, Connecticut
91. Urban Edge, Inc., Jamaica Plains, Massachusetts
92. Voice of the People, Chicago, Illinois
93. Walnut Hills Redevelopment Foundation, Cincinnati, Ohio
*94. Watts Community Labor Action Committee, Los Angeles, California
*95. West Harlem Community Organization, New York, New York
*96. Westside Housing Organization, Kansas City, Missouri
97. Whiteaeker Community Council, Eugene, Oregon
98. Youth Education and Health in Soulard (YEHS), St. Louis, Missouri
99. Young Israel Community Development Corporation, Los Angeles, California

---

*Denotes organization in the study sample.

Appendix B
Research Methods, Problems, and Prospects

Major Approaches

How was the information for this book obtained and analyzed? Initially, a long series of specific study questions and hypotheses, within the broad areas outlined in chapter 1, was formulated. Two principal approaches were then used to address them. The first was to collect and examine data contained in written documents available from the entire set of ninety-nine NDOs in the study. Because all study NDOs were recipients of grants under HUD's Neighborhood Self-Help Development program, they were required to answer a uniform set of questions about themselves, their project plans, and the progress they made. While not all of this information was in fact delivered, and its form varied, it served as a valuable base for important parts of our analysis.

In particular, written documents submitted by the full population of NDOs provided information about five topics.

- What are some basic characteristics of the NDOs under study—for example, age, size, location, ethnicity, programmatic history?
- What do NDOs' planned projects look like—for example, project type, expected scale, length, cost?
- What project work was actually carried out, and how did these accomplishments compare with expectations?
- What non-NSHD funds were obtained, and how did this fundraising compare with initial plans?

213

- To a lesser extent, how did NDO and project characteristics affect project results?

From grant-application and grant-award documents, we gathered the baseline parts of this information: NDO and project characteristics and intended project and leveraging outcomes. From progress reports submitted to HUD during the course of grants, plus our follow-up efforts, we determined what was actually being accomplished. A computer file was created containing a record of baseline and progress data for each study NDO; it was used extensively for the analysis presented in this book.

The second major study approach was to make site visits to a sample of thirty study NDOs that were selected randomly from the full group of ninety-nine.[1] Much vital study information is not of the type that is obtainable from written documents, especially documents that are provided by NDOs reporting on their own activities, from a long distance, and that are designed primarily to serve program operation rather than evaluation purposes.[2] On-site interviews with key actors in NDO work, coupled with direct observation of NDO projects and activities, thus provided the basis for analyses in several major study areas not well illuminated in written materials. Written information, nevertheless, served as valuable background in shaping the site visits.

Specifically, site-visit information was critical in four study areas:

- Describing more subtle characteristics of NDOs—for instance, staff skills, participation by boards of directors—that could only be observed by talking to actual participants.
- Measuring less-easily-apparent project outcomes such as who benefited, how residents participated, and where projects fit in broader strategies.
- Assessing how various factors contributed to project success or failure. Some of this analysis involved factors measurable for the full population, but much of it related to NDO characteristics observable only for places we visited. In addition, the process by which key factors affected project results was visible only from direct observation.
- Analyzing the growth in NDO capabilities during project work. Most capacity building was in characteristics (for example, learning by staff) not assessable from a distance either initially or as projects moved along.

---

1. Appendix A lists all NDOs in the full study population and identifies those in the sample.

2. HUD staff in the former Office of Neighborhood Development were, however, enormously helpful in trying to include requests for information useful to the evaluation in the reporting requirements.

We addressed these issues by talking with large numbers of people who worked in and with sample NDOs, early in NSHD project work and then again toward the end of projects. Drawing on answers to questions posed in the interview guides we prepared (see description following), we developed a series of case studies from which we could make broader conclusions.[3] Also, a second computer file was built for just the sample NDOs, containing quantifiable information from site visits, along with the data available for all ninety-nine NDOs. It was used to analyze many specific hypotheses.

Principal Tasks

Within each major study approach, a series of more specific tasks was also undertaken, relying on specific data sources described very briefly here. Further information on these tasks and data is available in the *Research Plan for the Study of the Impact of External Funding on Neighborhood Development Organizations*[4] and from the author on request; later sections of this appendix discuss some of the complexities encountered.

Consider first data collection and analysis for the full population of ninety-nine NDOs. At the outset of the study, information was drawn about NDOs themselves, and to some extent about their neighborhoods, from applications that each had submitted in seeking NSHD funds. From grant instruments negotiated between HUD and the grantees, information was then obtained about intended project outputs, fund leveraging, use of self-help, and scheduling.

During the course of project work, NDOs were to submit quarterly and final reports describing their activities. We utilized these to determine project tasks and outputs completed. Similarly, quarterly and final financial reports indicated, along with the progress reports, what non-NSHD funds had been obtained. We also used NDOs' formal requests for time extensions, for NSHD fund reallocation to other uses, and for changes in project scope to measure further aspects of project outcomes. Numerous NDO progress reports were unavailable to us, however, especially at the later stages of projects. Elimination of HUD's Office of Neighborhood Development and the resultant reorganization of the NSHD grant-monitoring functions intensified the usual problems of obtaining information from grantees. As a result, we made tele-

---

3. For reasons of confidentiality, the text of this report draws anonymously on the case studies for examples, but it does not present a single complete case-study report on each NDO separately and by name.

4. Mayer and Marshall 1981.

TABLE B.1

SAMPLE NDOS BY PROJECT TYPE

Project Type	Number of NDOs
Housing rehabilitation	14
Community development	2
Housing construction	2
Economic development	6
Commercial revitalization	5
Energy conservation and renewables	1

phone calls to about two-thirds of the NDOs we did not visit, in order to gain information on project and leveraging results, as well as on progress and revised expectations where projects were still incomplete. As already stated, information from these sources for the ninety-nine NDOs was coded and a computer file created for analysis. The file was used to generate findings of two types described throughout this book. The first group of findings is descriptive: of NDOs, projects, outcomes, leveraging, and so forth. The second is analytic: testing the relationship of NDO and project characteristics to project outcomes achieved.

Turning now to the study sample site visits, the sample NDOs were selected randomly from the study population, but after being grouped within categories of project types. Differing proportions of NDOs performing the various types of projects were selected. Housing rehabilitation projects were so numerous that had we not so stratified our selection process, too few examples of other kinds of work would have been included in the sample to allow adequate analysis of them. By oversampling other kinds of projects, a sample was obtained with the distribution of activities shown in table B.1.[5] Details of the sampling approach are described in the earlier-mentioned study research plan.[6]

Interview guides were developed for discussing NDO work with key actors at each site. The guides contained suggested questions of two main types. The most common types were direct questions explicity addressing a study issue—for example, questions asking people to give their opinion of the most important factors in the success (or failure) of their projects, or whether a specific factor seemed important in their experience, or whether a

5. Table B.1 lists projects by primary type of work. Some, in fact, involve mixtures of work type. (A few projects turned out to be of a different type than what we had been given to understand, based on written information at the time of the sampling.)
6. Mayer and Marshall 1981.

particular NDO capability was strong or growing. Other questions were more indirect—for example, asking NDO staff to identify the major steps in their project work. From the answers to such indirect questions, we made our own inferences—in the case cited here, about how knowledgeable staff were about development and how that knowledge had expanded during the course of NSHD activities.

Interview guides were designed for each of eleven categories of people we sought to interview at each site, one for the first visit and one for the second. Those interviewed included:

- NDO executive directors
- NDO NSHD project managers or development managers
- NDO financial managers
- NDO boards of directors
- NDO program planners
- Sources of funding (for NSHD projects primarily)
- Sources of technical assistance
- Contractors and/or joint venturers
- Local government officials
- Community volunteers
- Leaders of other community organizations in the immediate area

NDO executive directors provided primary guidance in determining the specific individuals to talk with, along with lists of key actors contained in grant applications. The range of actors interviewed yielded a diversity of perspectives that contributed greatly to the value of the site visits.

As already noted, we visited each NDO in our sample twice, generally for three days the first time and two the second. To the extent possible, the first visit was made near the beginning of NSHD work and the second near the end, to get optimal information on capacity building over time and on factors in success at various stages of work. First visits measured baseline capabilities, and second visits assessed capability changes; both visits addressed why projects were proceeding well or poorly. The study, however, started somewhat too late and ended somewhat too early to allow desired timing of visits to be fully realized. A few organizations were observed only once because their projects were well advanced by the time we were first able to get there, and some others were visited longer after their start-up or longer before their finish than we would have preferred.

We prepared full reports of each visit for each NDO. Major study issues were then analyzed by looking across the thirty specific situations for recognizable patterns. Analysis was partly qualitative—based on salient observations and examples from the site reports—and partly quantitative—describing NDOs and testing hypotheses about factors in their success or failure, in terms of variables enumerated for each organization. For quantitative analyses, each sample observation was weighted appropriately to compensate for the varying sampling proportions used for NDOs of differing project types. Much of the analysis combined the two approaches: for instance, identifying in the site reports interesting cases of capacity growth and then tabulating the most common capacity-building patterns among all thirty sample grantees.

Representing NDOs with the NSHD Population and Sample

It should be recognized that the full population of ninety-nine study NDOs is highly representative of but does not neatly reflect the characteristics of all such organizations in the country. The NSHD program selected grantees based on competitive proposals, using a lengthy set of criteria and standards. Four criteria were notable. First, organizations needed at least some history of service to their neighborhoods related to the development work they were proposing—either an established record in the same type of project or some demonstration of capability based on similar or closely allied work. Second, they had to demonstrate some technical and management capacity on their project team (staff, consultants, and so forth) sufficient to undertake their proposed projects; and these projects also had to be well along in planning. Third, they had to show that they were accountable to neighborhood residents and that proposed projects would serve low- and moderate-income members of the community. Fourth, they needed established relations with outsiders adequate to show real potential to garner other funds, as well as a sufficiently friendly relationship with local government to obtain limited approval of their proposed project.[7]

Thus to win NSHD grants, NDOs in general had to be further along in their efforts than neighborhood organizations just deciding, for example, to enter the development field.[8] At the same time, selection was, by design, not limited to the most sophisticated NDOs. The number of grants assured extension beyond that, as did the modest requirements regarding experience. The NSHD program was intended to help NDOs build more effective organizations. NDOs were not selected from the strongest down, but instead from

7. Local mayors had to agree to certify that NDO projects were consistent with localities' overall revitalization plans.

8. Some NDOs, however, were in development projects where for the first time they took prime responsibility as developers.

a broader field of NDOs with enough capacity to do the sometimes limited, sometimes more substantial projects they proposed, on behalf of their communities.

How well does the sample of thirty NDOs represent the population of all urban NSHD grantees? Owing to our reliance on the sample to analyze a variety of issues that could not be well examined except by actually visiting NDOs, it is important to be assured that the sample well represents the larger population. A series of statistical tests was performed to assess directly whether the sample provided an apt representation of all grantees. The findings unequivocally affirmed that the sample provided a highly accurate representation.

The sample was chosen from among eighty-seven of the ninety-nine total grantees, because at the time of sample selection it was unclear whether the remaining twelve grants would ultimately either be committed or committed in full. Since the sample was chosen by random drawing within strata of NDOs grouped by project type, its characteristics ought to have matched those of the eighty-seven. Appropriate weights would need simply to be attached to the sample observations to compensate for the fact that, by design, differing proportions of the NDOs in each stratum were selected. It was possible, however, that by coincidence of the draw the sample would not well approximate the study population from which it was drawn, in terms of various characteristics of NDOs and their projects. That possibility was tested by comparing the weighted characteristics of the sample with those of the eighty-seven NDOs, using characteristics that we could measure well from written documents or from information obtained by us in telephone calls for the entire group of study organizations.

It was somewhat more likely that the sample would match the eighty-seven NDOs from which it was drawn but not all ninety-nine grantees that we wanted ultimately to represent. This likelihood was raised by the fact that the twelve NDOs eliminated for sampling purposes showed some special early signs of trouble and/or were delayed in receiving NSHD funding commitments. The population including those twelve thus might have differed particularly in the level of successful project outcomes. We therefore tested the (weighted) characteristics of the sample against those of the full population of ninety-nine NDOs as well, again using information available for all grantees.

The sample and population were compared according to a total of eighteen different characteristics, including five measures of how NDO projects turned out (for example, the share of originally planned work that is complete) and thirteen measures of NDO characteristics (for example, the extent of past experience). Comparisons were made between sample and total population frequency distributions (for instance, what share of NDOs had small, medium, or large budgets in the sample and in the population) and, where appropriate, between sample and population means.[9]

For all eighteen characteristics, we found no significant differences between the sample and the larger NDO population (either of eighty-seven or ninety-nine). Indeed, some of the matches were remarkably close. The sample NDOs are somewhat more often located in smaller cities and have slightly more experience and funding on average, but not significantly so. The only noteworthy difference is that the full population of ninety-nine has more projects from the second of NSHD's two funding cycles, because all twelve NDOs excluded from sampling were in that later grantee group. Even that fact creates no statistically significant contrast between the sample and the total ninety-nine. The tests give us great assurance in using the sample in analyzing key study issues; that is, we can have substantial confidence in drawing inferences from the characteristics and experiences of the sample of thirty NDOs, in instances where needed information is available only for those organizations we visited.

Dealing with Research Complexities and Problems

As is typical in research projects of this magnitude, our study of NDOs encountered a variety of methodological challenges and difficulties. Some of these we had anticipated and had dealt with in the construction of our research design. Others were unexpected, in kind and/or extent. This section describes how some of the more prominent complexities were confronted and the lessons that were gleaned for the conduct of future research.

Obtaining Data

We were able to gather much of the data that we had intended from the outset to collect, from our anticipated sources. This was true for basic data about NDOs (obtained from grant applications); about projects and their intended financing (from grant instruments plus applications); and about NDO capabilities and growth, and factors in their success (from site-visit interviews). Having access to documents associated with NSHD grant-making processes was a great advantage, although we were not conducting a program evaluation; indeed, such linking of research on urban dynamics with repre-

---

9. Frequency distributions were compared using Chi-Square tests and means using t-tests, both at the .05 significance level.

sentative programmatic activity might usefully be made deliberate in other studies.[10]

Much less successful, as noted earlier, was our plan to obtain information on project progress and outcomes from quarterly reports that were to be submitted by NDOs. In their place, the telephone calls we made to most of the nonsample NDOs near the end of our study were an efficient, productive way to gather the needed data on project results. Telephone interviews allowed explicit communication (more so than did NDO written self-reporting) of actual outcomes compared with the intentions outlined in baseline materials. Furthermore, they enabled us to avoid assumptions we made for non-telephone-call NDOs, such as that if money was being spent from a specific source and we had no information to the contrary, then the amount of money actually obtained from that source equaled expectations. The results of our efforts recommend the use of telephone calls, structured by original statements of intent, to track program progress in similar studies in the future.

Another difficulty in obtaining data is related to study timing. Many projects were still unfinished when time for collecting outcome data ended. As indicated in chapter 3, this created some important problems for measuring the extent of project accomplishment and success. Actual outputs (such as houses rehabilitated) are really only well measured for projects on which work is finished, and this is especially true in instances where outputs are large and discrete (such as an apartment building under construction in which no units are likely to be complete until nearly all work is finished). We responded to this problem in several ways: by focusing on finished projects; by looking at expectations for unfinished ones; and by defining completion in terms of an index of tasks wholly or partly finished, adjusted by the share of grant period elapsed.

But none of these approaches is completely satisfactory. Projects finished relatively early may represent more efficient and successful work than the average, even once all projects are complete. Expectations about the outputs of unfinished projects may also prove to be wrong. Our percentage-of-tasks-complete variables are somewhat rough indices. Standardizing them by percentage of grant period elapsed makes finished and unfinished projects more comparable; but it assumes that projects should proceed very evenly over time, and it neglects the prospect of further productive work beyond originally scheduled deadlines. Structuring future comparable studies to ensure more uniform completion or near-completion of projects should produce improved outcome measures.

---

10. The link was, in our case, based on program-evaluation intentions, which changed after the NSHD program was eliminated.

Measurement Problems and Related Analytic Issues

We had some difficulty measuring a number of descriptors of NDOs, their environments, projects, and project outcomes. In some instances the measurement problems limited our ability to pursue potentially valuable analyses; but most of the initially defined issues of study interest could be and were addressed.

We had hoped to derive more descriptive information from NSHD grant applications and instruments concerning the total population of ninety-nine NDOs than was actually the case. Some basic information on size, history, and project activities was obtainable from these sources, although even in those instances, differences in NDO approach to applications made the data of sometimes uncertain comparability (particularly in budget size, for example, where NDOs differed in their treatment of project and pass-through monies). But our hopes of compiling information from grant applications and instruments about spin-off organizations, board selection processes, division of staff functions, and other internal matters (as well as some information on success factors from quarterly reports) proved unrealistic. When the information from these sources was compared with data obtained on site visits for those same items, the match was not sufficient to justify continued use of the study population data. We thereafter confined our attention to sample organizations in assessing such characteristics, and, given the substantial size of our sample, this approach was fully satisfactory. It is likely that written self-reporting would work well in comparable studies only if NDOs (or similar program actors) were sent highly structured questionnaires dealing explicitly with the questions of interest; again, telephone interviews would be a superior way of securing information from many organizations, supplementing the critical site visits without the cost of travel.

We also obtained considerably less systematic information on NDO environments than we would have liked. Statistical information supplied by NDOs about their neighborhoods was so disparate that no real cross-NDO analysis was feasible, whether for descriptive purposes, to statistically analyze neighborhood impacts on projects, or to control for neighborhood conditions in analyzing the impacts of other variables. It would have required an enormous effort for us to gather detailed, current, neighborhood data, even for sample neighborhoods—and might have been ultimately infeasible given the lack of up-to-date Census Bureau information. For both descriptive and analytic purposes, it would be instructive to take advantage of Census-based measures in a future study (before 1980 figures grow old). It should be noted, however, that site-visit interviews did allow us to make extensive observations specifically about the impacts of differing neighborhood conditions on project results.

A related problem was the inherent limit on our ability to examine directly the effects of national economic conditions and public policies on NDO projects. NDOs are quite similarly affected by national circumstances at any one moment. Only a study so lengthy that it could view the impacts of national conditions as they change would really suffice. However, again site interviews yielded substantial information about the impacts of these factors. And the rise in interest rates and the decline in federal funding during the course of NSHD projects also provided a special opportunity to view the effects of these changes. In addition to the sample observations, we were able to use information about all ninety-nine NDOs' initially planned sources of funding, and the impacts of those plans on actual leveraging and project outcomes, to assess many consequences of the national environment.

We were able to meet many of our objectives for measuring how projects turned out. Information seems solid about absolute levels of primary direct outputs, comparison of outputs and timing with project expectations, the distribution of project benefits, fund leveraging and its extent in relation to initial goals, use of self-help, the relationship of projects to neighborhood revitalization strategies, and project-related capacity building.[11] Written NDO self-reporting, telephone calls, and site visits all contributed to our information-gathering efforts. We expected to find few indirect project impacts and changes in basic NDO community conditions as a result of NSHD projects, and our expectations were realized.

There are three areas of project performance that deserve more study in future research, as mentioned briefly in chapter 3. First, we were unable to get reliable information about "other direct" outputs—notably jobs generated in activities such as housing rehabilitation where the rehabilitation goal was primary. Such outputs are often an important goal and result of NDO work, and to neglect them is to understate the productivity of NDO efforts. Regrettably, neither written reporting, telephoning, nor site visits produced solid data.

Second, we were unable to generate meaningful analyses of project costs per unit output. Problems were several and varied. In some instances, not all dollar expenditures we measured were actually elements of unit cost, although they occurred as part of project work. For example, housing-acquisition expenses were often mixed with the costs of rehabilitating the housing once it

---

11. This statement must be qualified by the problems of unfinished projects already discussed.

was acquired, preventing us from computing per-unit-repair expenditures. Projects often had multiple outputs, creating both practical and conceptual problems for unit-cost analyses. Some NDOs included the financing of closely related work in computing leveraged funds for NSHD projects; however, if they did not also include the outputs of those efforts, the unit costs we computed were misleading. Even a "finished project" may not have generated all eventual output and thus will show incorrect unit-cost results: for example, an economic development venture whose start-up costs are fully paid but whose total employment generated may grow for two more years. Funds for general support and administration are counted differently by various NDOs. To obtain useful unit-cost information, a major effort focused on that subject (beyond this study's level of emphasis) would have to be launched. And in order to use the information for productive comparisons, detailed attention to project conditions (extent of housing dilapidation before repair, and so forth) would have to be given.

A third area of project performance that we would have liked to have pursued further was to compare NDO performance with that of other actors doing similar work under similar circumstances. As indicated in the text, we were simply unable to identify (by queries to key actors in our first visits to sites) projects that were felt to be truly comparable to the efforts of our study NDOs. Thus we did not even get far enough to confront the substantial problems of making legitimate and careful comparisons. Again, a major effort in this direction would be required and still might not produce results, if we are right that few other actors undertake comparable work.

Making Sample Site Visits

Most actors we sought to interview on site visits were open and forthcoming in describing both the achievements and problems in developing their projects. The fact that NSHD program cancellation eliminated potential concern about evaluation for future funding probably contributed to these actors' forthrightness, although we have also met with generally good responsiveness in other, similar research. Some people within the organizations avoided discussing problem areas, however, which may have reduced our ability to assess success factors and capacity-building needs. We found that interviewing a large, varied set of actors inside and outside the organizations was important in fashioning a complete picture of project progress and its causes. We included some categories of people on our list of interviewees—such as architects or leaders of other community organizations—who most often have limited information on NDO work but occasionally contribute much to our understanding. We would also have benefited greatly from the guidance that

HUD project monitors might have provided us, but the limits on their knowledge about any given NDO narrowed as the monitoring process was reduced and turned toward program closeout and as monitoring responsibilities were repeatedly transferred from one individual to another.

Two other limitations on site-visit information should be noted. Clearance for our study's movement into the field was delayed by HUD review of the research project as administrations changed. One result was that our first visits to sites occurred after much project planning and packaging work was over for some NDOs, thus restricting our ability to study those processes. Some projects had completed much of that work even before becoming NSHD grantees. Another constraint worth considering is that NDO board of directors and staff-management functioning is easier to assess if the analysts can actually observe board and staff meetings. Site visits therefore might be timed to include direct observation, although scheduling in large-scale field efforts is already difficult without this further constraint.

Qualitative and Quantitative Data

A concern expressed in HUD's request for proposal for this study was the appropriate use of qualitative and quantitative information. Our original research design anticipated a balance among data of three types: traditional quantitative measures (for example, number of houses rehabilitated or dollars leveraged); explicit qualitative measures (for example, whether a project director's skills are strong or weak); and qualitative case-study information, especially material describing relationships between NDO characteristics and the organizations' performance and growth. Our intent was to provide statistical descriptions and analyses/hypothesis tests using the first two kinds of information, and narratives based on the third. Wherever possible, the approaches were to complement each other with respect to specific topics and issues.

This author believes that such a balance was effectively reached in the conduct of our study and is reflected throughout this book.[12] Our experience certainly supports the idea that the statistical and case-study approaches should continue in tandem in future studies of the work of urban actors and programs. It is hoped that our study will provide useful guidance in shaping such a complementary approach.

---

12. Note, again, that we promised confidentiality to individual site interviewees and indicated that no NDO would be identified by name as a strong or weak performer in our written reports for publication. We have maintained that confidentiality and do not believe it injured our ability to give detailed examples of important findings.

Multivariate Analysis

We had hoped to explore the potential for separating out statistically the effects of various factors in success using regression and/or related multivariate techniques. The fact that many key variables could be measured properly only for the thirty sample organizations made such an effort basically infeasible, because the set of candidate independent variables was so large relative to the number of observations.

The research did, however, incorporate two procedures to sort out relationships between explanatory variables and project outcomes. A primary purpose was to avoid reporting apparent linkages between one independent variable and project performance as seen in the many two-way tabulations reported throughout chapter 4, when in fact what appeared in the table was the result of coincidental correlation between that independent variable and another variable that really "caused" the project outcome. One of the procedures we used to avoid this was to compute three-way tabulations, controlling for powerful explanatory variables such as project type when testing links between outcomes and other variables. Chapter 4 cites a number of situations in which using controls affected our findings. More work could still be done with the present data in this area. The other step we used was to integrate the findings from site-visit case studies with the statistical analyses of factors determining performance, identifying truly causal relationships by tracing (through interview information) the ways key factors actually influenced project outcomes.

Directions for Future Research

Several valuable lines of future research are suggested by the limits and accomplishments of this study—some of which have already been noted here. Perhaps the most important such line of future research would involve a significant broadening of our focus. We developed a rich body of information about the performance of NDOs in specific projects, their immediate impacts, the reasons for success or failure, and the resulting NDO growth. And we found that NDOs are good project performers and that it is possible to improve their performance. Yet, while we took note of the substantial links between individual projects and broader NDO strategies for neighborhood revitalization, we did not try to assess the strategies themselves. Nevertheless, stabilizing and "turning around" neighborhoods are central NDO goals, along with providing direct and immediate project benefits to residents they serve.

What is of course required in order to assess strategies is a better understanding of neighborhood and urban dynamics. Along with this is needed greater specific attention (which our study was deliberately not designed to give) to the compatibility of NDOs' overall action plans and sequencing of specific projects with the conditions they face, as well as greater awareness of the ways NDOs generate and revise their strategies. While such a research recommendation may sound too general and overwhelming, it does suggest at least one approach that could be put into practice. A series of case studies might be undertaken in, say, several neighborhoods in a given city, in which the impacts over several years of actions by private and public actors and NDOs could be traced (and indirect impacts given special attention). The effectiveness of different plans of attack and of institutional actors in varying environments could be tested. Since action is often slow, the studies would not need to be constant but could involve less-expensive periodic monitoring, once baseline conditions were established. Or a stripped-down version of such an analysis might be accomplished retrospectively at a given time.

Several narrower areas of work are also suggested by our study. As already mentioned, 1980 Census Bureau data could be used to enhance current descriptions of NDO neighborhoods and therefore also the analysis of the neighborhood enviroment's role in project success as well as the analysis of other factors in success using neighborhood as a control. Given that our NSHD grantee observations neatly overlap and follow the period of Census-data collection, this work might simply be appended to our data file and analyses.

Additional work could also be done to establish the efficiency of NDOs relative to other actors in comparable work—in terms of unit costs, likelihood of completion, and so on. We have seen that NDOs deliver quite well on their promises, in the face of extremely difficult conditions. Still, it may be desirable to have on hand a small set of comparisons to others' performance, in deciding whether to greatly expand NDOs' roles in revitalization work. Further exploration would have to be made to establish whether sufficiently comparable non-NDO projects (which we did not find) do in fact exist elsewhere. The caveat, raised in our research plan, that others' projects must be similar enough to NDO efforts and that special NDO goals must be given adequate credit so that seeming "efficiency differences" are not actually differences in projects, would still apply.

Two final areas of needed research look specifically to current developments and to their implications for the future. We need to look over a longer term at the impacts of changes in federal funding and taxing policies on NDOs' work, in view of the fact that those impacts have been felt more fully in the period following our study work. We also may want to look systematically at the implications of change for the feasibility of various types of projects, the special assistance that may thus be needed to make them work, and the realistic potential for greater NDO self-sufficiency given the kinds of work such organizations do—rather than letting ideology about roles of public and private sectors and volunteerism obscure the true shape of opportunities and constraints. This book delineates numerous ways that impacts have already been and may be felt, as well as the resources that must be generated to allow NDO work to go forward. These lessons might be expanded upon to indicate more fully what they mean for effective conduct of specific projects and for the choice of future policy changes.

References

Abt Associates. 1973. An evaluation of the Special Impact Program: Final report. Cambridge, Mass. Mimeo.

Bratt, Rachel G., Janet M. Byrd, and Robert M. Hollister. January 1983. The private sector and neighborhood preservation. Cambridge, Mass.: Neighborhood Policy Research. Mimeo.

Cohen, Bernard. 1979. Growth: An agenda for the 1980's. Parts 1, 2. *City Limits* (New York) 4(7): 4, 5, 16–17; 4(8): 6, 7, 19, 20.

Cohen, Rick, and Miriam Kohler. 1983. Neighborhood development organizations after the federal funding cutbacks. Draft prepared for U.S. Department of Housing and Urban Development, Office of Policy Development and Research, Washington, D.C. Mimeo.

Friedman, Joel. 1981. Partnerships for community self-reliance. Draft prepared for U.S. Department of Housing and Urban Development, Office of Policy Development, Division of Community Conservation Research, Washington, D.C. Mimeo.

Hanson, Ranee, and John McNamera. 1981. *Partners*. Minneapolis: The Dayton-Hudson Foundation.

HUD. *See under* U.S. Department of Housing and Urban Development.

Litvak, Lawrence, and Belden Daniels. 1979. *Innovations in development finance*. Washington, D.C.: Council of State Planning Agencies.

McNeely, Joseph. 1982. Self-help community development: Life after Reagan. *Citizen Participation* (Boston) 3(3).

Mayer, Neil S., with Jennifer L. Blake. 1981. *Keys to growth of neighborhood development organizations*. Washington, D.C.: The Urban Institute Press.

Mayer, Neil S., and Sue A. Marshall. August 1981. *Research plan for the study of the impact of external funding on neighborhood development organizations*. Rev. ed. Washington, D.C.: The Urban Institute.

Moritz, Doug. 1979. Developing a Section 8 Substantial Rehab project: A case study. Prepared for *Neighborhood case studies*. U.S. Department of Housing and Urban Development, Washington, D.C.

National Center for Economic Alternatives. 1981. *Federal assistance to community development corporations: An evaluation of Title VII of the Community Services Act of 1974*. Washington, D.C.: NCEA.

National Commission on Neighborhoods. 1979a. *Neighborhood case studies.* Washington, D.C.: Government Printing Office.

National Commission on Neighborhoods. 1979b. *People building neighborhoods: Final report to the president and the Congress of the United States.* Washington, D.C.: Government Printing Office.

New World Foundation, The. 1980. *Initiatives for community self-help: Efforts to increase recognition and support.* New York: The New World Foundation.

Rosenbaum, Nelson, and Bruce L.R. Smith. December 1981. *Fiscal capacity of the voluntary sector.* Washington, D.C.: Center for Responsive Governance.

Salamon, Lester M., and Alan J. Abramson. 1983a. *The federal government and the non-profit sector: Implications of the Reagan budget proposals.* Washington, D.C.: The Urban Institute.

Salamon, Lester, et al. 1983b. "Serving community needs: The non-profit sector in an era of governmental retrenchment." Progress Report 3. Washington, D.C.: The Urban Institute.

Support Center, The. 1980. Summary of financial management needs assessment among neighborhood development organizations. Prepared for U.S. Department of Housing and Urban Development, Office of Policy Development and Research and Office of Neighborhood Development. Washington, D.C. Mimeo.

U.S. Department of Housing and Urban Development. 1978. *President's national urban policy report.* Washington, D.C.: Government Printing Office.

U.S. Department of Housing and Urban Development, Office of Neighborhoods, Voluntary Associations, and Consumer Protection. 1980. *Neighborhoods self-help case studies: Abstracts of reports on revitalization projects funded by the Office of Neighborhood Self-Help Development.* Washington, D.C.: Government Printing Office.

WIDENER UNIVERSITY
WOLFGRAM
LIBRARY
CHESTER, PA.